PIMENTOS & PIRI PIRI
PORTUGUESE COMFORT COOKING

CARLA AZEVEDO

whitecap

Whitecap Books is known for its expertise in the cookbook market,
and has produced some of the most innovative and familiar titles found in
kitchens across North America. Visit our website at www.whitecap.ca.

Edited by: Theresa Best and Tracey Bordian
Cover design: Andrew Bagatella
Interior design: Naomi MacDougall
Food photography: Ryan Szulc
Food styling: Nicole Young
Prop styling: Madeleine Johari
Proofreading: Jesse Marchand and Grace Yaginuma

Printed in Canada

Library and Archives Canada Cataloguing in Publication
Azevedo, Carla, 1959–
Pimentos and Piri Piri: Portuguese comfort cooking / Carla Azevedo.
Includes index.
ISBN 978-1-77050-190-4

1. Cooking, Portuguese. 2. Cookbooks. I. Title.

TX723.5.P7A94 2013   641.59469   C2013-900952-3

The publisher acknowledges the financial support of the Government of Canada
through the Canada Book Fund (CBF) and the Province of British Columbia
through the Book Publishing Tax Credit.

13 14 15 16 17   5 4 3 2 1

CONTENTS

INTRODUCTION

It's hard to believe that more than 20 years have slipped by since my first book, *Uma Casa Portuguesa: Portuguese Home Cooking*, was published. Three reprints later the book is still in demand. Now, having taken a break from cookbook writing and having changed professions, I am always surprised when someone recognizes me and asks, "Did you write the cookbook *Uma Casa Portuguesa?*"

Family, friends, neighbours, food lovers—they all want to know how to replicate the barbecued sardines, pork and clams, and custard tarts that they enjoy in restaurants and bakeries and in the homes of friends. Avid cooks looking to demystify sweet bread, cod croquettes, and other foods rarely featured in popular magazines refer to my book. I am always extremely proud when I hear that the bread or rice recipe they found in my book was exactly as their mother or grandmother had made.

Over the years, the proprietors of the Cookbook Store and the Portuguese Book Store in Toronto gently encouraged me to write a new book. Although I could not see it at the time, they knew there was still more to offer on the topic of Portuguese cooking. And so, not knowing what to expect, I looked to the Portuguese community and began to explore new recipes and seek out passionate cooks who could bring me new recipes.

I began asking complete strangers to cook for me. You can imagine the look I received when, for example, I asked a Portuguese woman at the fish store how she prepared the fish she purchased and if I could go to her home and watch her make it.

I quickly learned that many recipes are passed on by word of mouth amongst friends . . . *just add a little bit of this or that.* Many of the people I asked for recipes were politely dumbfounded when I would request more detailed instruction and first-hand observations. (Although I know a lot about Portuguese cooking, following an oral recipe without watching the preparation yourself is like cooking Chinese food when you've never had Chinese food before.)

After about five months I was rewarded: I met a woman determined to keep her food culture alive, a kind-hearted Portuguese reporter, and a talented and generous chef who all opened doors for me. They introduced me to new recipes and to people who could help me further explore Portuguese cooking for the purposes of my book.

Those who cooked for me insisted that I taste their renditions of classic Portuguese dishes, many of which I had included in my first book: Creamy Potato Purée and Greens (page 82), Cod in Cream Sauce (page 142), Duck with Rice and Madeira (page 182), and Pork and Clams Alentejo-Style (page 220), all essential Portuguese gastronomy. Watching and participating in these demonstrations was a necessary first step in reminding me of the essentials of Portuguese cooking. After the classics, the equally delicious and lesser-known dishes were brought forward. So many gems: Broad Bean Soup with Bacon (page 87), Whole European Sea Bass with Fresh Coriander and Lemon Dressing (page 160), and French Toast Slices in Port and Cinnamon Sauce (page 358). Later, I would come knocking with samples of matching dishes I had made in my own kitchen and was welcomed back and given a few pointers on how to make improvements. I learned a lot. I was pleasantly surprised to find how much.

I was more than pleased with all that I tasted and learned and am thankful to everyone who, despite their work and families and limited time to cook, made the effort to share recipes with me. It made my job much easier. Other than amazing food, I developed wonderful friendships with people who shared a part of themselves with me and who I highly respect. One food aficionado, Isabel Vieira, christened me the Portuguese Food Ambassador of Canada. I could not ask for a higher honour.

The recipes in this cookbook, as in my first cookbook, have been influenced by the world travels of the Portuguese. Portuguese people first came to Canada's shores looking to fish the cod off the Grand Banks in the early 1500s. Much later, in the 1950s, they began arriving in Canada for permanent residence. The country offered job opportunities and a prosperous new life for individual workers, and their families who followed soon after. All of this immigration has had an impact on Portuguese cooking in North America today.

The food of Portugal varies by region. In the north of Portugal, the climate is colder and landscape more mountainous, so hearty soups and fresh fish from cold mountain rivers are a large part of the diet. Port wine, which hails, famously, from the northern city of Porto, is found in both sweet and savoury dishes. Some typical recipes from the north are Tripe and Beans Porto-Style (page 230) and Trout Wrapped in Prosciutto with Pine Nut Sauce (page 158). The south is known for specialty dishes that include shellfish, fresh sea fish, almonds, fresh coriander, tomatoes, and peppers, in addition to rice grown in paddy fields. Some typical recipes from the south are Clams in Coriander Sauce (page 41) and Almond Tart (page 346). In spite of regional differences, however, many dishes are shared throughout Portugal.

In North America, the regional differences in Portuguese cooking are not as obvious. Far from home, from the farms, regional grocery stores, and authentic restaurants, Portuguese cooks embrace the more common, classic Portuguese dishes. As I researched my book, however, I became aware of the uniqueness of mainland Portugal and its cuisine and how it is subtly different from the cooking in the Azorean islands.

Interestingly, my first book is more reflective of the Azorean islands, since 20 years ago when it was first published the greater number of Portuguese immigrants to Canada hailed from that region. I was surprised, at first, when Portuguese from the mainland did not recognize some of the more traditional dishes in my book, even though they had the same name and included almost the same ingredients and cooking processes as mainland recipes. Mainlanders identified the addition of pimento paste (a preferred Azorean seasoning), hot sauce, and plenty of Hungarian paprika as Azorean. Although both mainland and Azorean seasonings centre on wine, bay leaves, and garlic, mainlanders view Azorean food as different from theirs.

In Toronto, Portuguese grocery stores were identified to me as either Azorean or mainland, and I was told that the markets fit the unique needs of each community. I was very curious and went to these stores to note the differences first hand. I found that one of my favourite mainland cheeses, Queijo Serra da Estrela, was not available in Azorean grocery stores (although they had plenty of the Azorean cheese São Jorge). Island-flavoured smoky chouriço and take-out foods that included seasoned fish and pork with hints of red (from the pimento paste) were sold instead. If you got to the stores early enough, you could also find flat cornbread, another popular island specialty (if it hadn't sold out yet).

The mainland Portuguese I met preferred to shop at Portuguese stores with a more European feel, and these shops lacked many of the Azorean take-out foods and highly seasoned sausages.

I quickly learned that changes had been taking place in the North American Portuguese communities since I wrote my first cookbook. There now seems to be a greater presence of immigrants from mainland Portugal. This has meant new foods and greater variety—a bonus for all who love food. In this book I celebrate the changes that have been unfolding in North America with recipes that include, for example, Watercress Soup (page 84), Pine Nut–Crusted Rosemary and Garlic Lamb Ribs (page 214), and Portuguese Pulled Pork (page 222).

Today's immigrants, much like the early explorers, have brought their own way of preparing foods to their new homeland and with an open mind have reinvented Portuguese cooking once again. Early explorers travelled to Angola, Mozambique, or Brazil, introducing Portuguese cooking to these cultures. They also brought back with them crops and spices and varieties of foods never before known to Europe. Oranges, sweet potatoes, and piri-piri hot peppers, to name a very few, changed the way the world eats today. Similarly but on a much smaller scale, the Portuguese who have immigrated to Canada in recent years are interacting with North American culture, new markets, and new neighbours and are experimenting in their kitchens without realizing they are doing so.

Many cooks have told me how they have been influenced by other cultures; how, for example, they loved the dried or fresh oregano used by their Greek neighbour and so decided to add it to their Portuguese beans. Or how marinades now include store-bought barbecue sauce or ketchup as a base, which they then enhance with a bit of pimento paste, bay leaves, and all the typical Portuguese seasonings. Ketchup and barbecue sauce, not so common in Portugal, have made life easier during barbecue season in North America and lent a hint of sweetness and body to the usual marinades. One friend made an amazing liver recipe that included an entire cup of ketchup, her mother's secret ingredient, which blended well with the wine and paprika that gave the dish a distinct Portuguese flavour. Another friend marinates her pork ribs Portuguese-style and then follows it with a store-bought cayenne pepper sauce. When she visits her family in Portugal, she brings five bottles to keep everyone supplied until her return. These items, not so common in Portugal and as a result used sparingly, are readily available and used in abundance in North American kitchens.

Over time, the lines can become blurred between an original Portuguese recipe and the North American changes to the traditional recipe. On more than one occasion I would hear "I do not remember what was done in my hometown anymore. It was so long ago when I left."

Irene Alves and Maria Lourdes, two of the new friends I made while researching this book, have adapted ingredients in their traditional Portuguese recipes to include garlic powder, balsamic vinegar, and prepared powdered salts. Another food friend, Isabel, who after moving here from Portugal worked as a cook for a vegetarian family, embraced different vegetables and curries she had never before tasted. Although still very traditional in the way she prepares many Portuguese-flavoured dishes that her husband craves, the dynamic nature of cooking, in addition to her general curiosity, has brought some exciting changes to her day-to-day cooking.

Although many people love to experiment, they still hold on to classic Portuguese flavours when they cook, especially for their families who might still desire dishes like their mothers, or grandmothers, made. One food aficionado, Olidia Hipolito, explained her food experience best: when she cooks some of her traditional dishes, her children smell their grandmother who had passed away and who taught Olidia how to cook. It was evident from being with Olidia in the kitchen that she was, in a small way, keeping their grandmother alive.

A great many of the recipes in this book, although dynamic and made from North American ingredients, are still uniquely Portuguese, reflecting the classic Portuguese flavours of olive oil, white wine vinegar, bay leaves, and paprika. However, this book is not a bible of authentic Portuguese cooking. Change is all around Portuguese cuisine. In this book, much like its predecessor, my goal was to capture the food as it came into contact with North

America. It is more a reflection of the amazing home cooks and chefs, and the numerous experts I was fortunate enough to encounter on my quest. These people adapt ingredients, and sometimes skills, to fit their environment and lifestyle. They use what they can find at their local grocery stores to make amazing meals that go beyond traditional dishes for a taste of something different.

I have learned a lot while gathering the recipes for this book. I have spent endless hours in the kitchens of restaurants and home cooks. I have felt the wholehearted support of many cooks along the way. I peeled hundreds of potatoes, soaked and scraped countless cod, and cleaned tons of sardines. I got to know the character of these ingredients intimately. If it were not for my husband's gentle reminder of a deadline, I would still be out there finding just one more recipe. I am confident that the recipes included in this book are outstanding—and the credit goes to all the cooks I have met along the way.

These recipes are a beautiful marriage of some of the treasures from my first book, *Uma Casa Portuguesa*, and all the new recipes I researched. This book also contains some excellent but subtle tips and suggestions that can improve your cooking quickly and easily. It's hard for me to believe, but I am happy to say that this book is even better than the first, and through it I wish to share my deep love and passion for Portuguese cooking. It is my hope that you, your friends, and your family will enjoy it.

ESSENTIALS OF PORTUGUESE COOKING
Techniques, Ingredients, and Utensils

One of the highlights of researching this book was observing one of the top Portuguese chefs in Toronto, José Alves. I watched him make some outstanding Portuguese dishes at his restaurant, Via Norte. The experience was inspirational. Each week after I left his kitchen my mind was brimming with recipes, techniques, and general food tips. I learned much from him. Most important was how to boost flavour as naturally and as simply as possible. I've tried to incorporate some of the methods I observed into the recipes in this book.

Often the Portuguese home cooks I met, short on time, would use powdered stocks and other seasoning packages as shortcuts to boost flavour. With some advance planning, however, the professional chef's techniques offered in this book can just as easily become part of your everyday cooking. Once you begin cooking like a chef and taste some of the full-flavoured results you can achieve, you won't want to cook any other way.

The following information should provide you with a good understanding of the ingredients, seasonings, and techniques involved in Portuguese cooking.

SEASON TO TASTE

A big part of Portuguese cooking includes adjusting the seasonings to taste. Many of the ingredients used in Portuguese cooking, such as cod, do not produce the same results every time. Tasting and judging for yourself becomes an extremely important skill, along with adjusting recipes to your family's preferences. If making Cod Carpaccio (page 54), for example, some people might prefer more olives, others coriander rather than parsley. The recipes contain distinctly Portuguese flavours, although there is lots of room for variation, such as in the Cod Carpaccio recipe. Look at the recipes as guidelines and, like the Portuguese, feel free to experiment with the ingredients to suit you and your family's taste. The dishes will still reflect Portuguese cuisine.

BUY THE FRESHEST AND THE BEST

Go shopping on a regular basis. Purchase fresh herbs, greens, meat, and fish. Build a relationship with the grocers in your neighbourhood, and get to know when their fresh produce or meats arrive. Quality ingredients can do most of the work for you in your meal preparations.

CREATE AND SAVE EVERY OUNCE OF FLAVOUR

In a professional kitchen, beef jus is made regularly once a week. Bones are roasted and added to a broth with vegetables and herbs to make a rich, delicious reduction. The addition of jus to steak sauce, meat dishes, risottos, and stews adds a robust flavour to entrées. When chefs run out of jus, they'll add a few spoonfuls of the pan juices of whatever meat they have roasting to their entrées just before serving them. You can apply the same flavour-enhancing skills to rice and vegetable dishes. If you don't have time to make a jus from scratch, you can also pump up flavour with a few tried-and-true kitchen tips.

Grill mushrooms earlier in the day and then sauté them with garlic just before making an earthy-flavoured risotto. Do not waste a drop of flavour. Reserve and return the cooking juices from the sauté pan of meat or roasted fish to enhance the flavour of side dishes such as grilled vegetables or rice. Add some of these drippings onto Sautéed Garlic Rabe Greens (page 261) or Cumin, Tomato, and Chouriço Beans (page 266). Gather and refrigerate or freeze the jus or stock of all the meats that you cook. Degrease and reserve your meat drippings from when you cook every day. Deglaze any bits of meat or vegetables left behind in pans with stock or wine and return them to your dish or set them aside for later use. You do not need very much to add richness to your cooking.

RUN AN EFFICIENT KITCHEN

Much of what I observed in professional kitchens can go hand in hand with how to run an economical and efficient home kitchen. Vegetables can be pre-cooked early in the day and then submerged in ice water to abruptly stop the cooking, refrigerated, and then warmed up just before serving. The liquid used to cook greens can be added to soups and rice (never throw it out—it is full of flavour). The stalks of greens, and bits and pieces of veggies not fit for serving, can be stored in an airtight container in the refrigerator and later combined and boiled with other vegetables to make outstanding soups. Red peppers, mushrooms, and pineapple can be roasted or grilled ahead of time and set aside, then brought back to life in minutes by sautéing them in garlic oil. In fact, roasting or grilling vegetables in advance to have on hand when preparing meals will add layers of flavour to your entrées. And when you partially precook vegetables, double the amount that you are making for one recipe and save the extra for later use.

You can also partially precook short-grain rice and then cool and refrigerate it until you are ready to make risotto or Coriander Rice (page 254). When needed, you can take the rice directly from the cold refrigerator and continue cooking it in a hot broth. Doing this gives a less-soggy result, as the cold rice does not absorb all the liquids as quickly as it might otherwise.

The flavour of many recipes is enhanced by time—simply being set aside to marinate and soak in the seasonings produces extraordinary results. Tomato Sauce with Port Wine (page 283) and Red Pepper and Olive Relish (page 284) made a day or two ahead only get tastier with time. Make use of fresh herbs—thyme, rosemary, parsley, and coriander—whenever possible. Fresh herbs add a subtle boost of flavour to fish and vegetables in particular. Puréed garlic and chopped parsley and coriander (chopping first and then washing is easier than chopping washed herbs) can be stored in the refrigerator or freezer, ready to drop into any recipe as needed.

Make some preparations during the weekend when you might have more time so that you can whip up your favourite dishes during rushed weekdays. If guests are expected, preparing as much as you can ahead of time will allow you more time to enjoy with family and friends. If short on time, make very simple dishes by grilling fresh trout or whole European sea bass—no marinating required—and dressing them up with homemade Piri-Piri Sauce (page 282) or Parsley Dressing (page 280). All of these preparatory steps will help to ensure that you (or any family member who likes to cook) are stocked and ready to make any of the recipes in this book quickly and easily.

BOOST FLAVOUR NATURALLY

Some easy but essential cooking techniques are crucial to producing perfect results almost every time. Professional chefs are not afraid to sauté onions and garlic until they are golden brown, to the moment of almost burning (a method called *refogado* by the Portuguese). Once I began applying this more time-consuming technique (about five extra minutes) to my cooking, I realized how important it was to the depth of flavour. Slow-cooking onions and garlic adds a touch of sweetness to dishes that is well worth the extra time. In addition, the precious fat renderings from sautéed bacon or sausage boost the flavour of onions, garlic, and tomatoes. When I discovered the delicious results made possible by these easy, natural methods, I introduced them to some of the recipes I had collected and, as a result, added another layer of flavour to these homestyle dishes. Rather than prepackaged stocks and other artificial or freeze-dried flavour enhancers, I decided to bring the flavour of well-prepared ingredients back into traditional dishes for some amazing results. The recipes in this book show you how you can capture the full flavours of Portuguese food and enjoy them in your North American kitchen.

COOKING TECHNIQUES

BAIN-MARIE (HOT WATER BATH) Fragile sauces and custards are often cooked in a *bain-marie*—partially immersed in water and cooked in the oven or on top of the stove to prevent drying out.

BARBECUING (ROTISSERIE) Cooking meat on a grill (using a propane barbecue or over hot coals) or rotating it over a spit is extremely popular in Portuguese homes and take-out delis. Portuguese restaurants that specialize in barbecuing are called *churrasqueira*.

BASTING Flavour and moistness are enhanced by periodically spooning cooking liquids and marinades over food during cooking.

CARAMEL-MAKING Sugar cooked until it reaches the liquid stage is used to coat countless Portuguese desserts. Cook the sugar in a heavy saucepan over medium-low heat, uncovered, for 10 to 15 minutes or until the sugar turns amber. Shake the saucepan occasionally, but do not stir. Watch the saucepan carefully.

FOLDING Folding keeps the air in light-textured desserts when batters are blended with beaten egg whites or whipped cream. Carefully pour the lighter mixture on top of the heavier mixture. With a rubber spatula, gently cut through the mixture to the bottom of the bowl and slide the spatula along the bottom and up the side, bringing some of the heavier mixture up and over with the spatula. Repeat the procedure until the light mixture is evenly distributed throughout the heavy one. Try not to tap or hit the side of the bowl, which will deflate the mixture.

KNEADING Kneading is necessary to work the dough for breads and puff pastry. Fold the dough over on itself and push it down and away from you. Turn the dough after each folding.

MARINATING Marinating tenderizes and flavours meat, poultry, and seafood. Cheaper cuts of meat marinated over an extended period can become just as tender as a lean and expensive cut. The Portuguese use aromatic marinades almost daily.

Refrigerate meat and fish if you will be marinating them for longer than 30 minutes. Larger pieces of meat such as roasts or whole chickens are often marinated for a few days in the refrigerator. Fish, on the other hand, can become tangy when marinated for a long time, especially if you are using large quantities of lemon juice or strong wine vinegar. Firm fish such as halibut and tuna and other fish steaks can be marinated for up to one to two hours. Flaky fish and fillets can be marinated for up to 60 minutes.

The more acidic the base (in particular homemade vinegar or wine), the stronger the effect. Some cooks dilute the vinegar, wine, or lemon juice with equal amounts of water. This allows you to marinate thinner cuts over a longer period and provides an even flavour.

For best results, immerse the meat in the marinating juices. Use your hands to rub paste-like marinades—such as pimento paste and garlic—into the meat. Placing the meat and marinade in a clean resealable plastic bag with the air pushed out is the most effective method.

MERINGUE-MAKING Meringue, egg whites beaten until stiff peaks form, is essential to many Portuguese desserts. This is called *castelo* by the Portuguese, which means to form castles or beating them so they look like castles in the air. A few basic hints will result in perfect meringues every time: keep the egg whites at room temperature; make sure there is no yolk in the whites; and use a deep, absolutely clean glass or porcelain bowl. Beat egg whites on low until foamy. Add sugar gradually. Set beater to high and beat the egg whites only until stiff peaks form. Overbeaten whites become dry and will not produce a light, airy dessert. Beat egg whites just before needed so they will keep their height.

PREHEATING I have omitted instructions for preheating ovens as an energy-saving measure. Most people (myself included) tend to keep the oven on for too long while attending to other things or while marinating the dish before putting it in the oven. In general, heat the oven to the desired temperature only about 10 minutes before putting it in the oven. (Set a timer for yourself if you think you might forget.)

REDUCING Reducing liquids in a saucepan thickens sauces and intensifies its flavour. To reduce, boil the sauce rapidly, uncovered, so the liquid evaporates. You may want to use this method to make sauces with degreased pan juices (if you do not have enough pan juices, add wine or stock to the pan), even in dishes where no sauce is called for.

INGREDIENTS

For guaranteed freshness, buy only enough dried herbs and spices to last a few months, and restock when you run out. Dried herbs and spices should stay fresh for six months after purchasing. Most spices can be purchased at grocery stores, stores specializing in ethnic cuisines (such as Indian, West Indian, or Portuguese), or bulk food outlets.

ALLSPICE The dried berry of the pimento tree is grown in the West Indies and is popular in some Azorean cooking. The taste is a perky combination of cloves, nutmeg, and cinnamon. It is used whole to season savoury foods or add flavour to marinades. You may want to wrap the berries in cheesecloth so that you can remove them easily after cooking. Substitute a pinch of ground allspice if whole allspice is unavailable.

ANISE SEED The dried seed of a plant belonging to the celery family is most often used in ground form. Only a pinch is required to provide an intensely sweet and aromatic licorice flavour. Anise is also used in small doses in baking; a pinch of anise seed can also be substituted for anise liqueur in cooking.

BAY LEAVES The dried leaves of laurel are often crumbled or added whole to flavour casseroles, stocks, stews, and sauces. It is added liberally to almost all savoury dishes. Choose bright-coloured, fresh-looking leaves with no imper-fections. Fresh, now more readily available in stores, is preferred.

BEANS   Dried beans play a major role in hearty Portuguese dishes. Beans are as much a Portuguese staple as rice and fish. It is easy to pull together a Portuguese meal with either precooked dried beans or canned beans. I add about ½ cup (125 mL) of beans to almost everything I make. Black-eyed peas, black beans, and navy beans are most often used in soups, stews, and salads. Choose blemish-free, firm beans.

Beans you soak and cook yourself are superior to canned beans, although canned beans can be a great last-minute time saver. To cook dried beans, rinse the beans, discarding any shrivelled or off-coloured ones. In a bowl, cover the beans with cold water and soak overnight. For faster results, in a large saucepan, cover the beans with water and boil for two minutes. Remove from the heat and let stand, covered, for one hour. Drain and rinse again before the next step.

Next, cover the beans with water and bring to a boil. Reduce the heat to low and cook at a gentle simmer, with lid slightly ajar, for 50 to 60 minutes, stirring occasionally. Beans should be cooked until almost done, when soft in the middle; taste to check for doneness. Store in the refrigerator for five to ten days or freeze for up to three months.

BEEF   Although the Portuguese have a culinary reputation for fish dishes, beef is very popular. Long, thin beef loin, flank steak, or tenderloin with or without bones, no more than three to four inches (8 to 10 cm) thick, are preferred over the traditional round roast because spices can more easily penetrate the meat. Marinating and slow-cooking produce dazzling results from less-expensive cuts. Sirloin or strip loin are best for grilling or pan-frying.

CHEESE   Cheese is often served with Portuguese breads as a traditional European ending to a meal. There are many cheeses, including *Serra da Estrela*, which has a creamy flavour similar to Oka cheese, a worthy substitute found in many Canadian markets. The semi-soft sheep's milk cheese with a smooth texture and mild tangy flavour is an excellent addition to a cheese platter. It pairs well with toasted almonds, figs, melons, and berries as well as Quince Marmalade Slices (page 290). It also is good in pressed or toasted sandwiches and melted in recipes with baked potatoes and bacon. The cheese can be difficult to find; ask your local grocers if they can order the Portuguese cheese for you.

Queijo fresco is a fresh, moist, creamy cheese. It is similar to a ricotta cheese in flavour, although a bit firmer in texture. This cheese is very perishable and should be refrigerated and used within three or four days. The Portuguese love to eat it on flat cornbread, crusty buns, or sweet egg bread with a bit of honey. At other times it is delicious simply with salt and pepper or with a bit of pimento paste or tossed into salads. There are two versions of the cheese: one made with cow's milk and the other with goat's milk. Both are excellent. Keep in mind that the moist cheese requires some draining before serving and using.

São Jorge is a sharp, tangy cheese that pairs nicely with any type of bread, but is especially tasty served as a *petisco* (snack) with Portuguese cornbread (and wine). It has a pungent odour and is best stored in the refrigerator covered in plastic wrap and double layers of foil. The taste is similar to sharp cheddar. São Jorge can be blended with Parmesan cheese and added to pasta and egg dishes or slivered and then tossed on greens with figs and prosciutto.

CHESTNUTS Simply boiled or roasted, chestnuts are served as a snack. Look for them in the fall and winter in ethnic grocery stores and vegetable and fruit markets. Pick firm, smooth, blemish-free chestnuts.

CINNAMON This spice comes from the bark of a tree that grows in Ceylon. Ground or whole cinnamon is used liberally to add colour and taste to savoury and sweet dishes. A pinch of ground cinnamon can be substituted for a cinnamon stick if sticks are unavailable, but note that a cinnamon stick gives you a more subtle flavour and allows you to control how much cinnamon flavour you would like to add to your dish. Simply remove the cinnamon stick or leave it in longer, to taste. Often home cooks combine cinnamon sticks with whole orange peel in desserts for a deeper homestyle taste.

CLOVES Nail-shaped cloves are the dried flower buds of the clove tree, grown in the East Indies. They are added whole to marinades and sauces to produce a spicy base for many Portuguese dishes. Ground cloves are added to sweet dishes. Cloves are especially favoured in Azorean cooking; they are added to dishes by the handful and are sometimes retrieved after cooking. You may want to tie the cloves in cheesecloth for easier removal. Substitute a pinch of ground cloves when whole cloves are unavailable.

COD   Salt cod is a staple of Portuguese cooking. Its is usually purchased in a large quantity then soaked and frozen in smaller quantities, to ensure that a cod dish is never too far away from the dinner plate.

The best place to purchase salt-dried cod is in a fish store or ethnic grocery store that has a high turnover of salt-dried cod. Get to know your fishmongers or grocers quite well, and get them to save some good pieces for you. Choose thick, meaty pieces. Keep in mind that bone-in cod will add more flavour. If you happen to have a very bony piece of cod, add an extra piece of dried fish to the soaking water to compensate. Most recipes are flexible, and if you have more or less than the amount of cod called for, the result will still be equally as good.

Make sure that you soak the dried cod long enough to remove as much salt as possible. Often one to three days is recommended for reconstituting the fish and this is only a rough time estimate. To prepare dried cod for cooking, place the cod in a large bowl with enough cold water to cover it completely. Cover the bowl in plastic wrap and refrigerate for 24 to 48 hours, changing the water two to three times a day, until the fish is spongy in texture and desalted. (Larger pieces of fish may take longer.) Although you can soak cod at room temperature, it is best to soak it in the refrigerator to avoid any potential for bacteria to grow. I prefer soaking cod for longer, breaking off and tasting a piece at intervals. If it seems leathery, continue soaking for another day. You have to taste and judge for yourself; the cod should be moist and spongy. If you do not soak it long enough, your dish will be inedible. Once the cod is desalted, drain off the water and rinse, and the cod is ready to use. If not using immediately, store soaked cod for up to two days in the refrigerator or for up to three months in the freezer.

There are endless Portuguese cod recipes, and although the price has gone up over recent years, a small piece of cod goes a long way. Try to use fillets and steaks of the same size for even cooking. Soaking may or may not flush out all the salt. Taste the dish during cooking and add salt only if necessary.

COLLARD GREENS   There is a long-standing controversy concerning the English name for the green-leafed cabbage the Portuguese call *couve*. It has been called collard greens, and has been called kale. It has also been described as Galician cabbage. It is a dark-green, flat-leafed vegetable and is often mistaken for the lighter-coloured, frilly-leafed cabbage. The taste is a cross between cabbage and spinach. Try to purchase collard greens at a Portuguese grocery store. In communities where it may be hard to find, you can substitute sturdy kale, green leafy cabbage, broccoli rabe or watercress (watercress can also be used in soups and as a salad base or garnish).

CORIANDER Fresh coriander grows abundantly all over the south of Portugal. It is used heavily in many dishes originating in the southern Algarve province, and it is rarely used in Azorean cooking. In the Azores, parsley is more familiar and accessible, and its milder taste is preferred by Azoreans. Since more Portuguese from the Algarve province have immigrated to North America in recent years, coriander is appearing more often in Portuguese home cooking (and thus appears more often in this book than it did in my first book, *Uma Casa Portuguesa*).

Bright-leafed fresh coriander can be mistaken for Italian parsley in appearance, but the taste is completely different—pungent and grass-like. Use fresh coriander as you do parsley, adding it to soups, stews, and roasts and to countless fresh salads. You can find fresh coriander in well-stocked supermarkets and in Chinese or Indian markets. It is also called Chinese parsley and cilantro. The seeds are strong-tasting and not used in Portuguese cooking.

CORN FLOUR Corn flour and cornmeal are milled by a process similar to regular wheat flour. Corn flour is simply ground cornmeal. The grainy-textured flour has no gluten, which is what gives wheat flour its strength and elasticity. Because of this, corn flour does not form a dough when mixed with water. To make breads you must mix it with wheat flour. It is used as a thickening agent and is popular in a number of hearty breakfasts and puddings.

The colour of the corn flour depends on the variety of corn—white or yellow—used in the milling. The colour called for in a recipe often is based on tradition, depending on what corn was grown in the region where the recipe originated.

CORNMEAL Corn kernels are milled to form a granular substance called cornmeal. Like corn flour, the different colours depend on the type of corn used—yellow or white. Stone-ground and regular cornmeal can be processed in a food processor for a finer consistency if preferred.

CUMIN Ground cumin is a staple in Portuguese kitchens. The pungent and aromatic spice is sprinkled in marinades and sauces. In the northern city of Porto, a steady supply is required to make the city's regional dish, Tripe and Beans Porto-Style (page 230). Cumin is a common spice used throughout the mainland and the Azorean islands. Portuguese cooks use only the ground spice, never the whole seed.

EGGS All eggs used in the recipes are large.

FAT In traditional Portuguese cooking, the preferred cooking oil is pig fat (i.e., lard), achieved by boiling down fatty pieces of pork. To cut down on fat and cholesterol, vegetable oils and butter are mostly used in the recipes in this book. However, if Portuguese-flavoured lard is available (usually flavoured with wine and garlic, similar to chouriço), I recommend using one or two teaspoons (5 to 10 mL) in place of some of the cooking oil. A small quantity of lard will lend a large dose of flavour.

FISH Buy the freshest fish possible. (Frozen fish is acceptable when fresh fish is unavailable.) Ask when your local fish market receives its fresh supplies and call before you go (sometimes schedules change).

The eyes of the fish should be completely clear, never cloudy or sunken. The flesh should be firm, spring back when touched, and smell fresh with no strong odour. Gills should be bright red. Check inside the fish and make sure there are no blood clots, no internal bruising, and no bones protruding.

Have the fishmonger gut and scale the fish.

To prepare a whole fish, using a sharp knife, cut both sides of the dorsal and anal fins. Pull out all the fins. Remove the head, if preferred. Small fish such as sardines, stickleback, and smelts can be cleaned the same way, although they are often cooked and served without cleaning. Heads are left on so the small fish can be held and eaten similar to corn on the cob.

FLOUR Buy sifted all-purpose flour so no additional sifting is required, and simply toss with the other dry ingredients.

GARLIC Portuguese cooking is laced with garlic, at times as much as one whole head, and the general rule is the more garlic, the tastier the dish. Do not be afraid of the large amounts, as the long cooking process produces a sweet flavour. The garlic cloves used in this book are medium to large. When buying, feel the heads and press firmly. Select firm cloves that are not empty or dried up. Store in the refrigerator or a cool, dark place until needed.

If you do not like the taste and after-effect of raw garlic in salad dressings, drop a clove in boiling water for one minute to blanch. Proceed with the rest of the recipe.

The best way to peel a clove is to press down on it with the flat side of a French knife. The skin should then come off easily.

LAMB This meat is often on the dinner table in northern Portugal. Aged lamb is preferred in stews; mutton or goat can also be substituted. Marinating is essential for tender results. Due to its availability in North America, more Portuguese from the Azores and other parts of Portugal are learning how to prepare lamb and including it in their diet.

LEMONS Freshly squeezed lemon juice is a base for marinades and, when combined with wine or beer, lends a superb flavour to meat and fish. Feel free to substitute lemon juice for white wine vinegar or for some of the wine or beer in marinades. Freshly grated lemon zest is a favourite flavouring in desserts; oranges are acceptable substitutes. When grating, avoid the bitter white part of the rind. Wash the lemon before using.

MINT This herb is used surprisingly little in Portuguese cooking, considering that it grows wild in almost every crevice in the Azorean islands. It is added whole to soups, loosely placed on rice while cooking, or used to garnish dishes.

NUTMEG Freshly grated nutmeg is used sparingly in savoury dishes and to add pizzazz to sauces. Whole nutmeg is available in most grocery stores. Freshly grated nutmeg packs more flavour than the powdered variety.

OCTOPUS Octopus can be purchased frozen and is often sold pre-cleaned in large supermarkets or ethnic grocery stores. Freezing actually tenderizes the octopus. Keep in mind too that it is easier to cut an octopus into pieces when it is partially frozen.

Cleaning octopus is easy, especially if you leave the skin on as the Portuguese prefer for added flavour and colour (I prefer skin on). If you prefer to remove the skin, do it after cooking; the purple skin detaches easily with a clean kitchen towel or your hands. If you would like to remove the skin before cooking, pull it off with a sharp knife; to scrape off any stubborn pieces, immerse the octopus in boiling water for a few minutes and then plunge it into a bowl of ice water.

To prepare the octopus for cooking, use a sharp knife to cut through the sac-like body of the octopus, separating the tentacles from the body. Pull open the body sac and discard the attached innards and stringy entrails. Pull out and cut away the hard beak in the centre of the tentacles and discard. Rinse the octopus under cold running water. The sac-like body of the octopus can be cooked and eaten in stews and salads along with the tentacles.

OLIVE OIL The olive oil used in Portuguese cooking and salad dressings is fruity with a robust olive flavour unlike virgin olive oils. You can purchase a number of Portuguese brands at grocery stores.

OLIVES The canned black olives or pimento-stuffed green olives you can easily find at grocery stores is what's usually served at a Portuguese home. In Portuguese restaurants, marinated black olives (*azeitona preta*)—similar to the Greek kalamata olives—are often served as a snack (*petisco*) with bread and cheese. Try the recipes for Popular Garlic Olives (page 64) and Orange and Cumin Olives (page 65), which pair nicely with São Jorge or Creamy Fresh Cheese (page 49) and Cornbread (page 304).

ONIONS All of the onions used in these recipes are medium-large. Yellow onions or Spanish onions are the most popular in everyday cooking. Choose a firm onion with no sign of sprouting or black mouldy spots. Store in a cool, dark place.

OREGANO Oregano is used liberally in Portuguese cooking. Dried oregano is used in a variety of preparations, such as in soups and stews and sprinkled over roasted and baked meats. It is also enjoyed on salads.

PAPRIKA The Portuguese call paprika *colorau* since it is used mainly to add colour to dishes. Unless specified otherwise, use sweet Hungarian paprika in the recipes in this book. Since my first book, *Uma Casa Portuguesa*, was published, I have found that some home cooks are beginning to use smoked Spanish paprika. It is used in Portuguese cooking to infuse a smoky and exotic kick to meals and you'll see it used in some of the recipes here. I like that it allows you to add lots of chouriço flavour and cut down on the actual amount of sausage (and as a result cut down on additional fat) in your dish. If you like, experiment by substituting smoked paprika when sweet paprika is called for.

PARSLEY The Portuguese have a passion for Parsley Dressing (page 280), a rich green sauce that is smothered on fish and boiled potatoes. Parsley is used generously to garnish foods. The flat-leaf Italian style is preferred. Keep a fresh bunch in a glass jar full of water, covered loosely with a paper towel and plastic bag, in the refrigerator.

PEPPER Coarsely ground black pepper is often added for seasoning, while whole or crushed peppercorns flavour marinades. To extract the flavour, crush the peppercorns with a mortar and pestle or heavy pot.

PEPPERS Bell peppers are the most popular peppers used for everyday cooking, although any type of sweet pepper can be used.

PIMENTO PASTE (*CALDA DE PIMENTO* OR RED PEPPER PASTE) This combination of peppers that have been boiled, ground, and salted is a tangy thick seasoning that is added liberally to Azorean dishes. The paste-like consistency makes it perfect for marinades, which is one of its prime uses.

The best place to purchase pimento paste is at a Portuguese grocery store; sweet and hot pimento pastes are available. The hot version is a blend of thin hot red banana peppers and long sweet shepherd peppers. If it is difficult to find, you can easily make your own (page 286), using more or fewer hot peppers according to your own taste. You can use shepherd peppers (available in the fall) or sweet bell peppers. To make a speedy version (when you don't have time to make it from scratch or store-bought pimento is not available), mix ¼ cup (60 mL) puréed grilled red peppers with two teaspoons (10 mL) salt.

In most of the recipes in this book, a mild pimento paste is called for. Use less piri-piri sauce if you are using hot pimento paste. Note that pimento paste is salty, so taste the dish before adding salt.

PIRI-PIRI PEPPER Piri-piri pepper, the explosive hot pepper from Angola and Mozambique, is hard to find. As a substitute, you can use the small red chilies known as Thai chilies, red hot chillies, or dried red chili flakes. If you cannot find these at your grocery store, substitute Tabasco or any hot pepper sauce.

PORK The Portuguese prefer to use fatty pieces of pork for a juicy and tender dish. For equally tasty results, trim off as much fat as possible or choose pork tenderloin and cook only until the meat is no longer pink. (Overcooked pork becomes tough and dry.)

Pork ear, feet, and tail are traditional additions to Portuguese stews and soups (mostly used in stews for added flavour); they have been eliminated from the recipes in this book.

PROSCIUTTO (*PRESUNTO*) Prosciutto is the dry-cured ham found in Italian grocery stores, called *presunto* by the Portuguese. Prosciutto can be used interchangeably with the presunto, which is coated in paprika but is otherwise similar in taste. Thin slices of the deli meat are served in sandwiches and to flavour cooking. Look for fresh moist pieces, and have the butcher cut it into very thin slices. Presunto bones are used to flavour soups or stews.

RICE The Portuguese consume rice almost daily. Usually short-grain rice is preferred; long-grain rice can be substituted for fluffier results. Use short-grain rice in desserts for a creamy texture. Since my first book was published, I have seen more risotto-style dishes in Portuguese restaurants. As a result, arborio rice is now more readily available in Portuguese grocery stores and prepared at home. Purchase and use the highest-quality arborio rice you can find. You can precook the rice until it is almost done; drain, cool, and refrigerate until ready to make the risotto. This preparation helps to avoid soggy rice.

One tip for cooking arborio rice is to heat the stock (or whatever liquid) on low keeping it close by as you are making your risotto. Also, stir the rice occasionally, allowing the rice and liquids to cook in between additions of stock at a lower simmer. When in doubt about doneness, taste to get the texture of the rice just right. Remove when the rice has a bit of bite remaining. Ladle some fresh stock onto the rice just before serving, as the rice will continue to cook and absorb most of the liquids.

ROSEMARY Rosemary is another mainland favourite, fast becoming more widely used in Portuguese cooking in North America. It is especially tasty when used to season roasted meats such as lamb and chicken. Fresh is preferred; chop it finely, combine it with finely chopped thyme, and sprinkle onto roasted meats and stews.

SAFFRON Saffron is used sparingly in Portuguese cooking. Soak it in cooking liquid before using. In Portuguese grocery stores, thick, colourful shredded saffron flowers are sold inexpensively and are used for garnishing.

SARDINES Sardines are most often purchased frozen, due to their availability. They keep well in the freezer and are easily defrosted, washed, and scaled. The fish is not usually gutted when grilled. At least one hour before you plan to grill sardines, sprinkle the fish with coarse salt and set aside in a colander or baking dish until ready to use. Just before grilling, rinse off the salt and pat dry with paper towels; if desired (most people leave the salt on the fish). Salting the fish before cooking, in this manner, will ensure that the sardines will have a firmer texture for cooking.

High heat is required to grill sardines so that they cook quickly and don't dry out (robbing them of their beautiful and delicious omega oil) or stick to the grill. Be careful not to burn them. The sardines' oil, extracted while cooking, drips onto the coals or gas and results in flare-ups, causing the sardines to burn if you don't remove them quickly. If you can, use a specially made fish grill that sandwiches four to five fish at a time and allows you to easily remove it during flare-ups. The fish grill also allows you to easily turn the fish over for the brief periods needed to cook them. (Cooking sardines over low heat for a longer period is a sure way to dry them out.)

SAUSAGES *Chouriço* is the most popular of the Portuguese sausages. The highly flavoured smoked pork sausage is seasoned with lots of garlic, paprika, wine, and pimento paste and smoked for 12 to 24 hours. In some stores that specialize in making chouriço, you can find regional specialties that provide variation in the spicing; for example, vinho verde (green wine) chouriço from northern Portugal or Azorean-style chouriço made with parsley and extra-hot pimento paste. (Spanish chorizo is not the same sausage as the Portuguese chouriço; however, where no chouriço is available, Spanish, Italian, or kielbasa sausages can be used instead.)

Chouriço is available sweet or hot. Hot is preferred because of the zesty perk it adds to dishes. Although it is already cooked, if you are serving it simply as a snack, you may want to grill, barbecue, or pan-fry it until warm and serve with bread. To store it, wrap the chouriço in an airtight bag and refrigerate for a few days or freeze for up to three months.

Linguiça is similar in taste to chouriço, though it is sometimes narrower. It can be referred to as homemade chouriço.

Morcela is a delicious sausage made of pig's blood. The reddish-brown links are flavoured with cinnamon; often, depending on the region, the sausage is stuffed with rice or breadcrumbs. Although not used often enough in cooking, it is a favourite side dish simply boiled or pan-fried.

Salpicão contains many of the same ingredients as chouriço, but it is cured and lightly smoked and is less fatty and is shorter and thicker in shape. It can be substituted for chouriço.

Lean smoked bacon pieces (*toucinho*) are often substituted for chouriço or used in Portuguese dishes in addition to chouriço for extra flavour.

SHELLFISH All shellfish should be bought alive, frozen, or already cooked.

Clams and mussels should be purchased tightly closed. If they do not close when tapped, do not buy them. Manila clams can be substituted for the cockles traditionally used in Portuguese cooking; use the smallest clams you can find. Scrub clams and mussels with a wire brush under cold running water to remove sand and grit, and pull the beards off the mussels. Discard any that do not open after cooking.

Crabs should be rinsed thoroughly under cold running water to remove any sand between the shell and legs. Smaller crabs are generally preferable.

Limpets are shellfish that attach themselves to rocks and cliffs by the water. They are often hard to spot because of their greyish-brown colour. They usually must be pried from the rocks with a sharp knife. Limpets are plentiful in the Azores. Simply rinse them and serve live, or barbecue briefly for a delicious and simple meal. Limpets can also be tossed into a rice dish or slathered with one of the delicious sauces from the sauces chapter.

Shrimp should be cooked in the shell for extra-tender and flavourful results. Simply pull off the legs and, using kitchen shears, cut each shrimp shell along the back. Pull out the intestinal vein, if desired, but leave on the shell and tail. Rinse under cold running water before using.

SQUID AND CUTTLEFISH Squid and cuttlefish can be used interchangeably; they are similar in taste and appearance and are both often identified by the Italian name *calamari*. Cuttlefish and jumbo squid are much thicker than the regular-sized squid more readily found in grocery stores. Cuttlefish has a slightly sweeter taste. Both are usually available pre-cleaned. If pre-cleaned, examine inside the sac for any attached entrails and discard them, and rinse well under cold running water.

You can clean the squid or cuttlefish yourself. Grab hold of the body and, using your fingers, grab the plastic-like backbone that is attached to the inside of the squid sac. Detach the bone and pull it out; all of the intestines should come out with it. Empty the sac by placing it upside down and squeezing from tip to bottom. Make sure the sac is empty and remove any remaining stringy entrails. If desired, pull off the purple skin and back fins (they should come off easily using your fingernail) and discard. Using a sharp knife, separate the tentacles from the rest of the body by cutting them off just above the eyes. In the centre of the tentacles you will find a hard black beak; remove it. Discard everything but the tentacles and sac. Rinse thoroughly before using. (Squid and cuttlefish can also be purchased cleaned and/or frozen. If buying frozen, partially defrosting it before using will make cutting an easier task. Examine inside the sac for any attached entrails and rinse well under cold running water before using.) If barbecuing large squid or cuttlefish, cut the body in three or four places in even intervals, without separating the pieces. These incisions will help ensure the molluscs cook evenly.

SWEET POTATOES The sweet potato, which is native to South America and the west Indies, is popular with Portuguese North Americans. The favourite preparation is simply boiled or baked. For a special occasion, slice into shoestrings and fry until golden brown.

TARO ROOT This dark-brown root vegetable is called *inhames* by the Portuguese. It is usually boiled until tender, peeled, and chopped and served as a side dish. It can be purchased at Portuguese, West Indian, and Chinese grocery stores.

THYME Fresh thyme is used to season roasted meats and stews. Fresh is preferred; chop finely and combine with finely chopped rosemary and sprinkle onto roasted meats and stews.

TOMATO Tomatoes are used liberally in Portuguese dishes. Often fresh or canned tomatoes are used in stews, which lends a full-bodied flavour. For the best flavour, use canned San Marzano tomatoes if you can find them.

VINEGAR Because wine is made in many Portuguese homes, homemade vinegar is usually readily available. Homemade vinegar adds a stronger and more pungent flavour than regular vinegar. Substitute store-bought red wine vinegar or balsamic wine vinegar. For a lighter flavour, use white wine vinegar. When added near the end of cooking, sherry vinegar will add a sweet finish to stews and other dishes.

WINE Both wine and beer play major roles in Portuguese cooking. Although the wine traditionally used in cooking is usually homemade, you can also use commercial wines. Often wine or beer are substituted for each other, although the flavour will be quite different. The wine used can vary according to the region; for example, vinho verde (green wine) is favoured in northern Portugal. If alcohol is a concern, remember that most of the alcoholic content of wine and beer is burned off during cooking.

Port and Madeira are dessert wines used in cooking as well as to end a special meal. Madeira is used in many savoury dishes, whereas the sweet-tasting port is more appropriate for flavouring desserts. Buy a bottle of tawny port for sipping after a meal; it goes well with many Portuguese desserts. Madeira and port can be used interchangeably; substituting other liqueurs will not give you the same results.

Aguardente means "firewater" and is moonshine that can still be purchased homemade in small towns in Portugal. Commercial Aguardente can be purchased in liquor stores specializing in Portuguese liquor. Substitute brandy if you cannot find it.

UTENSILS

Nothing more extravagant than regular kitchen utensils are required for Portuguese cooking. The essentials include a good skillet, chopping knife, stockpot, fine-mesh sieve to strain sauces, lots of wooden spoons, a barbecue for summer cooking, and a lot of resealable bags for marinating. A few more unusual utensils are noted below; some are for special uses. If you do not have them, you can make do without.

ALGUIDAR An *alcatra* (marinated roast) is prepared in a special earthenware pot known as an *alguidar.* The odd-shaped dish looks like a flowerpot and is used only for making and serving alcatra. You can use a regular roasting pan or baking dish with equally satisfying results, although the alguidar also makes a spectacular serving dish.

The alguidar must be seasoned two to three days before using it for the first time. Liberally rub the inside and outside walls of the dish with lard. Immerse the dish completely in cold water and soak for two to three days. Drain the water and clean off the lard with hot water. Add six whole potatoes and fill the *alguidar* to the brim with water. Place in a 400°F (200°C) oven and cook for one hour after the water begins to sparkle (it does not really come to a boil). If the water level goes down, replenish the dish. Discard the potatoes and water; the dish is now ready to use. For the first year, or if you do not use your dish regularly, soak the dish in water for a few hours or overnight before using. The dish is considered "broken in" when it has a deep-brown coating and is no longer a peachy clay colour.

CATAPLANA This clam-shaped cooking utensil from the Algarve region is used to cook Clams in Cataplana (page 100). The spectacular meal is brought to the table in this special pan, which when opened up provides a receptacle for the clamshells. A wok or large pot with a tight-fitting lid can be substituted.

Once only used for the clam dish, the cataplana is now used to cook a number of Portuguese dishes. Many tourists who return home with the copper dish are unaware that the shiny coating must be removed before using or the exterior will quickly tarnish. Scrub the dish liberally with paint and tarnish remover. The dish is often hung on the wall when not in use.

MOULDS A number of heat-resistant tin or clay moulds are used to make the delicious sweet and savoury desserts that the Portuguese are famous for. Any shape can be used, but the most popular are ring moulds. Individual serving moulds can also be used. Adjust the cooking times for smaller moulds. Test doneness with a toothpick; if it comes out clean, the dessert is cooked.

Cheese moulds are used for making homemade cheese. They look like small flour sifters with holes in the sides for draining the whey. You can also use perforated tuna cans or decorative baskets lined with cheesecloth.

MORTAR AND PESTLE Many cooks believe food does not taste the same unless you use a mortar and pestle to mash garlic and spices to a paste-like texture for marinades. If you do not have one, use a small bowl and the back of a spoon, or simply chop and blend ingredients in a bowl. Using a food processor or blender tends to liquidize the ingredients rather than mash them. If using a food processor, pulse the ingredients for short bursts to get a mash-like consistency.

APPETIZERS AND LIGHT DISHES

Acepipes e Pratos Ligeiros

Petiscos, appetizers or snack-type meals similar to Spanish *tapas*, are typically enjoyed with a glass of wine and in the company of friends and family. These small dishes range in complexity from simple yet tasty spreads served with bread to fluffy mini-omelettes and savoury pastries.

I like to keep a variety of Portuguese treats on hand in the pantry so that tasty *petisco* offerings are never more than a few minutes' preparation time away. A simple cheese platter can be made in a snap with blocks of Serra da Estrela or São Jorge cheese and some homemade Quince Marmalade Slices (page 290). Pieces of fresh or dried figs can be wrapped in thin slices of prosciutto ham and topped with spoonfuls of homemade Tomato Jam (page 288). Drizzle mild Creamy Fresh Cheese (page 49) with assertive and salty Red Pepper Pimento Paste Seasoning (page 286). Pan-fry sweet or spicy chouriço sausage or, for a more dramatic presentation often seen in Portuguese restaurants, flambé it tableside.

You can quickly prepare a fresh Portuguese salad by sprinkling slices of tomatoes and rings of onions and peppers with oregano. Serve the salad with olive oil and white wine vinegar alongside for drizzling, to taste. For a heartier salad, combine fresh baby broad beans (frozen if not in season) with grilled octopus and serve with an oil and garlic dressing. Or try fresh-tasting Cod Carpaccio (page 54) alongside Green Beans in Light Batter (page 52) for a light meal.

Some of the preparations, such as precooking octopus and soaking cod, can be done a few days ahead of time until you are ready to put your meals together. Other time-consuming *petiscos*, such as Cod Croquettes (page 44), and Shrimp Turnovers (page 38), can also be made ahead and frozen, then thawed and prepared just before guests arrive.

Add a homemade touch by making some of the *petiscos* in this section and combine them with some store-bought Portuguese treasures. Olive Paste (page 65) makes a subtle and hearty snack when spread thinly over toasted cornbread, and is a snap to make with or without homemade marinated olives. You can also top toast with Grilled or Marinated Sardines (page 57) and a helping of fresh-tasting Red Pepper and Olive Relish (page 284).

Serve some of these light dishes, such as Green Eggs (page 60), with a simple Portuguese salad and cornbread, and you will feel like you are in a sunny restaurant in the south of Portugal.

APPETIZERS AND LIGHT DISHES

Acepipes e Pratos Ligeiros

GREEN ONION AND PARSLEY MINI-OMELETTES

Tortas

MAKES 2 TO 4 SERVINGS

6 eggs

4 green onions (white and
    green parts), finely chopped

½ cup (125 mL) chopped
    fresh parsley

2 Tbsp (30 mL) corn flour

1 Tbsp (15 mL) dry breadcrumbs

1 tsp (5 mL) baking powder

½ tsp (2 mL) fine salt

1 Tbsp (15 mL) vegetable oil

Tortas—miniature omelettes—were a staple on the island of Pico during hard times when my mother-in-law was a girl. Farm-fresh eggs diluted with water could be stretched to feed the entire family. These simple Portuguese omelettes, with or without filling, are usually served with Parsley Dressing (page 280). If desired, you can also make one large omelette and cut it into wedges. This meal is usually paired with sweet potatoes, cornbread, and salad.

In a large bowl, beat the eggs until light. Gradually beat in the green onions and parsley.

In a separate bowl, combine the corn flour, breadcrumbs, baking powder and salt; beat into the egg mixture.

In a large skillet, heat the oil over medium-high heat. Spoon 2 Tbsp (30 mL) of the egg mixture into the skillet; use a spatula to help form a round 2 to 3 inches (5 to 8 cm) in diameter and ½ inch (1 cm) thick. Cook the omelettes in batches with no more than 4 in the skillet at once.

Using a spatula, lift the edges of the omelettes and tilt the skillet so that any uncooked egg mixture runs to the bottom. Cook for 2 to 3 minutes per side, until golden brown. Slide the cooked omelettes onto a warmed plate and transfer them to the oven to keep warm. Repeat with the remaining batter, stirring the mixture before forming into omelettes to prevent the corn flour from settling at the bottom. Add more oil to the skillet, if necessary.

As much as 1 cup (250 mL) flaked cooked cod or tuna or leftover meat can be added to the batter to make hearty omelettes that look like croquettes.

TOMATO AND EGG SPREAD

Pasta de Ovos e Tomate

These creamy eggs and tomatoes are delicious on baked potatoes, canned tuna, fried fish, or omelettes. After the spread has been refrigerated for a few hours, serve pâté-style on toast, topped with Pickled Peppers (page 221).

Purée the tomatoes in a food mill; discard the skin and seeds. Drain the excess juice from the tomatoes.

In a large heavy saucepan or Dutch oven, heat the oil over medium-high heat; cook the onion and garlic, stirring occasionally, for 3 to 5 minutes, until softened.

Add the puréed tomatoes and basil. Bring to a boil over high heat, stirring to scrape up any brown bits from the bottom of the pan. Reduce the heat to low and simmer, uncovered, for 1 hour, until reduced by half or thickened with no liquid remaining.

In a bowl, whisk the eggs, salt, and pepper. Add them to the tomato sauce, pouring in a thin stream and whisking briskly to combine well. Cook for 10 minutes, whisking often, until the sauce is thick and creamy and well blended. Taste and adjust the seasonings. If serving it as a spread, cover and refrigerate for 2 to 3 hours. Garnish with parsley and olives.

> When puréeing tomatoes, I prefer to use a food mill since it removes both the skin and seeds (which can be a little bitter) and this produces a sweeter spread.

MAKES ABOUT 3 CUPS (750 ML)

3 lb (1.5 kg) tomatoes

¼ cup (60 mL) olive oil

1 large onion, diced

1 clove garlic, diced

2 Tbsp (30 mL) chopped fresh basil

4 eggs, lightly beaten

½ tsp (2 mL) fine salt

Pinch coarsely ground
    black pepper

Chopped fresh parsley,
    for garnish

Chopped black olives,
    for garnish

CHOURIÇO PÂTÉ

Pâté de Chouriço

MAKES 4 TO 6 SERVINGS

8 oz (240 g) chouriço

1 red bell pepper

1 Tbsp (15 mL) Madeira or port

2 tsp (10 mL) olive oil

2 Tbsp (30 mL) chopped onion

1 small clove garlic, minced

10 black olives, pitted and roughly chopped

Fine salt and coarsely ground black pepper, to taste

Pitted black olives, for garnish

This delicate blend of chouriço, sweet red pepper, and plump olives captures the essence of Portuguese food. Easy to make, this spread is a wonderful appetizer or delicious snack. Any Portuguese sausage can be substituted for the chouriço. Serve with piri-piri sauce on thin slices of cornbread with extra black olives on the side.

In a small saucepan, cover the chouriço with water; bring to a boil over medium-high heat. Reduce the heat, cover, and simmer for about 5 minutes, until the chouriço is pink. Drain and set aside until cool enough to handle. Using a sharp knife, remove the skin and slice the chouriço into 1-inch (2.5 cm) pieces. Remove and discard any fat. Set aside.

Core the pepper, cut it in half lengthwise, and remove the seeds. Place the pepper on a baking sheet skin side up. Broil about 4 inches (10 cm) from the heat until the skin is blackened, 10 to 15 minutes. Transfer to a paper bag, seal, and set aside to cool. When cool enough to handle, peel.

In a blender or food processor, process the prepared chouriço just until the consistency of fine ground beef. Add the roasted pepper and Madeira and process with on/off pulses just until blended (be careful not to overprocess). Transfer to a bowl and set aside.

In a small skillet, heat the oil over medium heat; cook the onion and garlic for 2 to 3 minutes, until transparent. Transfer the onion and garlic with the cooking oil to the sausage mixture, add the olives, and mix with a wooden spoon until well blended. Taste and season with salt and pepper, if necessary. Pack into a small crock or individual ramekins. Garnish with olives (an olive per ramekin). Cover and refrigerate for up to 1 day.

SHRIMP TURNOVERS

Rissóis de Camarão

MAKES ABOUT 70 TURNOVERS

SHRIMP FILLING

2 lb (1 kg) large shrimp, in shells

4 cups (1 L) boiling water

1 tsp (5 mL) fine salt

Pinch coarsely ground
   black pepper

⅓ cup (80 mL) butter

2 onions, finely chopped

1 cup (250 mL) whole milk

1 Tbsp (15 mL) all-purpose flour

2 egg yolks

3 Tbsp (45 mL) lemon juice

2 Tbsp (30 mL) chopped fresh
   parsley

DOUGH

2 cups (500 mL) water

2 cups (500 mL) whole milk

Peel of 1 lemon

¼ cup (60 mL) butter

1 tsp (5 mL) fine salt

4½ cups (1.125 L) all-purpose flour

COATING

2 egg whites

3 eggs, lightly beaten

2 cups (500 mL) dry breadcrumbs

Vegetable oil for deep-frying

These savoury pastries are made from a dough that is partially cooked then rolled out and deep-fried. The pastry shell can be used for a number of different fillings, although these shrimp turnovers are the most popular.

TO MAKE THE SHRIMP FILLING In a saucepan over medium-high heat, add the shrimp to the boiling water. Add salt and pepper. Simmer for 2 to 3 minutes, until the shrimp turns pink. Using a slotted spoon, transfer the shrimp to a large bowl; reserve cooking water. Peel the shrimp and pull off the legs and tails; using a sharp knife, pull out the intestinal veins, if desired. Coarsely chop the shrimp.

In a large skillet, melt ⅓ cup (80 mL) butter over medium-high heat. Cook the onions for 3 to 5 minutes, until translucent but not browned. Stir in the shrimp. Cook for 1 minute and remove from heat.

In a small bowl, combine ¼ cup (60 mL) milk and 1 Tbsp (15 mL) flour until smooth; stir in the remaining ¾ cup (185 mL) milk and ⅓ cup (80 mL) reserved cooking water. Add to the pan with the shrimp and onion mixture and stir until well combined. Bring mixture to a boil over medium-high heat; reduce the heat and simmer gently, stirring occasionally, for 5 to 6 minutes, until slightly thickened. Slowly whisk egg yolks into the pan, stirring continuously for 1 minute. Stir in the lemon juice and parsley and cook for 1 minute. Taste and adjust the seasonings. Cover the surface of the mixture with waxed paper to prevent a skin from forming and set aside to cool.

TO MAKE THE DOUGH In a large, heavy pot over medium-high heat, bring the water, milk, lemon peel, butter, and salt to a boil. Reduce the heat to medium and stir in the flour with a wooden spoon (the heat will soften the dough). Cook for 5 minutes, stirring often, until a ball has formed and a spoon can stand in the centre. Remove from the heat and discard the lemon peel. Set the dough aside until cool enough to handle. For best results, handle the dough while still warm.

On a lightly floured surface, knead the dough until smooth. Divide into 5 equal pieces. Roll out one piece to a ⅛-inch (3 mm) thickness. (Wrap the rest in a damp kitchen towel or place in a resealable bag to keep moist and warm; if the dough becomes cold and difficult to handle, rub it with vegetable oil.)

TO ASSEMBLE THE TURNOVERS Using a 3-inch (8 cm) round cookie cutter, cut out circles. Place 1 tsp (5 mL) of the filling in the centre of each circle, leaving a ¼-inch (6 mm) border. Fold the dough over the filling to form a half moon and pinch the edges together gently but firmly. Place the half moons on a floured baking sheet. Repeat with the remaining dough and filling.

In a shallow dish, beat together egg whites with whole eggs. In another shallow dish or in a resealable bag, place breadcrumbs. One at a time, dip the half moons into the egg, then into the breadcrumbs, gently turning or shaking the turnovers to coat all over. (The turnovers can be frozen at this point.)

In a large skillet over medium-high heat, heat about a 1-inch (2.5 cm) depth of oil to 375°F (190°C). Fry the turnovers 5 or 6 at a time for about 2 minutes per side, until browned. Drain on a wire rack. Can be served warm or at room temperature. If serving warm, transfer to a baking sheet and warm in a 200°F (95°C) oven.

Uncooked turnovers can be frozen ahead of time and deep-fried (from frozen) just before serving (increase frying time by 2 to 3 minutes). Or, if desired, freeze cooked turnovers and reheat just before serving by spreading them out in a single layer on a lightly greased baking sheet and baking at 325°F (160°C) for 15 to 20 minutes.

SHRIMP AND PROSCIUTTO

Camarão e Presunto

MAKES 16 WRAPPED SHRIMP

16 large shrimp, in shells

¼ cup (60 mL) lemon juice

1 clove garlic, minced

2 Tbsp (30 mL) chopped
    fresh parsley

½ tsp (2 mL) fine salt

¼ tsp (1 mL) coarsely
    ground black pepper

8 thin slices prosciutto

Vegetable oil for deep-frying

¼ cup (60 mL) all-purpose flour

2 eggs, lightly beaten

½ cup (125 mL) dry breadcrumbs

These delicious appetizers—marinated shrimp wrapped in prosciutto—are so tempting that it is hard to limit yourself to just a few. For a striking presentation, alternate the shrimp with sliced cantaloupe on a bed of watercress. Most of this recipe can be prepared ahead of time, leaving you free to entertain your guests. Fry just before serving.

TO PREPARE THE SHRIMP Remove the shells and pull off the legs, leaving the tails on. Using a sharp knife, remove the intestinal vein, if desired. Rinse under cold running water and pat dry. Set aside.

In a large shallow bowl, mix the lemon juice, garlic, parsley, salt, and pepper. Add the shrimp to the marinade, turning to coat well. Cover and set aside at room temperature for 30 minutes or refrigerate for 1 hour, turning occasionally.

Cut each prosciutto slice in half. Remove the shrimp from the marinade, letting the excess marinade drip off and wrap each prosciutto half around the body of each shrimp, leaving the tail exposed. Hold the prosciutto in place with a toothpick inserted crosswise through the body. Discard the marinade.

In a skillet, heat a 2- to 3-inch (5 to 8 cm) depth of oil over medium-high heat. In a small, shallow bowl, beat eggs. In another shallow dish, place breadcrumbs. One at a time, dip each wrapped shrimp into the flour, the egg, and then dust with the breadcrumbs, gently turning to coat all over. Deep-fry shrimp in batches (no more than 5 or 6 at a time) for about 2 minutes per side, until lightly golden; add additional oil, if necessary. Using a slotted spoon, transfer the cooked shrimp to paper towels to drain. Serve warm or at room temperature.

CLAMS IN CORIANDER SAUCE

Amêijoas à Bulhão Pato

This classic appetizer is easy to prepare. Use the smallest Manila clams you can find and serve with crusty bread and a green salad. The pan juices of the clams mix with the coriander, creating a sauce that is perfect for drizzling over your finished dish.

Scrub the clams with a stiff brush under cold running water to remove surface sand and grit. Set aside.

In a large heavy saucepan, heat the butter and oil over medium-high heat until the butter melts. Add the garlic and cook for 1 minute, until soft. Add the clams, wine, bay leaves, salt, and pepper. Cover and cook for about 5 minutes, until the clamshells open. Discard any clams that do not open.

Add the coriander and stir. Ladle the clams into serving bowls and drizzle remaining liquid overtop. Serve immediately with lemon wedges.

MAKES 4 APPETIZER SERVINGS OR 2 MAIN-COURSE SERVINGS

2 lb (1 kg) Manila clams

2 Tbsp (30 mL) butter

2 Tbsp (30 mL) olive oil

4 cloves garlic, minced

⅔ cup (160 mL) dry white wine

3 bay leaves

¼ tsp (1 mL) fine salt

¼ tsp (1 mL) coarsely ground black pepper

½ cup (125 mL) chopped fresh coriander

Lemon wedges

OYSTERS ON THE HALF SHELL WITH ALMONDS

Ostras com Amêndoa

Oysters are usually eaten raw with a squirt of lemon. This recipe combines some favourite Portuguese ingredients for a spectacular appetizer.

TO CLEAN THE OYSTERS Scrub the oysters with a stiff brush under cold running water to remove surface sand and grit. Carefully shuck, trying not to spill their juice. Arrange the oysters on the half shell, side by side, on a baking dish. Set aside.

TO MAKE THE FILLING In a bowl, combine all of the filling ingredients. Place about 1½ tsp (7 mL) on top of each oyster.

TO MAKE THE TOPPING Combine breadcrumbs, cheese, and parsley; sprinkle over each oyster.

Bake on the top rack of a preheated 425°F (220°C) oven for 10 to 12 minutes, until heated through. Serve immediately with toast triangles.

TO ROAST A RED PEPPER

OVEN METHOD Using a sharp knife, cut the pepper in half lengthwise and remove the core and seeds. Transfer to a baking sheet skin side up. Broil about 4 inches (10 cm) from the heat until the skin blackens in parts, about 6 to 8 minutes. Plunge into ice water and set aside for about 5 minutes. Use a knife to scrape off the skin.

GRILL METHOD Grill the red pepper on high over direct heat (or about 4 inches/10 cm from hot coals) for 2 to 3 minutes per side or until blackened in parts. Plunge into ice water and set aside for about 5 minutes. Use a knife to scrape off the skin.

MAKES 18 OYSTERS

18 oysters

FILLING

½ cup (125 mL) butter, melted

3 Tbsp (45 mL) chopped unsalted, unroasted almonds

2 tsp (10 mL) dry breadcrumbs

2 tsp (10 mL) finely chopped roasted or raw red bell pepper

2 tsp (10 mL) anise liqueur

1 tsp (5 mL) lemon juice

1 green onion, chopped

Fine salt and coarsely ground black pepper, to taste

TOPPING

4 tsp (20 mL) dry breadcrumbs

4 tsp (20 mL) grated São Jorge cheese or sharp cheddar cheese

1 tsp (5 mL) chopped fresh parsley

COD CROQUETTES

Bolinhos de Bacalhau

MAKES ABOUT 60 CROQUETTES

2 lb (1 kg) salt cod

1 lb (500 g) potatoes, peeled (about 3)

2 Tbsp (30 mL) olive oil

1 large onion, finely chopped

3 eggs

½ cup (125 mL) chopped fresh parsley

1 Tbsp (15 mL) pimento paste (optional)

2 egg whites

Fine salt, to taste

2 eggs, lightly beaten

1 cup (250 mL) fresh breadcrumbs

Vegetable oil for deep-frying

There are a number of recipes for cod croquettes, but whipped egg whites make this version especially light. The pimento paste makes these croquettes distinctly Azorean; omit them if you prefer a more continental flavouring. These croquettes can be served as finger food, with bean salad and a green salad as a lunch or light dinner, or on a bed of lettuce as a first course. Serve with piri-piri sauce or Pimento Mayonnaise (page 224) for a splash of flavour and colour.

TO PREPARE THE SALT COD Place the cod in a large bowl with enough cold water to cover it completely. Cover the bowl in plastic wrap and refrigerate for 24 to 48 hours or longer, changing the water 2 to 3 times per day, until the fish is spongy in texture and desalted. (Larger pieces of fish may take longer.) Drain and discard the water.

TO PREPARE THE CROQUETTES In a saucepan, cover the prepared cod with fresh cold water; bring just to a boil over medium heat. Reduce the heat to low and simmer for 3 minutes (do not continue to boil). Drain and set aside until cool enough to handle. Remove the bones and skin and, using a fork, finely shred. Set aside.

In a saucepan over medium heat, boil the potatoes in water for about 20 to 30 minutes, just until tender. Drain and set aside until cool enough to handle. Finely dice the potatoes. Set aside.

In a saucepan, heat the oil over medium heat. Add the onion and cook, stirring occasionally, for 3 minutes, until tender.

In a large bowl, add the shredded cod, cooked potatoes, and sautéed onion and mix until just combined. One at a time, beat in the whole eggs, stirring well after each addition. Add the parsley and pimento paste and mix well. Set aside.

In a separate bowl, beat the egg whites until stiff peaks form. Fold into the cod mixture. Taste and add salt only if necessary.

Using your hands, carefully shape the mixture into 1-inch (2.5 cm) ovals or fingers to form the croquettes. In a small, shallow bowl, beat the eggs. In another shallow dish, place the breadcrumbs. One at a time, dip each croquette into the egg then roll in the breadcrumbs, gently turning to coat all over. Transfer to a greased baking sheet and refrigerate for 30 minutes.

In a large heavy skillet, heat vegetable oil to a depth of about 1 inch (2.5 cm) over medium-high heat. Cook croquettes in batches, 5 or 6 at a time, for 2 to 3 minutes per batch, until evenly browned and heated through. Turn often with a slotted spoon. Transfer the cooked croquettes to a plate lined with paper towels to drain. Keep warm in a 200°F (95°C) oven.

Serve warm, or cool completely and transfer to an airtight container and refrigerate for up to 5 days or freeze for up to 3 months.

Don't worry about making too many. The croquettes can be tucked into lunches and quickly disappear just sitting in the refrigerator. (They also freeze well.)

SHRIMP CROQUETTES WITH PINE NUTS AND LEMON SAUCE

Croquetes de Camarão

MAKES ABOUT 30 CROQUETTES

SAUCE

2 Tbsp (30 mL) butter

2 Tbsp (30 mL) all-purpose flour

1 cup (250 mL) hot whole milk

¼ tsp (1 mL) fine salt

1 tsp (5 mL) finely grated
lemon zest

4 tsp (20 mL) lemon juice

Pinch freshly grated nutmeg

Pinch coarsely ground
black pepper

1 egg yolk, lightly beaten

These croquettes are usually served on a bed of lettuce as a first course or snack. The pine nuts are an Alentejan influence, as the province has an abundant supply. Crisp on the outside and creamy inside, these croquettes should be eaten with a fork. Freezing as instructed makes the batter easier to work with. If you like, you can substitute crab or cooked ham for the shrimp. Reserve any leftover sauce to serve with the croquettes.

TO MAKE THE SAUCE In a small saucepan, melt the butter over medium heat; whisk in the flour. Reduce the heat to medium-low and cook, stirring constantly, for about 3 minutes, until smooth and golden but not browned. Whisk in the hot milk. Increase the heat to medium and bring to a boil; stir in the salt, lemon zest, lemon juice, nutmeg, and pepper. Reduce the heat to low and cook, stirring often, for 5 to 7 minutes, until slightly thickened.

Remove the saucepan from the heat and whisk in the egg yolk. Return the pan to the heat and whisk continuously for 1 minute, until the sauce is smooth and creamy. Taste and adjust the seasonings. If desired, strain. Cover the surface of the sauce with waxed paper to prevent a skin from forming and set aside.

TO MAKE THE CROQUETTES In a large bowl, toss the shrimp with the lemon juice and pepper. Set aside.

In a saucepan, heat the butter and oil over medium-high heat until the butter is melted. Sauté onion and garlic, stirring occasionally, for 3 to 5 minutes, until softened. Remove from the heat and set aside.

In a separate bowl, toss the bread with the milk. Set aside for 5 minutes, until the milk is absorbed. Using your hands, squeeze the bread and discard the milk (the bread should be wet but not soggy). Set aside.

Drain the shrimp and return it to the bowl. Add the prepared bread, the onion mixture, pine nuts, parsley, Madeira, nutmeg, piri-piri sauce, salt, pepper, and enough sauce to just moisten everything (the mixture should stick together when you form a ball). Taste and adjust the seasonings, if needed.

Spread the mixture evenly over a greased baking sheet and freeze until cold, about 1 hour. Using your hands, carefully shape the mixture into 2-inch (5 cm) ovals or fingers to form the croquettes. In a small shallow bowl, beat the eggs. In another shallow dish, place the breadcrumbs. One at a time, toss each croquette in flour, then dip each croquette into the egg and then roll it in the breadcrumbs, gently turning to coat all over. Transfer to a greased baking sheet. Chill in the freezer until the croquettes hold their shape, about 1 hour. Set aside at room temperate for about 30 minutes before frying.

In a large heavy skillet over medium-high heat, heat vegetable oil to a depth of about 1 inch (2.5 cm) to 375°F (190°C). Fry the croquettes in batches (5 or 6 at a time) for 2 to 3 minutes per batch, turning often with a slotted spoon, until golden brown and heated through. Transfer the cooked croquettes to a plate lined with paper towels to drain. Serve immediately.

CROQUETTES

3 cups (750 mL) chopped cooked shrimp

3 Tbsp (45 mL) lemon juice

¼ tsp (1 mL) coarsely ground black pepper

1 Tbsp (15 mL) butter

1 Tbsp (15 mL) olive oil

1 onion, chopped

2 cloves garlic, minced

3 slices bread, torn into pieces (about 6 oz/180 g)

½ cup (125 mL) whole milk

¼ cup (60 mL) pine nuts

½ cup (125 mL) chopped fresh parsley

2 Tbsp (30 mL) Madeira

¼ tsp (1 mL) freshly grated nutmeg

1 tsp (5 mL) piri-piri sauce or Tabasco sauce

½ tsp (2 mL) fine salt

Coarsely ground black pepper, to taste

½ cup (125 mL) all-purpose flour

2 eggs, lightly beaten

1 cup (250 mL) dry breadcrumbs

Vegetable oil for deep-frying

SPICY SHRIMP

Camarão com Pimentos

MAKES ABOUT 30 SHRIMP

1 lb (500 g) large shrimp, in shells

3 Tbsp (45 mL) pimento paste

3 Tbsp (45 mL) olive oil

2 cloves garlic, minced

1 tsp (5 mL) piri-piri sauce or
    Tabasco sauce

1 tsp (5 mL) white wine vinegar

1 bay leaf

1 tsp (5 mL) Worcestershire sauce
    (optional)

This rustic Azorean-style appetizer is full of flavour and easy to prepare. Use hot pimento paste for an extra spicy dish.

TO PREPARE THE SHRIMP Remove the shells and pull off the legs, leaving the tails on. Using kitchen shears, cut each shrimp shell along its back. Using a sharp knife, remove the intestinal vein, if desired. Rinse under cold running water and pat dry with paper towels. Transfer the shrimp to a resealable bag and place the bag in a large bowl.

In a small bowl, combine pimento paste, oil, garlic, piri-piri sauce, vinegar, bay leaf, and Worcestershire sauce. Pour the marinade into the bag, over the shrimp; seal the bag and gently turn it over to coat the shrimp. Refrigerate for 6 hours or overnight. Before cooking, let the shrimp stand at room temperature for 30 minutes.

In a well-greased baking dish, arrange the shrimp, with marinade, in a single layer. Transfer to the oven, 4 to 5 inches (10 to 12 cm) from the heat, and broil for 5 minutes. Turn the shrimp over, brush with the marinade in the pan, and broil for 2 to 3 minutes more, until the shrimp are pink and firm. Transfer the shrimp to a platter and brush each with some of the remaining baked marinade. Serve immediately with toast triangles.

CREAMY FRESH CHEESE

Queijo Fresco

This light Azorean cheese is traditionally spread on cornbread and served as a midday or after-drink snack with a side order of marinated olives and a glass of wine.

Be sure to make this ahead of time so the cheese will be spreadable (in 18 hours) or thick enough to slice (in two days). Drizzle pimento paste over the cheese for a kick of flavour and colour. It can also be served with Quince Marmalade Slices (page 290) and dusted with cinnamon as a sweet treat.

In a small bowl, dissolve the rennet tablets in water.

In a heavy saucepan over low heat, combine the liquid rennet and remaining ingredients. Using a wooden spoon, mix the ingredients thoroughly for about 5 minutes, until the salt is dissolved and the mixture lukewarm. To make sure the milk does not curdle, keep the temperature between 98° to 105°F (36.6° to 41°C), and do not boil. Immediately remove the pan from the heat, cover, and set aside in a warm place for 2 hours to allow the milk to form soft curds (the mixture should resemble yogurt).

Using a slotted spoon, transfer the curds into a 3-inch (8 cm) bamboo steamer lined with 2 layers of cheesecloth. (You can also use small baskets or other food-safe moulds with holes in the bottom and sides to allow the liquid whey to drain.) Fill the mould to the top, pressing down on the curds to allow excess whey to drain. Cover with cheesecloth. Set a small plate on top and press down to force the liquid whey out of the soft curds; discard the excess whey.

Method continues . . .

MAKES ABOUT 1 CUP (250 ML)

2 rennet tablets

2 Tbsp (30 mL) lukewarm water

4 cups (1 L) whole milk

1 tsp (5 mL) fine salt

CREAMY FRESH CHEESE
continued . . .

Set the mould on a dish to catch any liquid that continues to drain, and refrigerate for 24 hours (although it can be eaten after 18 hours if you prefer very soft ricotta-like cheese). Drain the excess liquid occasionally, especially in the first 2 hours. After 24 hours the cheese will be firm to touch and most of the excess whey will be drained. For a firmer cheese for serving and slicing, refrigerate for an additional day, continuing to drain whey until ready to serve (although liquid will be minimal). The cheese can be left to set for up to 3 days total.

To serve, remove the cheese from the mould and place on a decorative platter. Unused cheese may be stored in an airtight container and refrigerated for up to 4 more days.

Rennet tablets can be purchased at your local drugstore or at some specialty supermarkets.

When goat's milk is substituted for cow's milk, the cheese takes on a grassy flavour.

GREEN BEANS IN LIGHT BATTER

Peixinhos da Horta

MAKES 3–4 SERVINGS

10 oz (300 grams) green beans, tips removed

1 tsp (5 mL) fine salt

½ cup (125 mL) all-purpose flour

⅓ cup (80 mL) water

1 egg, separated

½ tsp (2 mL) each fine salt and coarsely ground black pepper, to taste

Vegetable oil for deep-frying

Peixinhos da Horta literally means "fish from the garden"—an apt name for these tempura-style green beans that resemble little fish when cooked. The beans are fried together, two to three pieces at a time, with the help of a light coating of batter. Serve these as a snack with piri-piri sauce for a dash of heat or with Cod Croquettes (page 44) for a light lunch or dinner.

In a saucepan, cook the green beans in water with 1 tsp (5mL) salt until tender-crisp, about 2 to 3 minutes (they will cook further once battered). Drain, pat dry with paper towels, and set aside to cool.

In a bowl, whisk the flour and water until a thick paste forms. Add the egg yolk, and salt and pepper and mix well. Set aside.

In a bowl, beat the egg white until stiff peaks form. Fold the egg white into the batter until just combined.

In a large skillet, heat vegetable oil to a depth of 1 inch (2.5 cm) over medium-high heat. Using your fingers, hold 2 or 3 green beans together and dip them in the batter, coating well. In batches (no more than 5 or 6 at a time), fry the green beans for about 1 to 2 minutes per side, until lightly golden. Using a slotted spoon, transfer the beans to a plate lined in paper towels to drain. Repeat until the beans and batter are all used up, adding more oil, if necessary. Serve warm.

> You can easily substitute asparagus or most any other thinly sliced vegetable in place of the green beans.

COD PANCAKES

Pataniscas de Bacalhau

These delicate and savoury cod pancakes were a hit with the Portuguese staff at my husband's office (my trusted taste testers). I developed this recipe watching Chef José Alves of Via Norte in Toronto make them (they are a staple in his kitchen). My taste testers directed me to increase the cod in the pancakes. As a result, my version of this dish is chock full of cod and confirms my belief that the Portuguese just can't get enough of the salted fish.

TO PREPARE THE SALT COD Place the cod in a large bowl with enough cold water to cover it completely. Cover the bowl in plastic wrap and refrigerate for 24 to 48 hours or longer, changing the water 2 to 3 times per day, until the fish is spongy in texture and desalted. (Larger pieces of fish may take longer.) Drain and discard the water and pat the fish dry with paper towels. Using a fork or sharp knife, remove the skin and bones from the cod and coarsely shred it; discard the bones and skin.

TO MAKE THE PANCAKES Transfer the cod to a work bowl. Add the onions and parsley, and mix well. Add the eggs, one at a time, mixing well after each addition. In alternating batches, gradually add the flour and the milk, and mix well. Add salt and pepper.

In a large heavy saucepan, heat oil to cover the pan by about ¼ inch (6 mm) over medium-high heat until very hot. Using a measuring cup, scoop the batter in ¼ cup (60 mL) portions onto the hot pan; immediately reduce the heat to medium-low (to keep the pancakes from browning too quickly). Cook the pancakes in batches (no more than 3 to 4 at a time) for 2 to 3 minutes, until the edges turn brown and the pancakes are golden on the bottom. Using a spatula, gently turn the pancakes over and cook for 2 to 3 minutes longer, until golden on the bottom. Transfer to a dish lined with paper towels, to drain. Repeat with the remaining batter. Serve warm.

When making these pancakes for myself, I add an extra ¼ cup (60 mL) of chopped fresh parsley and serve with a dollop of Red Pepper and Olive Relish (page 284) or Parsley Dressing (page 280).

MAKES 12 TO 15 PANCAKES

2 lb (1 kg) salt cod (approx.)

1 cup (250 mL) onions, minced

½ cup (125 mL) finely chopped fresh parsley

4 eggs

½ cup (125 mL) all-purpose flour

1 cup (250 mL) whole milk

¼ tsp (1 mL) each salt and coarsely ground white pepper (or to taste)

Vegetable oil for frying

COD CARPACCIO

Salada de Bacalhau

MAKES 4 SERVINGS

OIL AND VINEGAR DRESSING

½ cup (125 mL) olive oil (approx.)

3 Tbsp (45 mL) white wine vinegar (approx.)

3 cloves garlic, minced

Fine salt and coarsely ground black pepper, to taste

CARPACCIO

2 lb (1 kg) salt cod (approx.)

1 small red onion, finely chopped

1 cup (250 mL) cucumber, skin on, finely chopped

1 medium tomato, finely chopped and squeezed of juice

¼ cup (60 mL) black olives, pitted and chopped

¼ cup (60 mL) chopped fresh coriander or parsley

1 cup (250 mL) lettuce, shredded (Boston leaf lettuce or watercress)

Small loaf cornbread, cut into toasts or cubes

You and your friends will be transported to a Portuguese villa when you serve this marinated cod salad on cornbread toast brushed with garlic oil and a thin layer of Olive Paste (page 65). Although the cod in this recipe is flaked and not thinly sliced as in a beef or tuna carpaccio, the unusual use of raw cod makes it akin to a more traditional carpaccio dish. The raw salt cod is infused with Mediterranean warmth, and can easily be served as a salad on a bed of watercress or as a heartier meal tossed with legumes and served alongside crumbled or halved hard-boiled eggs.

Make this dish earlier in the day and set it aside to allow the cod and vegetables ample time to soak up the flavours. The secret to this dish is in the simple dressing: as the cod salad marinates and absorbs the dressing, taste it and add more oil and vinegar. Just before serving, toss the ingredients.

TO MAKE THE DRESSING Whisk together ⅓ cup (80 mL) of the oil, 2 Tbsp (30 mL) of the vinegar, and the garlic, and salt and pepper. Set aside. (The dressing can be made up to 48 hours ahead of time and refrigerated.)

TO PREPARE THE SALT COD Place the cod in a large bowl with enough cold water to cover it completely. Cover the bowl in plastic wrap and refrigerate for 24 to 48 hours, changing the water 2 to 3 times a day, until the fish is spongy in texture and desalted. (Larger pieces of fish may take longer.) Drain and discard the water. Using a fork or sharp knife, remove the skin and bones from the cod and coarsely shred it; discard the skin and bones.

TO MAKE THE CARPACCIO Transfer the cod to a work bowl. Add the onion, cucumber, tomato, olives, and coriander, mixing well after each addition. Spoon 2 to 3 Tbsp (30 to 45 mL) of the prepared dressing over the cod and vegetables, and mix to coat. Taste and add more dressing, if necessary. If all the dressing has been used, add the remaining 3 Tbsp (45 mL) oil and 1 Tbsp (15 mL) vinegar.

On a serving plate, arrange the lettuce and mound the cod in the centre. Serve with fresh cornbread cubes or cornbread toasts. Offer additional olive oil and vinegar on the side. The flavour of the carpaccio improves if the dish is made and set aside to marinate at least an hour before serving.

If serving this as a salad or main meal, cut the vegetables a little larger than called for in this recipe. If serving this as an appetizer, omit the lettuce and top the cod with extra pitted olives and a sprinkling of finely chopped coriander just before serving.

To serve as an appetizer, scoop 1 Tbsp (15 mL) of the cod salad onto cornbread toasts, brushing the bread with garlic-infused oil before toasting.

SARDINES THREE WAYS

Sardinhas Três Maneiras

Most Portuguese sardine lovers will tell you emphatically that there is only one way to eat sardines: grilled, with a squirt of lemon. I learned to make grilled sardines from an old friend, Executive Chef Manuel Vilela of Chiado restaurant in Toronto, and after eating a few this way, I can see why. Grilling brings out the full flavour of this much-loved fish.

I have included recipes for sardines prepared three ways: marinated raw, grilled, and crispy-fried in a golden batter—three reasons to fall in love with sardines all over again. Whichever way you choose to cook them, allow four to five sardines per serving.

MARINATED SARDINES

When it is too cold (and too much trouble) to grill, marinating sardines is a delicious option. If you marinate the fish overnight, you can eat them raw, though I prefer marinating cleaned and gutted sardines and then cooking them in a seasoned flour batter. Whole tiny sardines can be rinsed and briefly marinated, and then floured and deep-fried until they are crispy—perfect bite-sized treats served with a helping of Red Pepper and Olive Relish (page 284) or over top toasted Portuguese bread spread with a thin layer of Olive Paste (page 65).

Once a sardine is deboned it can be opened and laid flat. In a large baking dish, arrange about 12 sardines, skin side down, in a flat, even layer. Sprinkle with half of the garlic, parsley, coriander, and lemon juice. Top with salt, to taste. Sprinkle with half the chili pepper. Repeat in a second layer. Cover and refrigerate overnight. Serve with lemon wedges.

Recipe continues . . .

MAKES ABOUT 5 SERVINGS

About 25 sardines, cleaned, gutted, bones and heads removed, and tails trimmed

GARLIC HERB MARINADE

10 cloves garlic, minced

1 cup (250 mL) each chopped fresh parsley and coriander

¼ cup (60 mL) lemon juice

Fine salt, to taste

1 tsp (5mL) chili pepper

Lemon wedges, for garnish

MAKES ABOUT 5 SERVINGS

About 25 sardines, cleaned, gutted, heads and tails on, ends trimmed

Garlic Herb Marinade (see preceding recipe)

Fresh chopped parsley or coriander, for garnish

Lemon wedges, for garnish

GRILLED SARDINES

High heat is required to grill sardines so that they cook quickly and do not dry out or stick to the grill. (Do not place sardines over indirect heat for too long—this will dry the sardines and rob them of their beautiful and delicious omega oil.) Be careful not to burn them. The sardines' oil will drip during grilling and can cause flare-ups if you are not careful. If possible, use a specially designed fish grill that sandwiches 4 to 5 fish at a time and allows you to easily remove the fish during flare-ups. The fish grill also makes it easy to flip the fish while cooking. You can grill the sardines with or without the marinade.

TO MARINATE THE SARDINES In a large baking dish, arrange about 12 sardines in a flat, even layer. Sprinkle with half of the Garlic Herb Marinade. Repeat in a second layer of sardines and marinade. Cover and refrigerate for about 20 minutes.

TO GRILL THE SARDINES Grill the sardines in small batches (4 to 6 at a time) on high over direct heat (or about 4 inches/10 cm from the hot coals) for 3 to 4 minutes, until brown on the bottom and beginning to turn opaque. Using a lifter, carefully flip the sardines and grill for 1 to 2 minutes longer, until brown and opaque. Garnish with parsley or coriander (or both) and lemon wedges. Serve immediately.

SARDINES IN A GOLDEN BATTER

You can fry the sardines with or without the marinade.

TO MARINATE THE SARDINES In a large baking dish, arrange about 12 sardines in a flat, even layer. Sprinkle with half of the Garlic Herb Marinade. Repeat in a second layer of sardines and marinade. Cover and refrigerate for about 20 minutes.

In a shallow dish, season flour with salt and pepper. Dredge 5 or 6 sardines in the flour, coating completely; shake off the excess flour. Discard the remaining flour.

TO FRY THE SARDINES In a large skillet, heat about ¼ cup (60 mL) of the oil over medium-high heat. Fry the sardines in small batches (4 to 6 at a time) for 30 seconds to 1 minute per side, just until the sardines are no longer opaque and the edges turn golden brown. Gently turn the sardines over with a spatula and fry for 30 seconds to 1 minute, until cooked through. Drain on paper towels and keep warm. Repeat with the remaining sardines, adding oil, if necessary. Serve immediately with lemon wedges or a helping of Red Pepper and Olive Relish (page 284), piri-piri sauce, or Lemon Piri-Piri Sauce (page 282).

MAKES ABOUT 5 SERVINGS

About 25 sardines, cleaned, gutted, heads and tails on, ends trimmed

Garlic Herb Marinade (page 57)

1½ cups (375 mL) flour

Salt and coarsely ground black pepper, to taste

½ cup (125 mL) olive oil

Lemon wedges, for garnish

GREEN EGGS

Ovos Verdes

MAKES 8 SERVINGS

5 eggs

1 Tbsp (15 mL) olive oil

1 Tbsp (15 mL) white wine vinegar

6 Tbsp (90 mL) finely chopped fresh parsley

1 green onion (white and green parts), finely chopped

Dash piri-piri or Tabasco sauce, or to taste

Fine salt and coarsely ground black pepper, to taste

¼ cup (60 mL) dry breadcrumbs

Vegetable oil for deep-frying

Isabel Vieira, friend and fellow food lover, remembers preparing these eggs for her children when they were young, much like her mother did for her. Since the children were familiar with Dr. Seuss's *Green Eggs and Ham*, she of course served these eggs with a side of ham.

You will love these surprisingly simple and delicious eggs, traditionally served as a *petisco* (snack) with a variety of small plates, a green salad, and a glass of wine. These eggs can be dipped in piri-piri sauce, which is never too far from the Portuguese table.

In a large deep saucepan, place 4 eggs in a single layer and add enough cold water to come at least 1 inch (2.5 cm) above the eggs. Cover and bring to a boil over high heat. Turn off the heat and let stand, covered, for 20 minutes. Drain and run cold water over the eggs for 2 minutes. Peel the eggs. Using a sharp knife, slice each egg in half, lengthwise. Gently remove the yolk halves and transfer them to a small mixing bowl. Arrange the egg white halves on a separate plate and cover and refrigerate while you prepare the egg yolks.

Using a fork, mash up the yolks. Add the oil, vinegar, 3 Tbsp (45 mL) of the parsley, and the green onion, piri-piri sauce, and salt and pepper. Taste and adjust the seasonings. Spoon the egg yolk mixture back into the egg white halves, pressing down gently to secure a dense filling.

In a shallow dish, beat the remaining egg. In another shallow dish or resealable bag, combine the breadcrumbs and 2 Tbsp (30 mL) of parsley, and salt and pepper, to taste. One at a time, carefully dip the eggs into the egg wash and then into the breadcrumbs, turning carefully to coat all over. (At this point you can cover the eggs loosely in plastic wrap and refrigerate them until you are ready to cook them.)

In a skillet, heat vegetable oil to a depth of about 1 inch (2.5 cm) over medium-high heat. Cook the eggs in batches (3 to 4 at a time), using 2 forks to gently turn them over, for 1 to 2 minutes per side, until golden brown and heated through. Transfer the eggs to a wire rack to drain. Serve warm or at room temperature sprinkled with 1 Tbsp (15 mL) of the parsley.

Creative cooks spice up the fillings, sometimes by adding puréed tuna, cocktail shrimp, or pieces of finely diced cooked chouriço. If you decide to do the same, don't add more than 1 Tbsp (15 mL) of tuna, shrimp, or chouriço to the egg yolk filling or you'll overfill the egg halves.

SARDINE PÂTÉ

Paté de Sardinha

MAKES 3 TO 4 SERVINGS

⅓ cup (80 mL) + 1 Tbsp (15 mL) olive oil

¼ cup (60 mL) lemon juice or white wine vinegar

2 tsp (10 mL) finely grated lemon zest

2 cloves garlic, minced

2½ tsp (12 mL) smoked Spanish paprika (approx.)

1 small chopped piri-piri pepper (or to taste)

½ tsp (2 mL) fine salt

Coarsely ground black pepper, to taste

1½ lb (750 g) sardines, grilled, deboned, and mashed

3 Tbsp (45 mL) finely chopped fresh parsley or coriander

Thinly sliced red onions, for garnish

Chopped black olives, for garnish

1 hard-boiled egg, peeled and finely chopped, for garnish

I started experimenting with sardine pâté after my friend, Isabel Vieira, admitted that she could not bear to throw out leftover barbecued sardines and shared her recipe with me. Following her instruction, I removed all the skin and bones from the grilled sardines and layered the mashed fish with a helping of smoked paprika dressing. The resulting zesty sardine pâté tastes even better the next day for lunch, spread onto a Portuguese bun.

PIRI-PIRI SARDINE PÂTÉ

Whisk together ⅓ cup (80 mL) oil, lemon juice, lemon zest, garlic, 2 tsp (10 mL) of the paprika, piri-piri, salt, and pepper. Taste and add up to an additional ½ tsp (2 mL) paprika, if desired. Let stand for at least 20 minutes; whisk just before using.

In a small casserole dish or ramekin, arrange half of the sardines in a single layer and drizzle with half of the dressing. Top with the remaining sardines and cover with the remaining dressing. If necessary, add additional oil to cover the sardines. Sprinkle with parsley. Cover and refrigerate for 8 hours or overnight. Before serving, bring to room temperature. Enjoy overtop fresh or toasted bread or crackers garnished with onions, olives, and egg, if desired.

SARDINE PÂTÉ IN PORT

In a small skillet, heat the oil over medium heat; cook the onion, garlic, and bay leaf for 5 to 6 minutes, until beginning to brown. Add the tomato paste and cook for 1 minute. Add the port and cook for 2 to 3 minutes further, until the sauce thickens. Set aside to cool. Remove the bay leaf just before puréeing.

In a food processor, combine the port sauce, sardines, vinegar, butter, and piri-piri pepper and process with on/off pulses just until blended (be careful not to overprocess). (Alternatively, chop everything by hand and mix well.) Taste and adjust the seasonings with salt and pepper, if necessary. Sprinkle with parsley. Transfer to a small ramekin, cover, and refrigerate for 8 hours or overnight. Before serving, bring to room temperature and drizzle with olive oil, to taste. Enjoy overtop fresh bread or crackers.

2 Tbsp (30 mL) olive oil

1 onion, minced

3 cloves garlic, minced

1 bay leaf

2 Tbsp (30 mL) tomato paste

2 Tbsp (30 mL) port

1½ lb (750 g) sardines, cooked, deboned, and mashed

2 Tbsp (30 mL) white wine vinegar or lemon juice

3 Tbsp (45 mL) butter, softened

1 small piri-piri pepper, chopped

Fine salt and coarsely ground black pepper, to taste

3 Tbsp (45 mL) finely chopped fresh parsley

2 Tbsp (30 mL) olive oil, for drizzling

OLIVES

Azeitonas

MAKES ABOUT 6 CUPS (1.5 L)

6 cups (1.5 L) naturally cured
    black olives, with pits

⅓ cup (80 mL) olive oil

6 cloves garlic, minced

2 Tbsp (30 mL) balsamic vinegar
    or red wine vinegar

½ Tbsp (7 mL) dried oregano

½ tsp (2 mL) coarsely ground
    black pepper

Zest from ½ lemon, for garnish

½ lemon, thinly sliced, for garnish

Here are two unique recipes for marinated olives. Both will have a more pronounced flavour after being marinated for two or three days. Use either recipe to make Olive Paste, which is delicious spread over toasted cornbread.

POPULAR GARLIC OLIVES

Maria Lourdes runs a grocery store in Toronto called Popular Groceries with her husband, José, and their grown children. Maria, usually at the store, loves to offer her clients her homestyle seasoned garlic olives. Maria likes to add lemon zest to the olives just before serving so that they won't discolour. I like to add 1 Tbsp (15 mL) of chopped fresh thyme and rosemary to the olives before marinating. To intensify the flavour, you can also sauté the marinated olives on low heat for 20 minutes before serving. Before preparing this dish, be sure to rinse the olives really well to remove any salt residue.

Rinse the olives under cold running water, drain, and place in a medium-sized bowl. Set aside.

In a small bowl, make a paste with the remaining ingredients, excluding the lemon zest and lemon slices. Pour the paste over the olives and mix thoroughly. Taste and adjust the seasonings, if desired. Transfer to an airtight container and refrigerate for up to 2 days, stirring occasionally. Stir and taste again before serving; add more seasonings, if desired. Garnish with lemon zest and lemon slices. If not using immediately, transfer to an airtight container and store in the refrigerator for up to 1 week.

ORANGE AND CUMIN OLIVES

These olives are a regular dish at my friend Isabel Vieira's house. She likes to keep a constant supply to nibble on and linger over after dinner or to serve to friends who just drop by. I like to spoon these over pan-fried cod or plain steamed rice just before serving to add a splash of flavour.

Marinate these in a shallow airtight container or a resealable bag that allows all of the olives to be coated in the marinade. Squeeze the bag or shake the container occasionally to redistribute the delicious flavouring.

Rinse the olives well under cold running water, drain, and place in a medium-sized bowl. Set aside.

In a small bowl, make a paste with the remaining ingredients, excluding the orange slices. Rub the paste all over the olives, until well coated. Taste and add more seasonings, if desired. Transfer to an airtight container and refrigerate for up to 2 days. Stir and taste again before serving; add more seasonings, if desired. To serve, bring to room temperature, toss, and garnish with orange slices. Will keep for up to 1 week in the refrigerator.

MAKES 2½ CUPS (625 ML)

2½ cups (625 mL) black olives, stored in water

¼ cup (60 mL) olive oil

¼ cup (60 mL) fresh orange juice

1 Tbsp (15 mL) orange zest

2 cloves garlic, finely minced

½ tsp (2 mL) dried oregano

1 tsp (5 mL) ground cumin

½ tsp (2 mL) coarsely ground black pepper

1 small chopped piri-piri pepper

3 to 4 orange slices, thinly sliced, for garnish

OLIVE PASTE

You can use a variety of olives to make olive paste, as well as marinated olives. If using ripe olives in water, rinse and drain them well before using and season with garlic and herbs, to taste.

Combine olives with 2 to 3 Tbsp (30 to 45 mL) of olive oil (to desired consistency) and salt and pepper. Garnish with lemon wedges and chopped parsley. Will keep in the refrigerator for up to 4 days.

MAKES ABOUT ½ CUP (125 ML)

½ cup (125 mL) olives, finely chopped and pitted

3 Tbsp (45 mL) olive oil (approx.)

Fine salt and coarsely ground black pepper, to taste

Lemon wedges, for garnish

Parsley, for garnish

PEAS AND EGGS IN TOMATO AND RED PEPPERS

Ervilhas com Ovos, em Molho de Tomate e Pimentos Vermelhos

MAKES 4 SERVINGS

- 3 cups (750 mL) peas, fresh or frozen
- 4 slices thick fresh cornbread
- 3 Tbsp (45 mL) olive oil
- 1 large onion, diced
- 3 cloves garlic, minced
- 6 oz (175 g) chouriço, cut into ½-inch (1 cm) rounds, each round cut into halves or quarters
- ½ cup (125 mL) chopped fresh parsley
- 1 bay leaf
- 1 tomato, peeled, seeded, and chopped
- 1 Tbsp (15 mL) tomato paste
- 2 tsp (10 mL) pimento paste
- 1 cup (250 mL) dry white wine
- ½ cup (125 mL) water
- 4 eggs
- Fine salt and coarsely ground black pepper, to taste

Easily prepared with a few ingredients that are usually on hand in most Portuguese kitchens, this dish is tasty yet simple fare: eggs resting on slabs of fresh Portuguese cornbread surrounded by bright green peas, flecks of red tomatoes, and bits of browned onions and chouriço sausage. Fatima Toste, a busy author in Toronto's Portuguese community, makes this for family and friends who drop by for an impromptu visit.

If using frozen peas, place them in a colander under cold running water until defrosted; drain and set aside.

Place 1 piece of cornbread on each of 4 large serving plates and set aside.

In a large skillet, heat oil over medium heat. Add the onion, garlic, and chouriço and cook for 6 minutes, until the onion and garlic begin to turn golden brown. Add the parsley and bay leaf and cook for 1 minute. Add the tomato, tomato paste, pimento paste, and peas; bring to a boil, stirring to scrape up any brown bits from the bottom of the pan. Add the wine and water; stir well and simmer until the peas are tender and the sauce is thickened slightly, 3 to 5 minutes.

Remove the pan from the heat and shake to distribute the peas evenly over the bottom of the pan. Using a spoon, clear 4 evenly spaced openings in the pea mixture, each in a quarter section of the pan. Carefully crack an egg into each opening. Return the pan to the stove and cook over medium-low heat until the yolks begin to set and the egg whites begin to turn white. Use a spatula to jiggle under each egg to ensure they are not sticking to the pan. Cover with a tight-fitting lid or foil for the last few minutes of cooking to help cook the eggs to the desired doneness. Season with salt and pepper, to taste. To serve, carefully place 1 egg on each slice of cornbread and surround the egg with ladlefuls of peas.

For another version of this dish, substitute shelled and peeled broad beans for the peas and increase the amount of wine by ½ cup (125 mL). Place a thick slice of bread (day-old is best as it absorbs liquids without falling apart) on a serving plate and generously spoon over the broad beans. Top with the egg and some chopped mint.

QUINCE AND SERRA BITES

Tartes de Queijo da Serra e Marmelada

MAKES 24 TARTS

14 oz (400 g) Puff Pastry
(page 313)

6 oz (175 g) Serra da Estrela,
Oka, or Edam cheese

¼ cup (60 mL) quince
marmalade or fig jam

¼ cup (60 mL) piri-piri sauce
(approx.)

3 Tbsp (45 mL) chopped roasted
salted almonds or walnuts

Fresh thyme leaves, for garnish

Chopped figs, for garnish

Inspired by a Northern Portuguese sandwich called Romeo and Juliet that combines quince marmalade with a slice of Serra da Estrela cheese—two much-loved Portuguese favourites—these tarts pair nicely with a fruit platter to make a lovely appetizer course.

Grease 24 mini-tart tins and set aside. Divide the pastry in half and cover one half to keep it from drying out. On a lightly floured surface, roll out one portion of the dough to a ¼ inch (6 mm) thickness. Cut out twelve 3½ inch (9 cm) circles. Press each circle into each cup, trim excess. To prevent a soggy pie crust, blind-bake the crusts: Prick the prepared pie crusts all over with a fork, cover with foil, and fill with beans. Bake for 12 to 15 minutes in a preheated 400°F (200°C) oven then remove the beans and cool until ready to use.

Slice the cheese into 24 even pieces. Spoon about ½ tsp (2 mL) of the quince marmalade into each shell and top with cheese. Dot with about ½ tsp (2 mL) of the piri-piri sauce (or to taste). Sprinkle evenly with almonds or walnuts.

Bake on the top rack of a preheated 500°F (260°C) oven for 7 to 8 minutes or until the pastry is golden brown and the cheese is bubbling. Remove from the oven and while still hot, run a knife around the edge of the cups; let stand for only 5 minutes before removing the pastries. Cool on a wire rack. Repeat with remaining pastry and filling. If desired, garnish with fresh thyme leaves and chopped figs.

SOUPS

Sopas

The Portuguese make some outstanding soups fit for any occasion. The most popular is Creamy Potato Purée and Greens (page 82). I love its simplicity, so representative of Portuguese cooking. I always look for bits and pieces of chouriço, the gems at the bottom of the bowl that give the soup its trademark flavour (although the chouriço can easily be omitted for a vegetarian version). The potato base can be made ahead of time, the collard greens cooked separately, and the two brought together just before serving.

Most Portuguese soups, I learned, started out as peasant food. A variety of soups can be produced with minimal ingredients and work. Water or stock with fresh coriander, garlic, eggs, and a side of bread can feed a family in minutes. Bread and Egg in Garlic and Coriander Broth (page 78), Fresh Tomato and Bread Soup (page 80), and Seafood and Bread in Broth (page 77) are three such memorable classics.

Green soups, much like the above-mentioned Creamy Potato Purée and Greens as well as Watercress Soup (page 84), are enjoyed throughout the year. Portuguese cooks have learned to substitute any greens they can find for the collards. The potato base can also be varied; sweet potatoes, carrots, or turnips can be substituted for delicious results.

Warm soups are perfect for Canadian winters, chock full of hearty ingredients such as beans, greens, and rice. Bread Soup with Beef and Cabbage (page 83) and Broad Bean Soup with Bacon (page 87) are hearty, nutritious offerings sure to satisfy. Sometimes rice, pasta, and beans are added to make even heartier versions of classics.

Fresh Tomato and Bread Soup, mentioned previously, is a fresh-tasting blend of bread, tomatoes, and seasonings, a favourite in the summer months. Warm-weather soups are excellent accompaniments to Grilled Sardines (page 58) or Barbecued Cuttlefish (page 107).

More than one excellent cook I know insist that the secret to their homestyle Portuguese soups involves simple and fresh ingredients including aromatics like onion and garlic combined with a sweet-flavoured olive oil. These elements are manipulated over and over to make dozens of amazing one-dish meals.

SOUPS
Sopas

CHICKEN SOUP

Canja

MAKES ABOUT 8 SERVINGS

3 to 4 lb (1.5 to 1.8 kg) chicken
    bones or 1 whole chicken

12 cups (3 L) cold water

1 large onion

1 carrot

1 stalk celery

2 cloves garlic

3 sprigs fresh mint or parsley

Pinch fine salt

2 bay leaves

5 whole black peppercorns,
    crushed

Pinch saffron threads
    (about 4 to 6 threads)

½ cup (125 mL) long-grain rice
    or orzo pasta

Fresh mint leaves, for garnish

Lemon wedges, for garnish

The sweet fragrance of mint is intoxicating during the summer months in the Azores. Although mint grows wild all over the plush islands, it is used sparingly in cooking. Chicken soup is the exception. Fresh sprigs of mint are added to the simmering broth, and a mint leaf is used to garnish each serving.

Place the chicken bones or whole chicken in a large stockpot and cover with cold water. Bring to a boil over high heat. Skim off any scum from the surface. Reduce the heat to medium low and add the onion, carrot, celery, garlic, mint, salt, bay leaves, peppercorns, and saffron. Cover and simmer for about 2 hours, occasionally skimming off any scum during cooking.

Carefully strain the broth through a clean kitchen towel or a fine-mesh sieve lined with cheesecloth; discard the solids and reserve the chicken, if using. Transfer the broth to a clean stockpot and bring to a boil over medium-high heat. Add the rice and cook for about 15 minutes, until tender. Taste and adjust the seasonings with salt and pepper, if necessary.

Ladle the soup into bowls. Garnish with mint leaves and serve with lemon wedges on the side or add a few drops of lemon juice to each serving. If made with a whole chicken, chop up the chicken and serve it alongside.

A heartier adaptation of this soup calls for 4 oz (120 g) of roughly chopped chicken livers, added with the rice or pasta.

You are essentially making chicken stock here (before you add the rice). Use the stock as a base for rice dishes or for Creamy Potato Purée and Greens (page 82).

FISH STOCK

Sopa de Peixe

Seafood Stew (page 91) and Seafood and Bread in Broth (page 77) just don't taste the same unless they are made with this flavourful fish stock. Have some on hand in the fridge or freezer to add to rice dishes and soups for extra flavour or transform it into a delicious soup by adding some chopped green onion, rice, and shredded fish leftover from the bones.

Be sure to remove the fish bones after simmering for 40 minutes or the bones will break and the stock will become bitter. Avoid using freshwater fish, which makes the stock cloudy.

Place the fish bones in a large stockpot and cover with water. Bring to a boil over medium-high heat. Skim off any scum from the surface. Reduce the heat to medium-low, add the remaining ingredients, and simmer for 40 minutes. Using a slotted spoon, remove the bones and continue simmering for 80 minutes, occasionally skimming any scum from the top. Taste and adjust the seasonings with salt, if necessary. Carefully strain the stock through a clean kitchen towel or fine-mesh sieve lined with cheesecloth. Transfer to airtight containers and store in the refrigerator for up to 1 week or freeze for up to 3 months.

MAKES ABOUT 14 CUPS (6.5 L)

2 to 3 lb (1 to 1.5 kg) fish bones (halibut, cod, haddock, or sea bass)

24 cups (6 L) cold water

½ cup (125 mL) beer

1½ cups (375 mL) dry white wine

1 onion, chopped

1 clove garlic, crushed

2 Tbsp (30 mL) lemon juice

3 bay leaves

4 or 5 sprigs fresh parsley

1 tsp (5 mL) dried thyme

¼ cup (60 mL) whole black peppercorns, crushed

8 to 10 saffron threads

Pinch fine salt

CREAMY SHRIMP SOUP

Sopa de Camarão

MAKES 4 SERVINGS

1 lb (500 g) medium shrimp, in shells

6 cups (1.5 L) Fish Stock (page 75)

¼ cup (60 mL) butter

¼ cup (60 mL) olive oil

2 onions, finely chopped

1 carrot, finely chopped

1 sprig fresh parsley

2 Tbsp (30 mL) cognac

½ cup (125 mL) dry white wine

1 tomato, peeled, seeded, and chopped

Fine salt, to taste

2 Tbsp (30 mL) rice flour

⅓ cup (80 mL) whipping cream

Coarsely ground black pepper, to taste

Piri-piri sauce or Tabasco sauce, to taste

This creamy, rich seafood soup is a Portuguese favourite. Usually served at weddings, it's an elegant addition to any occasion. The secret to this dish is to leave the shrimp shells to simmer in the broth—it adds a deeper flavour. Serve as a first course, just enough to whet your appetite and leave room for dinner.

Rinse the shrimp under cold running water and pat dry with paper towels.

In a saucepan, cover the shrimp with the fish stock. Bring to a boil over medium heat and cook for about 5 minutes, until the shrimp are pink and firm when pierced with a fork. Remove the pan from the heat. Using a slotted spoon, transfer the shrimp to a dish. When cool enough to handle, pull off the legs and shells (leaving the tails on); reserve the shells and discard the legs. Remove the intestinal vein, if desired. Set the shrimp and stock aside and keep warm.

In a large skillet over medium-low heat, heat the butter and oil until the butter is melted. Cook the onions and carrot for 3 minutes. Add the parsley and reserved shrimp shells and cook, stirring occasionally, for 15 minutes. Add the cognac, wine, and tomato and simmer for 2 to 3 minutes. Remove from the heat and stir in the fish stock and salt.

In a small bowl, stir together the rice flour and whipping cream until smooth. Stir into the soup base and cook over medium-low heat, partially covered, for about 30 minutes, until thickened. Stir occasionally. Taste and adjust the seasonings with salt, if necessary.

Just before serving, strain the broth through a fine-mesh sieve; discard the solids. Ladle into soup bowls and top each serving with 6 or 7 reserved shrimp. Season with pepper, to taste. Serve with piri-piri sauce.

SEAFOOD AND BREAD IN BROTH

Açorda

The Portuguese passion for soups is apparent in the wide variety of recipes, from bean bases to vegetable purées and to both clear and chunky broths. There are also dozens of bread soups. *Açorda* is a classic bread and seafood soup, found in almost every restaurant in the Alentejan province of southern Portugal.

In a heavy saucepan, heat oil over low heat. Add the garlic and cook for 2 to 3 minutes, until softened.

Rinse the monkfish under cold running water and pat dry with paper towels. Using a stiff brush, scrub the clams and mussels under cold running water to remove surface sand and grit, and discard any that aren't tightly closed. Rinse the shrimp under cold running water and drain well. Transfer the monkfish, clams, mussels, shrimp, and fish stock to a large saucepan; cover and bring to a boil. Simmer for 5 to 7 minutes, until the clams and mussels open and the shrimp and monkfish are opaque and firm when pierced with fork. Discard any clams and mussels that haven't opened.

Remove the saucepan from the heat. Using a slotted spoon, transfer the seafood to a bowl; reserve stock. Remove the meat from the clams, mussels, and shrimp; discard shells. Return the prepared seafood to the stock. Add the piri-piri sauce and half the coriander. Reduce the heat to low and add the bread, a few handfuls at a time, stirring between additions. Add just enough to soak up the liquid—the mixture should be moist but not soupy. Taste and adjust the seasonings with salt and pepper.

Transfer the hot mixture to a decorative serving dish (perform the remaining steps at the dinner table). Break the eggs into a small bowl, and carefully slip over the bread and seafood mixture. Top with the crabmeat and add mustard. Quickly mix all the ingredients until well combined. Sprinkle with the remaining coriander. Serve immediately.

MAKES 4 APPETIZER SERVINGS OR 2 MAIN-COURSE SERVINGS

2 Tbsp (30 mL) olive oil

2 cloves garlic, minced

4 oz (120 g) monkfish, cut into 1-inch (2.5 cm) cubes

6 Manila clams

4 large mussels

12 large shrimp, in shells

1⅔ cups (310 mL) Fish Stock (page 75)

Dash piri-piri sauce or Tabasco sauce

2 Tbsp (30 mL) chopped fresh coriander

6 oz (180 g) day-old French or Italian bread, cut into 1-inch (2.5 cm) cubes (about 3 cups/750 mL)

Fine salt and coarsely ground black pepper, to taste

2 eggs

4 oz (120 g) cooked crabmeat

2 tsp (10 mL) Dijon mustard

BREAD AND EGG IN GARLIC AND CORIANDER BROTH

Sopa à Alentejana

MAKES 2 SERVINGS

4 slices day-old French or
    Italian bread, about ½ inch
    (1 cm) thick

3 cloves garlic, minced

Pinch fine salt

¼ cup (60 mL) finely chopped
    fresh coriander

2 Tbsp (30 mL) olive oil

2 cups (500 mL) boiling water

2 eggs

This popular green soup of the Alentejo province makes a simple, rustic meal. The frugal Portuguese have created many soups like this one that combine a light broth with day-old bread. This also makes a sensational soup course when followed by Spicy Shrimp with Beer and Garlic (page 109) and steamed rice.

Divide the bread slices between 2 soup bowls. Set aside.

In a saucepan, combine the garlic and salt. Stir in the coriander, oil, and boiling water. Bring to a boil over medium-high heat. Carefully break the eggs into a small bowl. Stir the boiling broth to create a whirlpool effect and carefully slip the eggs, one at a time, into the centre of the whirlpool. Reduce the heat to medium-low and simmer for 3 to 4 minutes, until the eggs are almost soft-cooked (the eggs will continue cooking in the broth). Using a slotted spoon, top the bread in each soup bowl with one poached egg. Taste the broth and adjust the seasonings with salt, if necessary. In each bowl, pour enough broth over the egg to cover the bread. Serve immediately.

FRESH TOMATO AND BREAD SOUP

Gaspacho

MAKES 6 SERVINGS

2 cloves garlic, minced

1 Tbsp (15 mL) fine salt

1 green bell pepper, seeded, cored, and coarsely chopped

3 large tomatoes, coarsely chopped

1 cucumber, peeled and coarsely chopped

5 cups (1.25 L) water

¼ cup (60 mL) white wine vinegar

2 Tbsp (30 mL) olive oil

2 Tbsp (30 mL) chopped fresh coriander

Pinch coarsely ground black pepper

4 oz (120 g) day-old French or Italian bread, cut into 1-inch (2.5 cm) cubes

Portuguese gaspacho originated with hungry farm workers who would toss this meal together in the fields with only a few ingredients on hand. This refreshing soup is a favourite in the summer months when tomatoes are at their peak and cooking is a chore. Paired with barbecued sardines, it makes a classic Portuguese summer meal. My friend Alexandra, a photographer, journalist, artist, single mom, and fellow food lover, shared her family recipe.

In a large serving bowl, mash the garlic and salt with a fork to form a paste. Add the green pepper, tomatoes, and cucumber. Use the back of a spoon to gently break up the tomatoes. Toss to mix well. Add water, vinegar, and oil and stir. Sprinkle with coriander and black pepper. Arrange bread over-top, cover, and let stand for about 20 minutes, until the bread is softened. Taste and adjust the seasonings with salt, pepper, and vinegar, if necessary. Serve immediately.

PUMPKIN SOUP

Sopa de Abóbora

In this hearty soup, the combination of sweet-tasting pumpkin and sweet potatoes are a perfect balance to the favourite Azorean seasonings of cinnamon, allspice, and cumin. This recipe prepares a perfect quantity for a family gathering, but can easily be cut in half, if desired. Other winter squash can be substituted for the pumpkin.

In a large saucepan or Dutch oven, combine the chouriço, bacon, onion, garlic, and stock. Cover and bring to a boil. Simmer over medium heat for 20 minutes. Skim off all scum.

Meanwhile, peel the sweet potatoes and quarter. Cut the pumpkin in half lengthwise, remove the seeds and skin, and cut into large cubes. Add the vegetables, cinnamon sticks, allspice, cumin, and salt to the saucepan. Simmer, covered, for 20 to 25 minutes, just until vegetables are tender. Discard the cinnamon and allspice. Using a slotted spoon, remove the chouriço and bacon, and chop the meat into bite-sized pieces; set aside and keep warm. (If desired, reserve some pumpkin and 4 cups/1 L of the broth to make a bread and cinnamon soup; simply add an equal amount of water to the soup base to compensate for the lost liquid. See more tips in the sidebar below.)

Transfer the pumpkin mixture to a food processor or blender and purée in batches, if necessary, until smooth. Return the soup to the saucepan and heat through. Taste and adjust the seasonings with salt, if necessary. Ladle into soup bowls. Serve with the reserved chouriço and bacon on the side. Sprinkle with ground cinnamon.

You can set aside 4 cups (1 L) of the broth (and any boiled pumpkin pieces) to make another Azorean favourite—bread and cinnamon soup. The next day, generously sprinkle a thick slice of crusty day-old bread with cinnamon. Place in a soup bowl and fill the bowl with reheated pumpkin and broth. Cover and let stand for 2 to 3 minutes before serving.

MAKES 10 SERVINGS

4 oz (120 g) chouriço, unchopped

8 oz (240 g) lean bacon or pork hock, unchopped

1 large onion, halved

1 clove garlic, crushed

10 cups (2.5 L) chicken stock

2 sweet potatoes

1 small pumpkin (about 4 lb/1.8 kg)

Two 1-inch (2.5 cm) cinnamon sticks

1 tsp (5 mL) whole allspice

2 tsp (10 mL) ground cumin

Pinch fine salt

Ground cinnamon, for garnish

CREAMY POTATO PURÉE AND GREENS
Caldo Verde

MAKES 8 TO 10 SERVINGS

8 cups (2 L) chicken stock
(see sidebar, page 74)

2 tsp (10 mL) fine salt

¼ cup (60 mL) olive oil

3 cloves garlic, minced

2 large onions, quartered

1½ lb (750 g) potatoes, peeled
and halved (about 4)

8 oz (240 g) chouriço

4 cups (1 L) water

2 cups (500 mL) finely
shredded collard greens

Creamy Potato Purée and Greens is a classic Portuguese dish that, for many, symbolizes the food of Portugal. It is easy to understand why the nutritious and easy soup is loved throughout the country. A light-tasting creamy potato base makes a delicious and lovely backdrop to the shredded collards. It is traditionally served with slivers of chouriço and a drizzle of olive oil. Vegetarians can omit the chouriço.

In a large saucepan, combine the chicken stock, 1 tsp (5 mL) salt, 2 Tbsp (30 mL) oil, garlic, onions, potatoes, and chouriço, and bring to a boil over medium-high heat. Reduce the heat to medium and cook for 25 to 30 minutes, until the potatoes are tender when pierced with fork.

In a separate saucepan over medium heat, combine the water, remaining 1 tsp (5 mL) salt, and the collard greens. Bring to a boil and simmer for 5 to 7 minutes, until bright green and tender. Drain the greens and transfer them to a large serving bowl. Set aside and cover to keep warm.

When the potato mixture is cooked, use a slotted spoon to remove the chouriço; slice it thinly and reserve. Transfer the potato mixture to a food processor or blender and purée it in batches until smooth. Pour the purée over the prepared collard greens and stir well to combine. Taste and adjust the seasonings with salt, if necessary.

To serve, ladle the soup into bowls and garnish each serving with a few slivers of chouriço and about 1 tsp (5 mL) olive oil drizzled over top.

Many Portuguese grocers have a manual shredder used only for collard greens (called *couves* in Portuguese). They will shred the collards on the premises for you. To shred your own collards at home, wash the leaves and trim the rough ends. Stack a few leaves and roll into a large cigar shape; using a sharp knife, slice as thinly as possible. Any unused shredded collards can be frozen for later use.

BREAD SOUP WITH BEEF AND CABBAGE

Sopa do Espirito Santo

This soup, literally translated as "soup of the Holy Ghost," is an Azorean specialty typically prepared in the spring. It is often made in large quantities and consumed after a day of festivities. A few hours before guests arrive, the bread and meat are strewn with fresh mint and the soup is tightly sealed with foil to allow the mint to infuse the dish. The resulting aroma makes it hard to wait for everyone to arrive to sit down and eat. Make sure that you use day-old bread—it's best for soaking up the broth without falling apart.

You don't need a special occasion to make this soup, it makes for a delicious and hearty main dish any time. Slow-cooking tenderizes inexpensive cuts of meat, until they melt in your mouth. Be sure to allow at least 30 minutes before serving for the finished soup to rest and take on the intoxicating scent of mint.

Place the beef in a large stockpot and cover with water. Bring to a boil over medium-high heat. Skim any scum from the surface. Add the wine, onion, garlic, salt, and allspice. Reduce the heat to low, cover, and simmer for 1 hour. Add the cabbage and potatoes and cook for 30 minutes, until the cabbage, potatoes, and beef are tender. Transfer the meat and vegetables to a serving plate, cut into serving pieces, and keep warm. Taste the broth and adjust the seasonings with salt. Set aside for about 15 minutes to allow the broth to cool slightly.

Line the bottom of a large soup tureen with both kinds of bread. Sprinkle the bread with the mint.

Using a spoon, degrease the broth and strain through a fine-mesh sieve. Pour 5 to 6 cups (1.25 to 1.5 L) of the broth over the bread and mint (enough to cover the bread), reserving the rest for later. Cover the tureen and set it aside for about 30 minutes, until the bread is softened, the liquid is absorbed, and the mixture is fragrant.

To serve, spoon the soup into individual bowls. Drizzle 1 cup (250 mL) of the reserved broth over the meat and vegetables. Serve the remaining broth on the side, if desired.

MAKES 6 TO 8 SERVINGS

2 lb (1 kg) cross rib beef roast or boneless cross rib steak with some fat

2 lb (1 kg) beef short ribs, in one piece

12 cups (3 L) cold water

½ cup (125 mL) dry red wine

2 onions, diced

3 cloves garlic, minced

Pinch fine salt

½ tsp (2 mL) whole allspice

½ head cabbage, quartered

1½ lb (750 g) potatoes, peeled and quartered

8 cups (2 L) day-old French or Italian bread, cut into 2-inch (5 cm) cubes

2 cups (500 mL) cornbread, cut into 1-inch (2.5 cm) cubes

1 cup (250 mL) chopped fresh mint

WATERCRESS SOUP

Sopa de Agrião

MAKES 6 SERVINGS

¼ cup (60 mL) olive oil (approx.)

1 large onion, chopped

1 large carrot, diced

2 bay leaves

4 cloves garlic (approx.)

4 oz (120 g) chouriço, or thick-slice
   Portuguese-flavoured bacon,
   or regular bacon, unchopped

2 small potatoes, peeled and diced

½ small turnip, peeled and diced

6 cups (1.5 L) chicken stock,
   vegetable stock, or water
   (approx.)

2 cups (500 mL) water

2 bunches watercress, trimmed

Fine salt and coarsely ground
   black pepper, to taste

Lemon wedges, for garnish

Olive oil, for drizzling

When fellow food lover and friend Isabel Antunes first came to Canada, she worked as a nanny for a vegetarian family. She learned to love a wide variety of vegetables and incorporated some of them into her diet. This soup, fast and easy to bring to the table, combines her passion for vegetables with a hint of classic Portuguese flavourings. Isabel will replace the carrots with whatever is in season, perhaps zucchini or squash, and for a boost of flavour and colour will sometimes use a small sweet potato instead of a regular potato. To make this soup vegetarian, omit the chouriço.

In a large saucepan or Dutch oven, heat 2 Tbsp (30 mL) oil. Add the onion, carrot, and 1 bay leaf and cook for about 8 minutes, until the vegetables soften and begin to brown. Add the garlic and chouriço and cook for about 2 minutes longer, until the chouriço begins to brown. Add the diced potatoes and turnip and cook for another minute, until well coated with oil. Add the stock, water, and another bay leaf. Bring to a boil over medium-high heat. Lower the heat to medium and simmer for about 10 minutes.

Meanwhile, prepare the watercress. Separate the stalks from the leaves to form two piles. Finely chop the leaves and reserve them (you should have about 2 ½ cups/625 mL). Finely chop the stalks (you should have about 2 cups/500 mL) and add them to the broth. Cook for about 20 minutes longer or until the potatoes and turnip are fork-tender.

Using a slotted spoon, remove the chouriço from the soup and cut it into small cubes; set it aside. Remove the bay leaves and discard them.

Transfer the vegetables and broth to a food processor or blender and purée in batches until smooth. Return the puréed mixture to a pan; if you find that the soup is too thick, add up to 1 cup (250 mL) stock to reach the desired consistency. Add the reserved watercress leaves and cook over medium heat, stirring often, for 3 to 5 minutes, just until the watercress is bright green and tender. Stir in the reserved chouriço. Taste and adjust the seasonings with salt and pepper.

(Alternatively, you can steam the watercress before adding and not purée the soup. In a separate pan, cover the watercress leaves in water, add salt, and steam until tender-crisp. Drain and, using you hands, squeeze as much water from the leaves as possible; set aside. In a large pan, add 1 Tbsp/ 15 mL of oil and 1 clove of garlic, minced; cook for 1 minute over medium heat. Add the watercress leaves and toss to coat evenly; cook for about 1 minute. Transfer the watercress to the soup. Stir, add the reserved chouriço, taste, and adjust the seasonings with salt and pepper.)

To serve, ladle the soup into individual bowls and garnish each with a few drops of olive oil and the lemon slices.

FISH SOUP ALENTEJO-STYLE

Sopa de Peixe à Alentejana

MAKES 4 TO 6 SERVINGS

1½ lb (750 g) extra-large
    shrimp, in shells

10 cups (2.5 L) Fish Stock
    (page 75)

3 Tbsp (45 mL) olive oil

1 onion, chopped

3 cloves garlic, minced

¼ cup (60 mL) tomato paste

3 potatoes, peeled and chopped

3 carrots, cut into 1-inch (2.5 cm)
    pieces

¼ cup (60 mL) white wine

3 bay leaves

4 whole black peppercorns,
    crushed

¼ cup (60 mL) chopped fresh
    parsley

2 tsp (10 mL) fine salt

2 cups (500 mL) toasted
    cornbread, diced, for garnish

¼ cup (60 mL) chopped fresh
    coriander, for garnish

¼ cup (60 mL) olive oil,
    for drizzling

I like to use a variety of fish bones to produce a rich base for my fish stock. Find out what your fishmonger has available and experiment with flavours. I like to include shrimp in the stock when I'm making this particular recipe. Carefully strain the stock through a clean kitchen towel or fine-mesh sieve lined with cheesecloth just before using in this soup.

TO PREPARE THE SHRIMP   Using kitchen shears, cut each shrimp shell along the back. Pull out the intestinal veins. Remove the legs but leave the shell and tail on each shrimp. Rinse under cold running water and pat dry with paper towels.

In a large stockpot, bring the fish stock to a boil. Add the prepared shrimp and simmer, partially covered, for about 6 minutes, until the shrimp are cooked. Using a slotted spoon, transfer the shrimp to a bowl and set aside until cool enough to handle. When cool, shell the shrimp and cut into bite-sized pieces; discard the shells. Set aside and keep warm.

In a large pot, heat the oil over medium heat. Cook the onion and garlic until golden, about 6 minutes. Add the tomato paste and cook for 3 to 4 minutes or until the mixture turns a deep red. Adjust the heat, if necessary, to prevent the mixture from burning. Add the potatoes and carrots and cook for 2 to 3 minutes. Add about 7 cups (1.75 L) of fish stock and wine, bay leaves, peppercorns, parsley, and salt and bring to a boil. Cook until the potatoes and carrots are tender, 30 minutes. Remove the bay leaves. Transfer the mixture to a food processor or blender and purée in batches. Taste and adjust the seasonings with salt and pepper. Return the purée to the pot and add up to 3 cups (750 mL) more of fish stock, until the desired consistency is reached. Bring the soup to a boil, add the shrimp meat, and cook for 2 to 3 minutes, until the soup is heated through.

To serve, ladle the soup into individual bowls and top with cornbread and coriander and a drizzle of oil.

BROAD BEAN SOUP WITH BACON

Sopa Puré de Favas com Bacon

This heartwarming dish is nourishing any time of the year. I like to make it in big batches and store it in the freezer for a quick and hearty dinner after work. It is also an excellent starter topped with coriander, olive oil, and cornbread croutons. If you prefer a chunkier dish, omit puréeing the soup.

In a large saucepan or Dutch oven, heat 2 Tbsp (30 mL) of the oil. Add the onion, garlic, ¾ cup (185 mL) coriander, bay leaves, bacon, and chouriço and cook until the onion begins to turn golden brown, 8 to 10 minutes. Add the broad beans, potato, and carrot; cook for 1 minute longer. Add 8 cups (2 L) of the stock, cover, and bring to a rolling boil over high heat. Reduce the heat to medium and uncover. Maintaining a rolling boil, cook until the potatoes, broad beans, and carrots are tender and the soup is slightly reduced, 10 to 12 minutes. Using a slotted spoon, transfer a handful of broad beans to a bowl and set aside. Remove the bacon and chouriço, chop into bite-sized pieces, and set aside. Discard the bay leaves.

Working in batches, transfer the soup to a food processor or blender and purée until smooth. Return the soup to the saucepan; if the soup is too thick, add up to 1 cup (250 mL) stock or water to reach desired consistency. Taste and adjust the seasonings with salt, if necessary. Heat through.

To serve, ladle into individual bowls and top each with the reserved bacon, chouriço, and broad beans. Sprinkle with the remaining coriander, top with cornbread cubes, and drizzle with the remaining oil. Season with pepper, if desired.

I often use frozen broad beans for this, as fresh broad beans are only available during the spring. Parboil frozen beans for 90 seconds, then plunge them in ice water. Using a sharp knife, remove and discard the outer brown skin. With fresh broad beans, parboil for 30 seconds and use a sharp knife to remove the shells and skins.

MAKES 6 TO 8 SERVINGS

3 Tbsp (45 mL) olive oil

1 large onion, chopped

4 cloves garlic

¾ cup (185 mL) + 2 Tbsp (30 mL) finely chopped fresh coriander

3 bay leaves

4 oz (120 g) lean bacon, unchopped

4 oz (120 g) chouriço, unchopped

1½ lb (750 g) broad beans, shelled and skinned

1 potato, peeled and chopped

1 carrot, peeled and chopped

9 cups (2.25 L) chicken stock or water (approx.)

Fine salt, to taste

2 to 3 slices thick cornbread, toasted and cut into cubes, for garnish

Coarsely ground black pepper, to taste, for garnish

FIERY SEAFOOD CORNMEAL SOUP FROM CAPE VERDE

Sopa de Marisco e Farinha de Milho de Cabo Verde

MAKES 3 TO 4 SERVINGS

- 1½ lb (750 g) mixed fish and seafood (about 4 clams or 4 mussels, 8 large shrimp, and 2 to 3 pieces of monkfish or other fish, as desired), cut into large pieces
- 4 cloves garlic, minced
- 2 Tbsp (30 mL) finely chopped fresh parsley
- 1 tsp (5 mL) dried oregano
- 2 bay leaves
- 1 tsp (5 mL) coarse salt
- 3 Tbsp (45 mL) olive oil
- 2 onions, chopped
- 1 yellow bell pepper, seeded and chopped
- 6 chili peppers, seeded and chopped
- 3 tomatoes, chopped
- 7 cups (1.75 L) Fish Stock (page 75) or clam juice (approx.)
- ¼ bunch coriander, rinsed, ends trimmed and stems tied into a bouquet with butcher's twine
- ¼ cup (60 mL) finely chopped fresh coriander
- ½ cup (125 mL) fine yellow cornmeal
- Fine salt and coarsely ground black pepper, to taste
- 2 to 3 Tbsp (30 to 45 mL) lemon juice (approx.)

This soup is believed to be a version of a dish created by fishermen off the west coast of Africa. On Cape Verde, where fish and shellfish are in abundance, this soup includes bits of clams, mussels, tuna, shrimp, lobster, squid, octopus, and barnacle.

This soup is spicy. It's made with hot chili peppers and finished with a hot pepper vinegar sauce. Ana Julia Sanca, a friend and poet, was raised on this soup and loves it so much that she dedicated a poem to her childhood nanny, Antonia, who ground the cornmeal for this soup almost daily. Ana keeps a batch of homemade hot sauce in her refrigerator at all times for dishes like these. The following recipe is inspired by Ana's version of Cape Verde Soup and includes her Cape Verde Hot Sauce.

Rinse the fish and seafood under cold running water and pat dry with paper towels. Transfer to a resealable bag and add half the minced garlic and the parsley, oregano, bay leaves, and coarse salt. Seal the bag, gently mix to ensure everything is well coated, and refrigerate for 8 hours or, if time allows, overnight. Bring to room temperature for 30 minutes before using.

In a large heavy saucepan, heat the oil over medium-high heat; cook the onion, yellow pepper, chili pepper, and remaining minced garlic, stirring occasionally, for 8 to 9 minutes, until the vegetables begin to brown and soften. Add the prepared fish and seafood with marinade and cook for 2 to 3 minutes, stirring well to coat. Add the tomatoes and cook a further 2 to 3 minutes, stirring to scrape any brown bits from the bottom of the pan. Add 6 cups (1.5 L) of the fish stock and the coriander bouquet; cover and bring to a boil over medium heat. Reduce the heat to medium-low and simmer, partially covered, for 6 to 8 minutes, until the fish and seafood are cooked through. Be careful not to overcook the fish and seafood. Using a slotted spoon, transfer the fish and seafood to a bowl and keep it warm for adding back into the soup later.

Increase the heat to medium and bring the soup to a boil. Add the cornmeal in a slow, steady stream to prevent clumping; stir until combined, about 1 minute. Reduce the heat to low and bring to a low simmer. Cook, partially covered, until the cornmeal is tender, about 6 to 7 minutes; stir occasionally to prevent the cornmeal from scorching. Taste and adjust the seasonings with salt and pepper.

Just before serving, remove the coriander and bay leaves. Chop the reserved seafood into bite-sized pieces and add to the soup. Sprinkle with fresh coriander and up to 3 Tbsp (45 mL) lemon juice, to taste. Note that the cornmeal will quickly thicken the soup; if you prefer a thinner soup, add up to 1 cup (250 mL) of hot fish stock to reach the desired consistency just before serving. Serve with Cape Verde Hot Sauce, if desired.

CAPE VERDE HOT SAUCE

Combine all of the ingredients in a small jar. Shake and set aside in the refrigerator until ready to use. Bring to room temperature for 15 minutes, shake well, and strain through a fine-mesh sieve before using. The hot sauce will keep in the refrigerator for up to 14 days.

> When I'm not using freshly caught unfrozen seafood, I toss in additional shells or fish bones (wrapped in cheesecloth and butcher's twine) to the fish stock. The shells and fish bones further enrich the flavour of the stock and are easily removed.

MAKES ABOUT 1½ CUPS (375 ML)

CAPE VERDE HOT SAUCE
½ cup (125 mL) white wine vinegar
½ cup (125 mL) white wine
½ cup (125 mL) lemon juice
8 to 10 hot chili peppers, seeded and chopped
4 cloves garlic
4 bay leaves
2 to 3 sprigs fresh thyme
5 to 6 whole black peppercorns, crushed
Peel of 1 lemon
2 Tbsp (30 mL) olive oil
½ tsp (2 mL) fine salt

SEAFOOD STEW

Caldeirada de Marisco

This dish is an ode to all of the different *caldeirada* and *cataplana* dishes I encountered while researching this book. *Caldeirada* is a fish stew cooked in a large pot. *Cataplana*, also a fish stew but thicker and tomato-basted, is usually cooked in a clam-shaped cooking vessel with a latch to trap the steam produced during cooking. If you don't have one, a regular pot with a tight-fitting lid traps the steam just as well. Both caldeirada and cataplana share garlic, onion, and potatoes laced between layers of fish and shellfish. They can be made with either only one type of fish, such as squid, cod, or sardines (see Sardine Stew on page 163), or with a combination of shellfish and firm fish.

The finished stew is usually brought to the table with the seafood and vegetables layered, much like it was assembled. The following recipe includes an optional cream sauce finish that makes it perfect for a special occasion. If you serve this layered, in the traditional style, omit the last step and before serving set the dish aside for about 20 minutes, covered, to allow the flavours to meld.

TO PREPARE THE FISH Under cold running water, rinse the grouper, monkfish, sea bass, and skate fish. Place on a plate or platter, sprinkle both sides with ½ Tbsp (7 mL) coarse salt, and set aside for about 1 hour. Rinse the fish again and pat dry with paper towels. Set aside.

TO CLEAN THE SHELLFISH Using a stiff brush, scrub clams and mussels under cold running water to remove surface sand and grit. Remove beards attached to mussels. Discard any clams or mussels that are not tightly closed.

Using kitchen shears, cut each shrimp shell along the back. Pull out the intestinal veins. Remove the legs but leave the shell and tail on each shrimp. Rinse the shrimp under cold running water and pat dry with paper towels.

Method continues...

MAKES 6 TO 8 SERVINGS

8 oz (240 g) grouper

8 oz (240 g) monkfish

8 oz (240 g) sea bass

8 oz (240 g) skate fish

3 Tbsp (45 mL) coarse sea salt

6 clams

6 mussels

6 shrimps, in shells

8 oz (240 g) squid

1 red pepper, seeded, cored, and halved

10 Tbsp (150 mL) olive oil

3 onions, sliced

8 cloves garlic, minced

1 cup (250 mL) tomato sauce

3 tomatoes, peeled, seeded, and chopped

6 bay leaves

2 sprigs fresh thyme, chopped

1½ lb (750 g) potatoes, peeled and sliced into ½-inch-thick (1 cm) pieces

6 Tbsp (90 mL) lemon juice

Fine salt and coarsely ground black pepper, to taste

¼ cup (60 mL) + 2 Tbsp (30 mL) port (approx.)

¾ cup (185 mL) white wine (approx.)

1 cup (250 mL) clam juice

4 or 5 sprigs fresh parsley

Ingredients continue on page 94...

SEAFOOD STEW

(continued)

TO PREPARE THE SQUID Grab hold of the body and, using your fingers, grab the plastic-like backbone that is attached to the inside of the squid sac. Detach the bone and pull it out; all of the intestines should come out with it. Empty the sac by placing it upside down and squeezing from tip to bottom. Insert your baby finger in the sac to make sure it is empty and remove any stringy entrails attached or otherwise. If desired, pull off the purple skin and back fins (they should come off easily using your fingernail) and discard. Using a sharp knife, separate the tentacles from the rest of the body by cutting them off just above the eyes. In the centre of the tentacles you will find a hard black beak; remove it. Discard everything but the tentacles and sac. Cut the squid sac into thick rings and cut the tentacles in half. Rinse under cold running water and pat dry with paper towels. Set aside.

TO ROAST THE RED PEPPER Grill the red pepper on high over direct heat (or about 4 inches/10 cm from hot coals) for 2 to 3 minutes per side or until somewhat blackened. Plunge into ice water and set aside for a few minutes. Use a knife to scrape off the skin. Slice the pepper into ½-inch-thick (1 cm) strips. Set aside.

Using a knife, scrape off and discard any salt that has not dissolved on the grouper, monkfish, sea bass, and skate fish. Cut each fish into 3 to 4 pieces and set aside.

In a skillet over medium heat, heat 3 Tbsp (45 mL) of the oil. Add the onion and garlic and sauté for 8 to 10 minutes, until evenly browned. Reduce the heat, if necessary, and stir often to prevent the garlic from burning. Remove from the heat and set aside.

In a large pot, seafood kettle, or Dutch oven, layer one-third of the onion mixture, ⅓ cup (80 mL) of the tomato sauce, one-third each of the fresh tomatoes and roasted red pepper, 2 Tbsp (30 mL) oil, half of the bay leaves, and half of the thyme. Top with the clams and mussels. Cover with half of the potatoes, 2 Tbsp (30 mL) of the lemon juice, and salt and pepper, to taste. Top with another third of the onion mixture, ⅓ cup (80 mL) of the tomato sauce, another third each of the fresh tomatoes and roasted red pepper, the remaining potatoes, and 2 Tbsp (30 mL) of the lemon juice. Cover with fish, shrimp, and the remaining onion mixture, tomato sauce, fresh tomatoes, and roasted red peppers. Sprinkle with 2 Tbsp (30 mL) of oil, and the remaining 3 bay leaves and thyme. Season with salt and black pepper, to taste. Drizzle with the remaining 2 Tbsp (30 mL) lemon juice, ¼ cup (60 mL) port, ½ cup (125 mL) white wine, and the clam juice. Add the parsley and cover.

Simmer over low heat, partially covered, for about 10 minutes, shaking the pan periodically. If required to keep the stew from drying up, gradually add up to an additional ¼ cup (60 mL) white wine, 2 Tbsp (30 mL) port, and 3 Tbsp (45 mL) oil (enough liquid to just cover the top layer of fish). Gently shake the pan; do not stir it (you do not want to disrupt the layers).

Continue cooking for 10 to 20 minutes further, until the fish is opaque and flakes easily when tested with a fork and the potatoes are tender. Cover and set aside for 20 minutes.

Remove the parsley and discard. Serve immediately.

Method continues . . .

SEAFOOD STEW
(continued)

2 Tbsp (30 mL) whipping cream

¼ cup (60 mL) chopped fresh
    coriander

Piri-piri sauce, to taste

TO MAKE AN OPTIONAL CREAM-BASED SAUCE Using a slotted spoon, carefully transfer the fish and shellfish to a large warmed serving dish. Discard any shells that do not open. Scoop out the potatoes and vegetables and add to the fish. Keep warm. Remove and discard the bay leaves then return to the pot to the heat, bring to a boil, and add the cream and coriander. Boil rapidly for 2 to 3 minutes or until the sauce thickens to desired consistency. Taste and adjust the seasonings with salt and pepper. Add piri-piri sauce, if desired, or serve it alongside. Pour the thickened sauce over the fish and serve.

I like to use roasted red peppers instead of the expected fresh for a smoky, sweet flavour boost. I sometimes omit the potatoes and instead pour the fish and robust sauce over slices of cornbread to soak up the tantalizing broth. There is plenty of room for variation. Toss in some fresh herbs and add the fish of your choice to make this dish uniquely your own (just be sure to keep the clams on the bottom, and layer sturdy and oily fish on the top).

Excellent for entertaining, you can make most of this dish ahead of time and have a simmering pot ready just before guests arrive (with or without the cream finish).

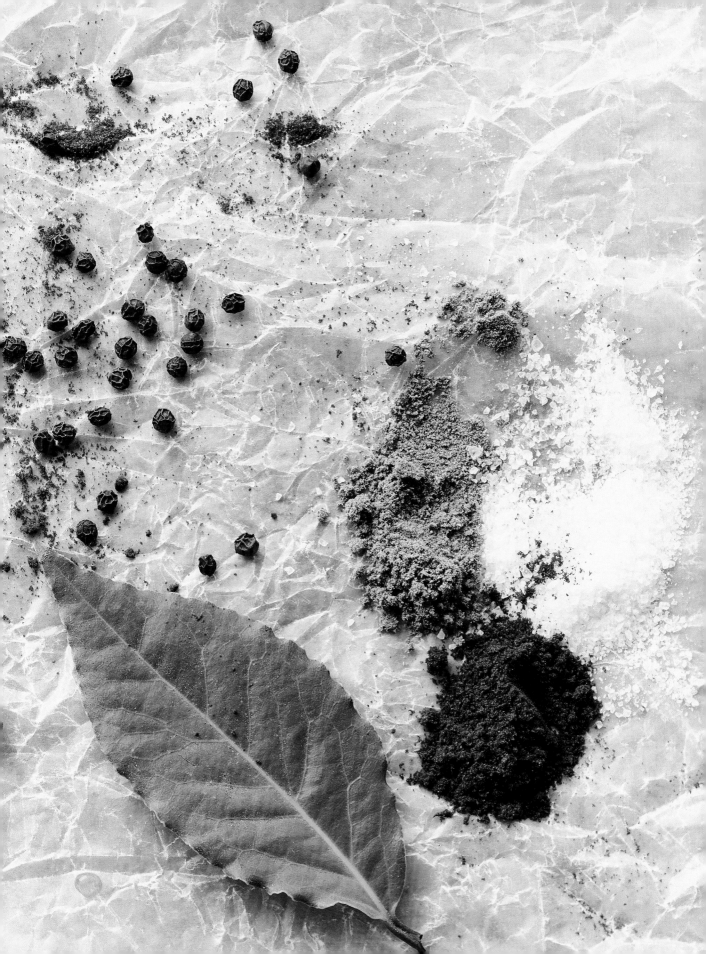

SEAFOOD

Mariscos

Whether from the Azores, Mozambique, Cape Verde, or mainland Portugal, the Portuguese love seafood. In fact, they love all things from the sea and are masters at drawing out every last drop of flavour, sometimes from unexpected places. On more than one occasion I've enjoyed the treasure of dried-up seaweed (fried with garlic and pimento paste) brought back by a family member from a recent trip to the Azores. And at a small restaurant in a costal village in Portugal, my husband and I observed staff eating what looked like a pile of mashed potatoes. After further investigation, we got to taste the unusually textured and light-tasting octopus eggs a fisherman had just brought in from his day's catch.

In North American kitchens far from the sea, the Portuguese are just as happy using frozen seafood. Frozen cuttlefish, squid, and gigantic octopus are savoured in a variety of dishes—the Portuguese are *passionate* for octopus, preferring the ones from Portugal or Moroccan waters for overall taste and superior cooking results. Large octopus is usually simmered over low heat until tender. And almost every part is used. Bits of tentacle and flecks of purple skin flavour the broth used to make rich dishes like Octopus Rice (page 126). Octopus meat is grilled, roasted, or briefly pan-fried in a simple garlic oil. And cuttlefish is fast becoming one of my favourite seafoods as it delivers a depth of flavour and tolerates a simmering pot. Adding cuttlefish to stews such as White Beans and Cuttlefish in a Cumin and

Port Tomato Sauce (page 114) infuses a comforting flavour that you'll return to again and again.

In my North American kitchen, I have discovered simple methods to deepen seafood flavours naturally. Bringing every little sea morsel to the kitchen, much like farmers who consume every bit of their pigs from nose to tail, curbs waste and layers flavour. Clever cooks can create flavourful meals without using the more popular (and expensive) crab, lobster, and shrimp by combining just a few inexpensive shellfish, such as one or two clams or mussels, with oily fish to boost flavour and nutritional value.

Seafood is a decadent treat that cooks up quickly and makes an indulgent meal any day of the week. Clams in Cataplana with Pork, White Wine, and Coriander (page 100) or Spicy Shrimp with Beer and Garlic (page 109) are just a couple of the seafood dishes you can easily make at home. Juicy tomatoes, fresh herbs, aromatic onion and garlic, and homemade stock can help to make outstanding seafood stews, soups, and rice. Get to know your local fishmonger to find out how you can purchase the freshest ingredients. Check out ethnic grocery stores that specialize in seafood. Be sure to have plenty of crusty Portuguese bread on hand to dip into the flavourful sauces these dishes produce.

SEAFOOD

Mariscos

CLAMS IN CATAPLANA WITH PORK, WHITE WINE, AND CORIANDER

Amêijoas na Cataplana

MAKES 4 APPETIZER SERVINGS
OR 2 MAIN-COURSE SERVINGS

2 lb (1 kg) Manila clams

¼ cup (60 mL) olive oil

4 oz (120 g) pork tenderloin, cubed

1 onion, chopped

3 cloves garlic, minced

1½ cups (375 mL) peeled, seeded, and chopped tomatoes

½ red bell pepper, seeded, cored, and diced

4 oz (120 g) chouriço, sliced into ½-inch (1 cm) pieces

1 bay leaf

½ tsp (2 mL) fine salt

¼ tsp (1 mL) coarsely ground black pepper

½ tsp (2 mL) dried oregano

¼ tsp (1 mL) piri-piri sauce or Tabasco sauce

½ cup (125 mL) dry white wine

¼ cup (60 mL) chopped fresh coriander

2 slices prosciutto, coarsely chopped

A *cataplana*, a hinged clam-shaped cooking vessel, is so popular in the Algarve beach resorts that dozens of dishes have been named after it. If you do not have a cataplana, use a wok or a large pot with a tight-fitting lid and carefully cover the lid with a kitchen towel; do not uncover the pot while cooking.

Using a stiff brush, scrub the clams under cold running water to remove any surface sand and grit. Discard any clams that are not tightly closed. Set aside.

In a large heavy saucepan or Dutch oven, heat the oil over medium heat; cook the pork for 2 to 3 minutes, until browned, and transfer to a dish; reserve. Add the onion and garlic and cook, stirring occasionally, for 3 to 5 minutes, until softened. Add the tomatoes, red pepper, chouriço, bay leaf, salt, pepper, oregano, and piri-piri sauce; simmer for 7 to 10 minutes, until slightly thickened.

Transfer half of the tomato mixture to the bottom of the cataplana. Arrange the clams overtop and cover with the remaining tomato mixture. Tightly secure the cataplana lid and simmer over medium-high heat for 5 minutes. Flip the cataplana over and unlatch it; add the reserved pork and the wine and sprinkle with the coriander and prosciutto. Tightly secure the cataplana lid and cook until the shells open and the pork juices run clear when pierced with fork, 5 to 8 minutes (check for doneness after 5 minutes of cooking and continue cooking if meat is still pink). Discard any clams that have not opened. Serve immediately, directly from the cataplana.

In Portugal, cockles are used to make this dish, but Manila clams are tasty substitutes.

GOLDEN CRÊPES STUFFED WITH CRAB

Crepes de Caranguejo

MAKES ABOUT 24 CRÊPES

CRAB FILLING

2 Tbsp (30 mL) vegetable oil

1 small onion, finely chopped

1 clove garlic, minced

4 oz (120 g) crabmeat, diced

½ cup (125 mL) dry white wine

¼ tsp (1 mL) fine salt

¼ tsp (1 mL) coarsely ground
     white pepper

1 bay leaf

1 cup (250 mL) cold whole milk

2 Tbsp (30 mL) cornstarch

CRÊPES

3 eggs

1 ¾ cups (435 mL) whole milk

¾ cup (185 mL) all-purpose flour

½ tsp (2 mL) fine salt

1 Tbsp (15 mL) vegetable oil
     (approx.)

COATING

2 eggs

1 cup (250 mL) dry breadcrumbs

½ cup (125 mL) butter

¼ cup (60 mL) chopped fresh
     parsley, for garnish

These Portuguese crepes are dipped in egg and breadcrumbs and briefly fried until golden. They are usually eaten sandwich-style, as a *petisco* (snack). They also make an elegant dinner when served in a pool of White Sauce (page 278). Use the crêpe recipe to wrap a variety of fillings, such as prosciutto and cheese, in place of the crab. The crêpes can also be stuffed with fruit and ice cream and topped with Port Sauce (page 292) and toasted pine nuts.

TO MAKE THE CRAB FILLING In a large heavy saucepan or Dutch oven, heat the oil over medium-high heat. Cook the onion and garlic for 3 to 5 minutes, until softened. Add the crabmeat, wine, salt, white pepper, and bay leaf. Simmer over medium-low heat, stirring occasionally, for about 5 minutes, until the wine is reduced by half.

In a small bowl, combine the cold milk and cornstarch; gradually pour it into the crab mixture, stirring constantly. Cook until the sauce is thickened and smooth. Discard the bay leaf and set aside.

TO MAKE THE CRÊPES In a large bowl or blender, beat together the eggs and milk; blend in the flour and salt. Cover and let stand at room temperature for 20 minutes.

In a 6-inch (15 cm) crêpe pan or skillet over medium-high heat, heat the oil. When the oil is nice and hot, add about 2 Tbsp (30 mL) of the batter to the pan. Swirl to coat the pan, then pour the excess back into the bowl. Cook the crêpe for about 1 minute per side, until lightly browned on both sides, turning once.

Transfer the crêpe to a wire rack to cool. Repeat with remaining batter, adding more oil if necessary. (If making ahead, stack the crêpes between sheets of waxed paper, wrap in foil or plastic wrap, and refrigerate for up to 1 week or freeze for longer storage.)

Spoon about 1 Tbsp (15 mL) of the crabmeat filling onto each crêpe. Fold up the sides and roll up spring-roll fashion; secure with a toothpick. Set aside to cool completely.

TO MAKE THE COATING In a shallow dish, beat together the eggs. In another shallow dish, place the breadcrumbs. One at a time, dip the cooled crêpes into the egg wash and then into the crumbs, turning or shaking to coat all over.

In a heavy skillet, melt the butter over medium-high heat. Add the prepared crêpe and cook for about 1 minute, until golden brown, turning once. Repeat with the remaining crêpes, adding more butter to the pan if necessary. Wipe the excess crumbs from the skillet if you find they are browning.

Serve hot or at room temperature sprinkled with chopped fresh parsley.

AZOREAN-STYLE CRAB IN THE SHELL

Caranguejo à Açoreana

**MAKES 4 APPETIZER SERVINGS
OR 2 MAIN-COURSE SERVINGS**

1 crab (3 lb/1.5 kg) or
    2 small crabs

4 cloves garlic, minced

2 Tbsp (30 mL) tomato paste

2 Tbsp (30 mL) white wine vinegar

2 tsp (10 mL) pimento paste

½ tsp (2 mL) ground allspice

1 bottle beer (12 oz/355 mL)

3 Tbsp (45 mL) olive oil (approx.)

2 onions, chopped

½ tsp (2 mL) fine salt

¼ cup (60 mL) chopped
    fresh parsley

In North American–Azorean homes, long after the Christmas Eve dinner dishes have been cleared, everyone has room for this traditional late-night holiday snack. Cooked earlier in the day, the crab has been soaking in a fragrant sauce; it is quickly reheated and served hot. Half the fun is savouring the last morsels by swishing a little wine around in the bowl-like shell. If you are using a live crab, precook for five to ten minutes before marinating.

Using a stiff brush, scrub the crab thoroughly under cold running water to remove any sand between the shell and legs. Pat dry with paper towels. Transfer to a resealable bag and place in a large bowl. Set aside.

In a bowl, combine the minced garlic of 3 cloves, tomato paste, vinegar, pimento paste, allspice, and beer. Pour the marinade into the bag with the crab. Seal the bag and gently turn to coat well. Set aside for about 20 minutes, turning several times. Remove the crab from the marinade, letting the excess drip off, and set aside; reserve the marinade.

In a large heavy saucepan or deep skillet, heat the oil over medium-high heat. Cook the onion and remaining garlic for 5 to 8 minutes, until evenly browned. Add the crab and cook for about 5 minutes on each side, until the shell is lightly golden. Add the reserved marinade and salt to the saucepan, cover, and bring to a boil. Reduce the heat to medium and simmer for about 15 minutes (less for small crabs), until the shell is bright red, turning the crab over after 10 minutes. Remove the pan from the heat and let cool for 10 minutes. For a stronger flavour, cover the saucepan and set it aside for 30 minutes then reheat the crab in the marinade just before serving.

If you are using 1 large crab, disassemble it before serving. To do this, hold the crab firmly and pull off the top shell; set it aside. Pull or scrape off the spongy gills on both sides of the soft stomach and discard. Turn the crab over; break off the triangular apron and mouth parts. Turn the crab over again and discard the soft stomach and entrails. Holding the crab on each

side where the legs are, crack the crab in half along the centre of its body. Fold it in half and twist to separate the two halves of the body. Break off the legs and claws. Reassemble the crab on the serving dish and sprinkle with parsley. Present the sauce in the top shell.

If you are using small crabs, serve them whole. Sprinkle with parsley and serve the sauce on the side.

BARBECUED CUTTLEFISH

Chocos na Brasa

Cuttlefish have a thicker skin than squid, but they are very similar in taste and general appearance. Although squid is best stuffed, cuttlefish stays tender in barbecues and stews. This recipe calls for cuttlefish, but you can use squid if that is what you have on hand. If you are using squid, choose large ones, which will be thicker skinned and more suitable for grilling.

Choose between a perky lemon piri-piri sauce or an onion and parsley dressing, or simply drizzle with a few drops of lemon or oil and vinegar. Serve on a bed of watercress, if desired.

TO PREPARE THE CUTTLEFISH OR SQUID Rinse the cuttlefish or squid under cold running water. Grab hold of the body and, using your fingers, grab the plastic-like backbone that is attached to the inside of the squid sac. Detach the bone and pull it out; all of the intestines should come out with it. Empty the sac by placing it upside down and squeezing from tip to bottom. Make sure the sac is empty and remove any remaining stringy entrails. If desired, pull off the purple skin and back fins (they should come off easily using your fingernail) and discard. Using a sharp knife, separate the tentacles from the rest of the body by cutting them off just above the eyes. In the centre of the tentacles you will find a hard black beak; remove it. Discard everything but the tentacles and sac. Rinse thoroughly before using. (Cuttlefish can also be purchased cleaned and/or frozen. If buying frozen, partially defrosting it before using will make cutting an easier task. Examine inside the sac for any attached entrails and rinse well under cold running water before using.) If barbecuing large squid or cuttlefish, cut the body in three or four places in even intervals, without separating the pieces. These incisions will help ensure the molluscs cook evenly.

Method continues...

MAKES 4 SERVINGS

8 cuttlefish or large squid

½ cup (125 mL) Lemon
    Piri-Piri Sauce (page 282)

ONION AND PARSLEY DRESSING

¼ cup (60 mL) olive oil

1 Tbsp (15 mL) white wine vinegar

2 tsp (10 mL) finely chopped onion

1 Tbsp (15 mL) chopped fresh
    parsley

Fine salt and coarsely ground
    black pepper, to taste

BARBECUED CUTTLEFISH
(continued)

Grill the cuttlefish on high (or about 4 inches/10 cm from hot coals) for 2 to 3 minutes, until browned on the bottom. Carefully turn it over and grill for 2 to 3 minutes longer, until browned and a fork easily pierces the meat (if you are using squid, it may require less cooking time than the cuttlefish). Transfer the cuttlefish to a plate and keep warm.

Meanwhile, make the Lemon Piri-Piri Sauce or dressing (or prepare them ahead of time).

TO MAKE THE ONION AND PARSLEY DRESSING Combine the oil, vinegar, onion, parsley, and salt and pepper.

Spoon the sauce or dressing over the grilled cuttlefish, or serve alongside, and enjoy immediately.

SPICY SHRIMP WITH BEER AND GARLIC

Camarão à Moda do Minho

Even in the northern Minho region, renowned for its beef and lamb, the Portuguese have a talent for delicious and simple seafood dishes like this one. Cook the shrimp with the shells on to seal in flavour and tenderness. Serve this with collard greens and Milk Bread (page 307).

TO PREPARE THE SHRIMP Using kitchen shears, cut each shrimp shell along the back. Pull out the intestinal vein. Remove the legs but leave the shell and tail on each shrimp. Rinse under cold running water and pat dry with paper towels. Set aside.

In a saucepan, heat the oil over medium-low heat. Cook the garlic, stirring occasionally, for 2 minutes, until softened. Add the prepared shrimp and cook for 1 minute on each side. Stir in the beer, wine, piri-piri sauce, paprika, and salt; bring to a boil over medium-high heat. Cover and cook for about 2 minutes, until the shrimp are pink and firm when pierced with a fork. Remove from the heat and set aside, covered, for 15 minutes. If desired, strain the sauce through a fine-mesh sieve before serving. Garnish with lemon wedges.

MAKES 4 APPETIZER SERVINGS OR 2 MAIN-COURSE SERVINGS

8 oz (240 g) large shrimp, in shells (about 12)

3 Tbsp (45 mL) olive oil

4 cloves garlic, minced

1 cup (250 mL) beer

2 Tbsp (30 mL) dry white wine

2 tsp (10 mL) piri-piri sauce or Tabasco sauce

½ tsp (2 mL) paprika

½ tsp (2 mL) fine salt

Lemon wedges, for garnish

SQUID STUFFED WITH CHOURIÇO AND SHRIMP

Lulas Recheadas

MAKES 4 TO 6 SERVINGS

10 medium-sized squid

5 Tbsp (75 mL) olive oil

1 Tbsp (15 mL) butter

3 onions, chopped

5 cloves garlic, minced

4 oz (120 g) chouriço, fat removed, finely diced

4 oz (120 g) shrimp, shelled and deveined

1¼ cups (310 mL) peeled, seeded, and chopped tomatoes or tomato sauce

1¼ cups (310 mL) dry white wine

2 bay leaves

2 Tbsp (30 mL) chopped fresh parsley, for garnish

2 Tbsp (30 mL) chopped fresh coriander, for garnish

Squid is slippery and has a very tiny opening, which makes it impossible to stuff without making a big mess. But the rich flavours of the squid, olive oil, chouriço, and seasonings make this dish well worth the finicky chore of stuffing it.

TO PREPARE THE SQUID Rinse the squid under cold running water. Grab hold of the body and, using your fingers, grab the plastic-like backbone that is attached to the inside of the squid sac. Detach the bone and pull it out; all of the intestines should come out with it. Empty the sac by placing it upside down and squeezing from tip to bottom. Make sure the sac is empty and remove any remaining stringy entrails. If desired, pull off the purple skin and back fins and discard (they should come off easily using your fingernail; it is not necessary to remove the skin from the tentacles). Using a sharp knife, separate the tentacles from the rest of the body by cutting them off just above the eyes. In the centre of the tentacles you will find a hard black beak; remove it. Discard everything but the tentacles and sac. Rinse thoroughly before using. (Squid can also be purchased cleaned and/or frozen. If buying frozen, partially defrosting it before using will make cutting an easier task. Examine inside the sac for any attached entrails and rinse well under cold running water before using.) Finely chop the tentacles. Repeat with the remaining squid. Pat the squid dry with paper towels and set aside.

TO MAKE THE FILLING In a saucepan over medium heat, add 2 Tbsp (30 mL) of the oil and the butter and heat until the butter melts. Add two-thirds of the onions and half of the minced garlic and cook over medium heat for 8 to 10 minutes, until evenly browned, reducing the heat and stirring often if necessary. Add the chouriço, shrimp, and squid tentacles and cook over medium heat for about 10 minutes, until softened. Let cool. (The filling can be prepared ahead of time. Will keep in the refrigerator for up to 2 days.)

TO MAKE THE SAUCE Meanwhile, in another saucepan over medium heat, add

2 Tbsp (30 mL) of the oil and the remaining onion and garlic, and cook for 6 to 8 minutes, just until the onions are translucent but not browned. Add the tomatoes, wine, and bay leaves and bring to a boil over high heat. Boil for about 5 minutes, until reduced by one-third, stirring occasionally. (The sauce can be prepared ahead of time. Will keep in the refrigerator for up to 4 days.)

TO STUFF THE SQUID Using a small dessert spoon or your hands, carefully stuff about 2 Tbsp (30 mL) of the filling into each squid sac. Be careful not to overstuff or the sacs will pop open. Secure the openings with a toothpick and set aside.

In a skillet over medium-high heat, heat the remaining 1 Tbsp (15 mL) of oil. Add the prepared squid and cook, turning to brown all sides, for about 1 minute per side. Add the tomato sauce, cover, and bring to a boil over medium heat. Cook for about 15 minutes, tightly covered, until the squid is tender and heated through. Sprinkle with parsley and coriander and serve.

If you make the stuffing and sauce in advance, the flavour improves. Many Portuguese cooks add a finely diced carrot and a cup of bread- crumbs to make the dish less meaty. If you do this, you will have enough stuffing for about five additional squid.

GRILLED OCTOPUS IN RED PEPPER AND OLIVE RELISH

Polvo com Pimenta Vermelha e Azeitonas Picadas

MAKES ABOUT 6 SERVINGS

1 large octopus, 6 to 8 lb (2.7 to 3.5 kg)

¾ cup (185 mL) olive oil (approx.)

20 cloves garlic

1 onion, quartered

12 bay leaves

4 cloves garlic, finely diced

1 cup (250 mL) Red Pepper and Olive Relish (page 284), for garnish (Lemon Piri-Piri Sauce, page 282, or Parsley Dressing, page 280, is also delicious)

1 lemon, cut into wedges, for garnish

¼ cup (60 mL) chopped fresh parsley, for garnish

¼ cup (60 mL) chopped fresh coriander, for garnish

When my husband first tasted grilled octopus in red pepper and olive relish, he claimed it was the best octopus he had ever tasted. Chef José Alves of Via Norte in Toronto showed me how to achieve tender results. He insists quality ingredients are the hallmark of producing good food. I witnessed this when I volunteered in his kitchen for a few hours almost every week for more than two years. He was not afraid to return anything that did not meet his high standards. Known for his talent preparing fish, he has fresh fish shipped to his kitchen twice a week to ensure that his customers are satisfied.

Chef Alves cooks his octopus from frozen and leaves the skin on, which lends a purplish hue to the cooking broth (reserve the water to make Octopus Rice, page 126). If you prefer to clean and remove the skin before cooking, follow the directions provided below. You can also remove the skin after cooking easily with a clean dish cloth or your hands. Look for large frozen octopus at ethnic grocery stores or ask your fishmonger to order some for you.

TO PREPARE THE OCTOPUS Rinse the octopus under cold running water. Using a sharp knife, cut through the sac-like body of the octopus, separating the tentacles from the body. Pull open the body sac and discard the attached innards and stringy entrails. Pull out and cut away the hard beak in the centre of the tentacles and discard. Cut the hood into 4 pieces and set aside. Peel the skin from the body sac and tentacles. (Alternatively, to loosen the skin, parboil the octopus for 2 minutes and then plunge it into cold water; use your fingers or a knife to peel away the skin. If it can't be completely removed, repeat the parboiling process.) Rinse the octopus under cold running water and pat dry. Note that frozen octopus is usually already cleaned of its entrails and other inedible pieces, but it's always a good idea to check before cooking.

In a large stockpot, heat ½ cup (125 mL) of the oil over medium-high heat; add the 20 whole cloves of garlic, onion, and bay leaves and cook, stirring occasionally, for 8 to 9 minutes, until the vegetables begin to brown and soften. Add the octopus and continue cooking for 2 to 3 minutes, until well coated. Cover the octopus with boiling water and simmer for about 45 to 60 minutes, until a fork just pierces the sides of the largest tentacles. (Keep in mind that the octopus will be cooked further.) Using a slotted spoon, transfer the octopus to a bowl and set aside. (You can now refrigerate the octopus until ready to use. It will keep for up to 4 days.)

In a saucepan large enough to fit the octopus, heat ¼ cup (60 mL) of the oil over medium heat. Add the diced garlic and cook, stirring occasionally, for about 3 minutes, until softened. Set pan aside.

Grill the octopus on high (or about 4 inches/10 cm from hot coals) for 3 to 4 minutes, until browned on the bottom, brushing it in intervals with up to ½ Tbsp (7 mL) of oil. Carefully turn over the octopus and grill for 3 to 5 minutes longer, until grill marks appear. Remove from the grill.

Add the grilled octopus to the pan with the oil and garlic, toss to coat well, and heat over medium heat for about 1 minute, shaking the pan to prevent the octopus from sticking to the bottom. Flip the octopus and cook for 1 minute longer to coat. Transfer the octopus to a serving plate and top with 2 to 3 Tbsp (30 to 45 mL) of Red Pepper and Olive Relish (or your condiment of choice). Serve the remaining relish on the side. Taste the octopus and adjust the seasonings with salt and pepper just before serving.

If desired, you can omit the relish and garnish the octopus with a squirt of lemon and a sprinkling of parsley and coriander.

José prefers octopus fished off of the Moroccan coast (and Portuguese when available). In the summer, when octopus is in demand, he boils it in advance and keeps it refrigerated for a day or two. You can do the same: refrigerate the cooked octopus for up to 48 hours ahead of time and keep it covered until ready to use. Grill the octopus just before serving and toss with the Portuguese seasonings while still hot.

WHITE BEANS AND CUTTLEFISH IN A CUMIN AND PORT TOMATO SAUCE

Feijão Branco com Chocos

MAKES ABOUT 4 SERVINGS

2½ lb (1.25 kg) cuttlefish, cleaned

4 cups (1 L) water

1 tsp (5 mL) salt (approx.)

1½ cups (375 mL) collards, broccoli rabe, or cabbage (stems and coarse ribs discarded), cut crosswise and chopped

3 Tbsp (45 mL) olive oil

3 oz (90 g) bacon, quartered

4 oz (120 g) chouriço, cut into 2 or 3 pieces

2 onions, chopped

4 carrots, finely chopped

4 cloves garlic, minced

2 cups (500 mL) peeled, seeded, and chopped tomatoes

1 Tbsp (15 mL) tomato paste

1 cup (250 mL) canned white kidney beans (or dried, soaked, and cooked)

1 Tbsp (15 mL) ground cumin

¼ bunch parsley, ends trimmed and stems tied into a bouquet with butcher's twine

2 bay leaves

1 small chili pepper, chopped

¾ cup (185 mL) dry white wine

3 Tbsp (45 mL) white port (approx.)

1 cup (250 mL) Fish Stock (page 75) or clam juice (approx.)

Fine salt and coarsely ground black pepper

½ cup (125 mL) chopped fresh coriander

This dish reflects two Portuguese passions: fish from the sea and hearty beans grown on the land. Both provide excellent sustenance and, together with Portuguese seasonings of wine, garlic, onion, tomatoes, cumin, and port, make for a full-flavoured yet inexpensive fish stew.

TO PREPARE THE CUTTLEFISH Rinse the cuttlefish under cold running water. Grab hold of the body and, using your fingers, grab the plastic-like backbone that is attached to the inside of the squid sac. Detach the bone and pull it out; all of the intestines should come out with it. Empty the sac by placing it upside down and squeezing from tip to bottom. Make sure the sac is empty and remove any remaining stringy entrails. If desired, pull off the purple skin and back fins (they should come off easily using your fingernail) and discard. Using a sharp knife, separate the tentacles from the rest of the body by cutting them off just above the eyes. In the centre of the tentacles you will find a hard black beak; remove it. Discard everything but the tentacles and sac. Rinse thoroughly before using. (Cuttlefish can also be purchased cleaned and/or frozen. If buying frozen, partially defrosting it before using will make cutting an easier task. Examine inside the sac for any attached entrails and rinse well under cold running water before using.) Chop into bite-sized pieces. Rinse the cuttlefish under cold running water and pat dry. Set aside.

In a large pot, combine the water, salt, and the collard greens. Bring to a boil and simmer for 5 to 7 minutes, until bright green and tender. Drain and set aside.

In a large heavy saucepan or Dutch oven, heat the olive oil over medium-high heat. Add the bacon and chouriço and cook to brown the meat and render the fat, about 10 minutes. Transfer the meat to a cutting board, cool, and chop; set aside.

Discard all but 3 Tbsp (45 mL) of the fat in the pan and heat over medium-high heat. Add the onion and carrots and cook, stirring often, until lightly browned, about 7 to 8 minutes. Stir to scrape up any browned bits from the bottom of the pan. Add the garlic and cook for 1 to 2 minutes, until the garlic and vegetables are evenly browned. Reduce the heat, if necessary, and stir often to prevent the garlic from burning. Add the tomatoes and crush them slightly with the back of a spoon; cook until the sauce is thickened and the liquids dry out, 6 to 8 minutes. Add the tomato paste and cook for 3 to 4 minutes longer, until the mixture reaches a deep-red colour. If the paste is browning too quickly, reduce the heat as needed.

One at a time and stirring after each addition, add the cuttlefish, reserved bacon and chouriço, beans, cumin, parsley bundle, bay leaves, and chili pepper. Continue cooking for 5 to 7 minutes, until a thick, flavourful sauce forms. Add the white wine, port, and about ½ cup (125 mL) of the fish stock; bring to a boil over medium-high heat and cook for 7 to 10 minutes, until the cuttlefish is almost cooked. If the liquids are drying up too quickly, add up to ½ cup (125 mL) stock and reduce the heat to medium-low. Partially cover and cook for 3 to 6 minutes further, until the cuttlefish is fork-tender. Add the prepared collard greens and cook, stirring to combine well, until warmed through. Remove the pan from the heat; taste and adjust the seasonings with salt and pepper. Remove and discard the bay leaves and parsley bundle.

To serve, sprinkle with coriander and serve over a bed of rice or potatoes.

Cuttlefish is a more flavourful and hardier fish than the thin-skinned squid and, as a result, is perfect for this stew. For best results, use the largest cuttlefish you can find (substitute large squid if you can't find cuttlefish).

AUNT EMILIA'S SQUID

Lulas' da Tia Emilia

MAKES 6 TO 8 SERVINGS

2 to 3 lb (1 to 1.5 kg) extra-large
   squid

2 Tbsp (30 mL) lemon juice

Zest from 1 lemon

1 tsp (5 mL) fine salt

¼ tsp (1 mL) coarsely ground
   black pepper

¼ cup (60 mL) butter

2 Tbsp (30 mL) olive oil

2 onions, minced

7 cloves garlic, minced

1 cup (250 mL) finely chopped
   fresh parsley

2 bay leaves

1 Tbsp (15 mL) all-purpose flour

2 cans tomato paste
   (5.5 oz/156 mL each)

1½ cups (375 mL) dry white wine

2 tsp (10 mL) Dijon mustard

½ tsp (2 mL) ground nutmeg

2½ cups (625 mL) Fish Stock
   (page 75) or chicken stock
   (approx.)

¼ cup (60 mL) port

⅔ cup (160 mL) parboiled
   long-grain rice

2 eggs

½ cup (125 mL) finely chopped
   fresh parsley

This squid casserole makes an elegant dish for entertaining. It can be made ahead of time and heated up to a golden, bubbly finish just before serving. Making this dish earlier in the day will allow more time for the port wine to impart its irresistible rich flavour to the tomato and squid sauce.

TO CLEAN THE SQUID Grab hold of the body and, using your fingers, grab the plastic-like backbone that is attached to the inside of the squid sac. Detach this backbone and pull this out with all the intestines. Empty the squid sac (tube) by placing it upside down and squeezing it from tip to bottom. Use your fingers to make sure the sac is empty. Using a sharp knife, cut off the tentacles just above the eyes separating the tentacles from the rest of the body. In the center of the tentacles you will find a hard black beak; remove and discard it. Discard everything but the tentacles and the squid sac. It is best not to pull off the skin as it will give the sauce its flavour. Using a sharp knife, cut the sacs into ½-inch (1 cm) rings. Rinse under cold running water and pat dry with paper towels. Transfer the cleaned squid to a dish; add the lemon juice and lemon zest, salt, and pepper and mix well. Set aside at room temperature for about 30 minutes to marinate.

In a large saucepan or Dutch oven over medium-high heat, melt the butter with the oil. Add the onion and garlic and cook, stirring occasionally, for 8 to 9 minutes, until the vegetables begin to brown. Add the parsley, bay leaves, and squid with lemon juice, stir, and continue cooking for about 5 minutes. Sprinkle with flour and cook over medium-low heat, without browning, for about 3 minutes, stirring constantly. Whisk in the tomato paste, wine, mustard, nutmeg, and 1½ cups (375 mL) of the stock. Bring to a boil over medium-high heat. Reduce the heat to low and cook, partially covered, at a low simmer for about 25 minutes, until the squid is easily pierced with a fork and the sauce is reduced by a quarter. Stir occasionally to prevent the squid from sticking to the bottom of the pan and add ½ to 1 cup (125 to 250 mL) more stock if the sauce dries up.

(If the squid cooks too quickly, use a slotted spoon to remove it and set it aside. Once the sauce is reduced, you can return the squid to the pan and continue with the recipe.)

Increase the heat to high, add the port, and bring to a boil; cook a further 4 to 5 minutes, until the alcohol burns off. Remove from the heat and, if time allows, set it aside for 15 to 20 minutes to marinate. Taste and adjust the seasonings with salt, pepper, and additional mustard and nutmeg, to taste.

Meanwhile, cook the rice according to package directions. Set aside to cool.

Grease a 9- × 13-inch (3.5 L) baking dish and arrange half of the rice in one even layer. Reserve about 1 cup (250 mL) of the tomato and squid sauce for serving. Top the rice with half of the remaining sauce, using the back of a fork to help cover the rice completely. Repeat with a layer of the remaining rice and top with remaining sauce. (You can make this ahead up to this point. Loosely cover it with foil and set aside at room temperature for up to 3 hours, until ready to use, or cover and refrigerate for up to 24 hours. Bring to room temperature before baking.)

About 30 minutes before serving, lightly beat the eggs and evenly pour over the squid casserole. Bake in a preheated 375°F (190°C) oven for 10 to 15 minutes, until bubbling and golden and the squid is heated through. Set aside to cool for 15 to 20 minutes. Sprinkle with parsley and serve with the reserved tomato and squid sauce.

My friend Olidia Hipolito always doubles the tomato and squid sauce in this recipe—family members, she says, cannot help but sneak bites of squid when they think she's not looking. Doubling this recipe ensures there is enough left for suppertime.

MOZAMBIQUE CURRIED SHRIMP

Camarão à Moda de Moçambique

MAKES 4 TO 6 SERVINGS

1 lb (500 g) large shrimp, in shells

3 Tbsp (45 mL) olive oil

1 Tbsp (15 mL) butter

1 large onion, finely chopped

3 cloves garlic, minced

2 bay leaves

1 small piri-piri pepper, seeded and finely chopped

1½ cups (375 mL) chopped tomatoes

2 to 3 Tbsp (30 to 45 mL) curry powder (approx.)

1 tsp (5 mL) paprika

1 cup (250 mL) coconut cream

2 Tbsp (30 mL) lemon juice

Fine salt, to taste

Growing up as a child in Mozambique was not any different than life in Portugal as a young adult, says Clara Abreu, Portuguese reporter and newscaster for OMNI News. In both countries the grocery stores and restaurants sold Portuguese goods and Portugese prepared foods. The only significant difference was on Sunday. On Sundays in Mozambique, curried shrimp bubbled away in almost every cooking pot in the country. Off the coast of Africa, shrimp is abundant, so it is a natural accompaniment to the blend of coconut and curry spices found here, in Clara's dish. It's a very versatile curry, and a variety of seafood or chicken can be substituted for the shrimp.

This curry blend from Mozambique includes sweet paprika, a Portuguese staple. Since most store-bought curry blends do not include paprika, I like to add Spanish paprika to the following recipe.

TO PREPARE THE SHRIMP Using kitchen shears, cut each shrimp shell along the back. Pull out the intestinal vein. Remove the legs but leave the shell and tail on each shrimp. Rinse under cold running water and pat dry with paper towels. Set aside.

In a large Dutch oven, heat the oil and butter over medium-high heat until the butter is melted. Cook the onion, garlic, bay leaves, and piri-piri pepper, stirring occasionally, for 8 to 9 minutes, until the vegetables begin to brown and soften. Adjust the heat, as necessary, to prevent the garlic from burning. Add the tomatoes, about 2 Tbsp (30 mL) of the curry powder, and the paprika and bring to a boil over medium-high heat. Simmer for 6 to 8 minutes, until thickened. Add the shrimp and cook, over medium-high heat, for 1 to 2 minutes, until opaque.

Method continues . . .

MOZAMBIQUE CURRIED SHRIMP
(continued)

Add the coconut cream to the curry sauce and bring to a boil over high heat. Reduce the heat to low and cook for about 15 minutes, removing the shrimp once cooked, after about 5 minutes. Shell the shrimp and set it aside. (Wrap the shells in cheesecloth and return them to the cooking pot for a stronger shrimp flavour.) Continue cooking the curry sauce for 10 minutes further or until the sauce is reduced by half. Return the reserved shrimp to the curry and cook until heated through. Taste and add up to 1 Tbsp (15 mL) curry powder, if desired. Sprinkle with lemon juice and season with salt, to taste. Serve with rice.

When you shell the shrimp, don't toss out the shells. Wrap them in cheesecloth and return them to the curry for heightened seafood flavour. The shells can continue flavouring the stew until the last moment. Remove the wrapped shells just before serving.

MUSSELS IN TOMATO CURRY SAUCE

Mexilhão com Molho de Tomate

These mussels smothered in a curry tomato sauce take on an irresistibly sweet taste. For a spicier version, double the piri-piri sauce. Be sure to have lots of bread on hand to absorb the spicy and savoury juices. You can also toss this fresh-tasting sauce with rice or pasta.

Using a stiff brush, scrub the mussels under cold running water and remove the beards. Discard any mussels that are not tightly closed. Set aside.

In a large heavy saucepan, heat the oil over medium heat. Cook the leeks, red pepper, and garlic for 6 to 8 minutes, just until the leeks are softened. Add the tomatoes, bay leaf, curry powder, wine, and piri-piri sauce, and salt and pepper, to taste. Simmer for 10 to 15 minutes, until thickened. Add the mussels, stirring well to coat. Cook, covered, over medium heat for 5 to 7 minutes, until the mussels open. (Discard any that do not open.) Taste and adjust the seasonings, as desired (adding more curry if you prefer a stronger flavour). Remove the bay leaf. Sprinkle with the coriander and parsley and serve immediately.

MAKES 4 APPETIZER SERVINGS OR 2 MAIN-COURSE SERVINGS

2 lb (1 kg) mussels

3 Tbsp (45 mL) olive oil

2 leeks (white and green parts), cut in 3-inch (8 cm) pieces

½ red bell pepper, seeded, cored, and chopped

3 cloves garlic, minced

1½ cups (375 mL) tomato sauce or peeled, seeded, and chopped tomatoes

1 bay leaf

1 tsp (5 mL) curry powder (approx.)

1 cup (250 mL) white wine

½ tsp (2 mL) piri-piri sauce or Tabasco sauce

Fine salt and coarsely ground black pepper, to taste

3 Tbsp (45 mL) chopped fresh coriander

3 Tbsp (45 mL) chopped fresh parsley

OCTOPUS BAKED IN BEER SAUCE

Polvo Assado em Molho de Cerveja

MAKES ABOUT 3 TO 4 SERVINGS

1 octopus, 3 to 4 lb (1.5 to 1.8 kg)

BEER SAUCE

⅔ cup (160 mL) beer

3 Tbsp (45 mL) olive oil

4 Tbsp (60 mL) pimento paste

4 Tbsp (60 mL) tomato paste

2 onions, chopped

3 cloves garlic, minced

2 tsp (10 mL) paprika

¼ tsp (1 mL) coarsely ground
black pepper

½ tsp (2 mL) dried red chili flakes
(optional)

¼ tsp (1 mL) dried oregano

2 lb (1 kg) small new potatoes,
scrubbed (about 12)

Aromatic Portuguese flavourings are thick in the air when octopus in beer sauce is baking. You can use large octopus tentacles instead of a whole octopus.

TO PREPARE THE OCTOPUS Rinse the octopus under cold running water. Using a sharp knife, cut through the sac-like body of the octopus, separating the tentacles from the body. Pull open the body sac and discard the attached innards and stringy entrails. Pull out and cut away the hard beak in the centre of the tentacles and discard. Cut the hood into 4 pieces and set aside. Chop the tentacles into 2-inch (5 cm) pieces (this is easier to do if the octopus is partially frozen). Rinse the octopus pieces under cold running water and pat dry with paper towels. In a greased 11- × 7-inch (2 L) baking dish, arrange the octopus in a single layer. Set aside.

In a small bowl, combine the beer, oil, pimento paste, tomato paste, onions, garlic, paprika, pepper, chili flakes, and oregano. Pour the sauce over the octopus. Cover and bake in a 400°F (200°C) oven for 45 to 50 minutes, turning and basting twice.

Meanwhile, in a saucepan, parboil the potatoes for 5 minutes. Transfer the potatoes to the pan with the octopus and stir to evenly cover with the sauce. Bake, uncovered, for 20 to 25 minutes longer, basting often, until a fork easily pierces the side of a larger tentacle and the potatoes are tender and golden brown. Using a slotted spoon, transfer the octopus and potatoes to a serving platter. If desired, transfer the sauce to a saucepan, pour off the fat, and boil over high heat for 3 to 4 minutes, until reduced by half.

To serve, pour the sauce or pan juices over the octopus and potatoes.

This dish can also be made without the potatoes and served with rice. For a more flavourful dish, parboil the potatoes separately and add them halfway through cooking so they don't rob you of the savoury juices that give the octopus its full flavour.

OCTOPUS THREE WAYS

Polvo Três Maneiras

One Sunday morning Fatima Silva, a friend I made who cooked for me almost every Sunday morning for about a year, bought plenty of octopus to make a few extraordinary dishes for me. She got up early to prepare the octopus and cook it just until tender. Like most Portuguese, Fatima savours every ounce of the delicious octopus. She simmers the octopus, reserving the purple broth and the small ends of tentacles to make moist and flavourful Octopus Rice. The chunkier tentacles are saved to make Octopus Salad and Octopus in a Light Batter. All three recipes are provided here. (If not making the rice immediately, reserve the broth to make the rice at a later date.)

1 large octopus, about
    6 to 8 lb (2.7 to 3.5 kg)
1 onion, quartered
2 bay leaves

TO PREPARE THE OCTOPUS Using a sharp knife, cut through the sac-like body of the octopus, separating the tentacles from the body. Pull open the body sac and discard the attached innards and stringy entrails. Pull out and cut away the hard beak in the centre of the tentacles and discard. Rinse the octopus under cold running water and pat dry. (Note that frozen octopus is usually already cleaned of its entrails and other inedible pieces, but it's a good idea to check it before cooking.)

Place the octopus in a large stockpot and cover with water. Bring to a boil over medium-high heat. Skim off scum floating at the top. Reduce the heat to medium, add the onion and bay leaves, and simmer for about 45 to 60 minutes, until a fork just pierces the side of the large tentacles (keep in mind that octopus will undergo further cooking for the rice and crispy batter dishes). Remove the octopus from the water and set aside until cool enough to handle; reserve the cooking water. When cool, chop the thicker pieces into 3- to 4-inch (8 to 10 cm) lengths. Reserve the smaller pieces, closer to the the end of the tentacles, as well as any bits of octopus left in the water, for the Octopus Rice. Reserve half the thick pieces for the Octopus Salad and the other half for Octopus in a Light, Crispy Batter. If not using immediately, transfer the reserved octopus to an airtight container and refrigerate for up to 4 days.

Recipe continues…

OCTOPUS SALAD

1 to 2 lb (500 to 1 kg) cooked
    thick octopus pieces, reserved

1 red bell pepper

1 cup (250 mL) broad beans,
    blanched, shelled, and skinned

½ cup (125 mL) finely chopped
    parsley or coriander

1 red onion, finely chopped

2 cloves garlic, minced

½ cup (125 mL) olive oil (approx.)

3 Tbsp (45 mL) white wine vinegar
    (approx.)

Fine salt and coarsely ground
    black pepper, to taste

¼ cup (60 mL) black olives,
    for serving

Cornbread, cut into 1-inch (2.5 cm)
    cubes, for serving

OCTOPUS SALAD

Using a sharp knife, chop the reserved (larger) octopus pieces into bite-sized pieces, place in a large serving bowl, and set aside.

Using a sharp knife, cut the red pepper in half lengthwise and remove the core and seeds. Transfer to a baking sheet skin side up. Broil about 4 inches (10 cm) from the heat until the skin blackens in parts, about 6 to 8 minutes. Plunge into ice water and set aside for about 5 minutes. Use a knife to scrape off the skin, dice, and transfer to the serving bowl with the octopus. (You can prepare the red peppers up to 24 hours ahead of time, cover, and store them the refrigerator.)

Add the broad beans and, one at a time, add the parsley, onion, and garlic to the octopus, stirring well after each addition. Add ⅓ cup (80 mL) of the oil, 2 Tbsp (30 mL) of the wine vinegar, and salt and pepper, to taste. Mix well. If the octopus becomes dry, add up to 3 Tbsp (45 mL) more oil and 1 Tbsp (15 mL) more vinegar, to taste. Set aside at room temperature for 30 minutes before serving to allow the flavours to infuse the octopus.

Toss the octopus before serving, taste, and add additional oil, vinegar, and salt and pepper, to taste. Serve with black olives and cornbread cubes.

The secret to the Octopus Salad, says Fatima, is the generous amount of oil, as the octopus tends to absorb it over a very short time. Dress the salad with oil and set it aside until ready to eat. Before serving, stir the salad and, if necessary, add a drop or two more oil. Serve additional oil and vinegar on the side.

Recipe continues . . .

MAKES ABOUT 3 TO 4 SERVINGS

OCTOPUS RICE

¼ lb (125 g) cooked small
   octopus pieces (tentacle ends),
   reserved

¼ to ⅓ cup (60 to 80 mL) olive oil
   (approx.)

1 onion, chopped

8 ½ cups (2.125 mL) reserved
   octopus cooking water

2 bay leaves

1½ cups (375 mL) long-grain rice

5 or 6 sprigs fresh parsley

½ tsp (2 mL) fine salt (or to taste)

½ cup (125 mL) finely chopped
   coriander (approx.)

OCTOPUS RICE

If you would prefer not to have loose octopus bits in your rice, strain the reserved cooking water and discard any loose pieces of octopus.

In a large saucepan or deep skillet, heat about 2 Tbsp (30 mL) of the oil over medium heat. Cook the onion, stirring often, for about 5 minutes, until softened and golden brown. Add ½ cup (125 mL) of the reserved octopus cooking water, reserved octopus pieces, and bay leaves. Simmer, partially covered, for about 5 minutes, until fragrant. Pour in the remaining 7½ cups (1.875 L) of octopus cooking water; bring to a boil. Reserve the remaining ½ cup (125 mL) octopus water for serving.

Add the rice, parsley, and salt and stir to coat well. Reduce the heat to medium-low. Simmer, covered, for 8 to 10 minutes, until the rice is al dente. The liquid should not be significantly reduced. The rice should be moist with at least ½ inch (1 cm) of the cooking liquid still covering it. Remove the bay leaves and parsley and discard. Add the coriander and stir. Taste and adjust the seasonings with salt, if necessary.

To serve, scoop a heaping cup (about 250 mL) full of rice with cooking liquid in individual serving dishes. The broth should pool around the rice. If the rice is dry, top with some of the reserved octopus cooking liquid. Drizzle each dish with a few spoonfuls of olive oil and serve immediately. (If covered and left too long, the rice will swell and the liquid will be absorbed.)

> I prefer to keep the octopus skin on during and after simmering; it makes these dishes tastier. Note that salt is not added to the octopus while it's cooking. Octopus tends to have a briny, salty taste of its own, so it's best to season the finished dish to taste.

OCTOPUS IN A LIGHT CRISPY BATTER

If desired, using your fingers, a clean dish cloth, or a sharp knife, remove the skin from the (larger) reserved octopus pieces. Cut each piece lengthwise but not all the way through (if the pieces are not large enough to cut in this manner, use whole pieces). Open each piece like a book and flatten slightly. Set aside.

In a bowl, whisk the eggs, flour, salt, pepper, and enough ice water to form a thick batter.

In a large skillet, heat a 1-inch (2.5 cm) depth of vegetable oil over medium-high heat. Dip the octopus in the batter, coating it all over. In batches (no more than 3 or 4 pieces at a time), cook the octopus for 1 to 2 minutes per side, until lightly golden. Using a slotted spoon, transfer the octopus to paper towels to drain. If necessary, add more oil to the pan. Taste and adjust the seasonings with salt and pepper.

Transfer the octopus to a serving plate and drizzle with Parsley Dressing or Lemon Piri-Piri Sauce. Serve with parsley and lemon slices.

> Large octopus is available in speciality ethnic stores or ask your fishmonger to order one for you. One large octopus should be enough to make all three of the recipes here. If you cannot find a 6- to 8-pound (2.7 to 3.5 kg) octopus, you can purchase smaller octopuses and reduce the cooking time to 40 to 45 minutes or until a fork just pierces the side of the large tentacles. Larger pieces of octopus will undergo further cooking in the above deep-fried recipe.

OCTOPUS IN A LIGHT
CRISPY BATTER

1 to 2 lb (500 g to 1 kg) cooked
thick octopus pieces, reserved

3 eggs, lightly beaten

1 cup (250 mL) all-purpose flour
(approx.)

½ tsp (2 mL) fine salt

½ tsp (2 mL) coarsely ground black
pepper

1 to 2 Tbsp (15 to 30 mL)
ice water (approx)

Vegetable oil for deep-frying

Fine salt and coarsely ground
black pepper, to taste

Parsley Dressing (page 280)
for garnish

Lemon Piri-Piri Sauce (page 282),
for garnish

½ lemon, cut into wedges,
for garnish

½ cup (125 mL) finely chopped
fresh parsley, for garnish

FISH
Peixes

The Portuguese love fish. This is evident in the variety of offerings at Portuguese fish stores and restaurants. Grouper, monkfish, skate, and tuna are pan-fried, grilled, or roasted. The less-familiar (to the Portuguese) but equally loved European sea bass and trout appear as well, and can be prepared with little effort, grilled to perfection and lightly doused with a lemon and herbal dressing. Adaptive Portuguese cooks have brought their simple and fresh methods to North American kitchens. Easy and full of rich flavour and healthy omega oils, these recipes are just one more reason to bring fresh fish into your own kitchen.

Salt cod is in a special fish category of its own. Although I always knew the passion the Portuguese had for cod, I didn't really appreciate that passion until I started collecting recipes for this book. I was sure I had collected all of the important cod recipes for my first book, *Uma Casa Portuguesa*. I was wrong. In fact, I had to turn away numerous cod recipes originally intended for this book. (I think I could write a cookbook made up solely of Portuguese cod recipes!)

Regardless of which part of Portugal a family comes from, whether very close to an abundance of fresh fish or not, dried salt cod is an important part of their diet. One Portuguese-born friend who summers in the fresh fish–rich Alentejo province passed on her mother's cooking tip for salt cod: soak the cod as usual and freeze each piece individually. This way you can make a cod dish within a few hours of defrosting one of the cod pieces. Another friend brought me to her favourite Portuguese grocery store where the staff used a jigsaw to cut up cod and packaged portions individually. I listened as she and the clerk discussed how to best use up the individual pieces of cod. The thinner, bonier pieces on the side would be used for cod balls, cod pancakes, and cod tarts, and the meaty pieces boiled or grilled.

In spite of the tremendous variety of cod recipes, I am often told that there is nothing better than cod simply boiled with vegetables (for example, Baked or Boiled Cod Dinner, page 146). Chefs and home cooks alike encouraged me to prepare the famous dried fish this way. However it's done, boiled or grilled cod, accompanied with steamed vegetables, is a favourite year round. To reinfuse the cod's moist, tasty flavour, drizzle a garlic-infused olive oil that has been gently warmed in a *bain-marie* (hot water bath) over the fish and vegetables just before serving. White wine vinegar, additional finely chopped fresh garlic (for braver taste buds), and salt and pepper also lend zip.

Sardines, another Portuguese favourite, have been embraced by North America, which has discovered their health benefits and ocean sustainability. Sardines are an inexpensive treat. They are often frozen on board the fishing trolleys moments after they are caught.

Although I have included seven excellent sardine recipes in this book, Portuguese cooks probably won't use them, as they prefer to simply grill sardines with a squirt of lemon or oil and vinegar. This classic preparation has been seared into the Portuguese psyche and is so ancient and so good that most people just do not see the point of enjoying the fish any other way.

Most sardine aficionados insist that the fish must be eaten on a thick slab of cornbread to sop up the sardine's delicious juices. My friend Domingos Marques, a grilled-sardine enthusiast, explained how to do this: once you have eaten all the meat on one side, you then turn the sardine over and enjoy the other side. He uses the same piece of cornbread to polish off four or five sardines, saving the cornbread to eat last, which at that point is saturated with flavour—a heavenly piece of bread worth waiting for.

Not only is fish a great health food, but prepared Portuguese-style it makes a simple and very tasty meal. Try Azorean favourite Stickle-back in Onion Dressing (page 140), elegant Cod and Potato Soufflé (page 148), or delicious Peppercorn and Garlic–Crusted Tuna (page 156). They will quickly become your favourites.

FISH

Peixes

FISH STEAKS IN PIMENTO AND BACON SAUCE

Alcatra de Peixe

MAKES 6 TO 8 SERVINGS

4 lb (1.8 kg) fish steaks (halibut, grouper, conger eel, tilefish, or snapper), about 1 inch (2.5 cm) thick

2 cups (500 mL) dry white wine (approx.)

2 Tbsp (30 mL) white wine vinegar

2 Tbsp (30 mL) pimento paste

1 Tbsp (15 mL) tomato paste

1 Tbsp (15 mL) paprika

1½ tsp (7 mL) whole allspice

1 tsp (5 mL) ground cumin

½ tsp (2 mL) dry mustard

1¼ tsp (6 mL) coarsely ground black pepper

3 Tbsp (45 mL) olive oil

3 onions, sliced

5 cloves garlic, minced

½ cup (125 mL) chopped lean bacon

3 tomatoes, sliced

1 red bell pepper, seeded, cored, and sliced

6 sprigs fresh parsley

½ tsp (2 mL) fine salt

½ cup (125 mL) whipping cream

½ cup (125 mL) chopped fresh parsley

An *alguidar* is a flowerpot-shaped earthenware dish traditionally used to make *alcatra*, marinated roast beef, although nowadays anything cooked in an alguidar is known as an alcatra dish. Besides being good for cooking roasts, the high-sided dish allows fish to be piled on top of each other. As alguidars may be difficult to find, cook this dish in a baking dish; this will require less cooking time but more careful attention.

Large conger eel steaks provide the best flavour for this dish but are not easy to find. You can substitute other fish steaks, such as halibut, grouper, tilefish, or snapper; just make sure that all of the pieces are the same thickness for even cooking. Adjust the cooking time according to the thickness of fish (about 10 minutes per 1-inch/2.5 cm thickness of fish); remove and set aside any fish pieces that cook first. Keep the dish covered while making the sauce to prevent the cooked fish from drying out. Clams and Rice (page 252) and steamed sweet potatoes or taro root are traditional accompaniments.

Rinse the fish steaks under cold running water and pat dry with paper towels. Set aside.

In a resealable bag placed in a large bowl, combine 1½ cups (375 mL) wine, wine vinegar, pimento paste, tomato paste, paprika, allspice, cumin, mustard and 1 tsp (5 mL) pepper. Add the fish to the marinade, seal the bag, and carefully turn to ensure everything is well coated. Refrigerate for 8 hours or, if time allows, overnight. Bring to room temperature at least 30 minutes before using. Drain the fish, reserving the marinade, and transfer to a greased alguidar or a baking dish large enough to hold the fish steaks in one layer.

In a small saucepan, heat the oil over medium-high heat; cook the onion and garlic, stirring occasionally, for 3 to 5 minutes, until tender. Add the bacon and cook for 3 to 4 minutes, until golden. Add the reserved marinade and bring to a boil, stirring to scrape up any brown bits from the bottom of the pan. Cook for 2 to 3 minutes, until fragrant.

Pour the sauce over the fish steaks; the sauce should just barely cover the fish. Add up to ½ cup (125 mL) additional wine, if necessary. Add the tomatoes, red pepper, parsley, salt, and remaining ¼ tsp (1 mL) pepper. (If using an alguidar dish, layer 2 steaks of fish in the bottom, top with some sauce, add one-third of the tomato slices, one-third of the red pepper, and 2 sprigs of parsley, and season with salt and pepper. Repeat twice. Drizzle any remaining sauce overtop.)

Bake in a preheated 400°F (200°C) oven for 7 to 8 minutes, uncovered, basting frequently with the marinade. Carefully turn over all of the pieces and cook 5 minutes longer or until the fish flakes easy when tested with a fork.

Transfer the fish to a serving plate and keep warm. Using a spoon, degrease the sauce and, if desired, strain into a small saucepan, reserving the red peppers and tomatoes for garnish. Bring the sauce to a boil over medium-high heat and simmer gently until reduced by one-third. Add the cream and simmer until slightly thickened. Add the parsley.

Arrange the fish and reserved red peppers and tomatoes on a serving dish. Spoon some sauce over the fish and serve the extra sauce on the side.

BAKED FISH IN CURRY AND WHITE WINE

Peixe Assado com Molho de Caril

MAKES 6 SERVINGS

3 to 4 lb (1.5 kg to 1.8 kg)
   whole fish (grouper, sea bass,
   or whitefish), gutted

Fine salt

2 lb (1 kg) potatoes, peeled and
   sliced paper-thin (about 6)

3 large cloves garlic, thinly sliced

¼ cup (60 mL) olive oil

1½ tsp (7 mL) paprika

1 Tbsp (15 mL) curry powder

¼ tsp (1 mL) whole cloves

2 bay leaves

2 onions, sliced

1 cup (250 mL) dry white wine

1 large tomato, sliced

4 slices prosciutto

1 red bell pepper, seeded,
   cored, and thickly sliced

¼ tsp (1 mL) whole black
   peppercorns, crushed

A subtle dose of curry blends with the more traditional Portuguese flavourings of olive oil, garlic, paprika, and white wine to make this rich-tasting fish dish. Use one large fish or two smaller ones, adjusting the cooking time to allow for 10 minutes per 1-inch (2.5 cm) thickness of fish. Serve accompanied by Mixed Green Salad (page 240) and cornbread.

TO PREPARE THE FISH Using a sharp knife and working from its tail toward its head, remove the scales from the fish. Cut both sides of the dorsal and anal fins; pull out all of the fins. Rinse the fish under cold running water and pat dry with paper towels. Make 3 shallow diagonal cuts about ¼ inch (6 mm) deep along both sides of the fish. Sprinkle both sides with salt.

Generously grease a baking dish large enough to hold the fish and potatoes. Arrange the potatoes in an even layer on the bottom. Insert the garlic slices into the cuts you made in the fish, about 1 or 2 slices per cut. Arrange the fish over the potatoes. Sprinkle with 2 Tbsp (30 mL) oil, ½ tsp (2 mL) paprika, 1½ tsp (7 mL) curry powder, a pinch of cloves, 1 bay leaf, and half of the onion. Pour ½ cup (125 mL) of wine overtop and add the tomato. Roll the prosciutto into cigars and tuck them into the corners of the pan. Arrange the red pepper slices over the tomatoes and sprinkle with the peppercorns. Cover.

Bake in a preheated 450°F (230°C) oven for 10 minutes per 1-inch (2.5 cm) thickness of fish. Halfway through cooking, remove the dish from the oven and carefully turn the fish over. Top the other side with the remaining 2 Tbsp (30 mL) oil, 1 tsp (5 mL) paprika, 1½ tsp (7 mL) curry powder, a pinch cloves, 1 bay leaf, the remaining onion, and ½ cup (125 mL) wine. Uncover fish in last minute or so of cooking to brown. The fish is done when it flakes easily when pricked with a fork. Transfer the fish to a platter and arrange the potatoes around the fish.

Degrease and strain the pan juices through a fine-mesh sieve. Drizzle over the potatoes and fish and serve.

MARINATED FISH STEAKS IN SPICY WINE SAUCE

Peixe com Molho Fervido

For a light and quick summer meal, barbecue or grill fish after marinating in these bold Azorean flavours. Pimento paste lends a strong peppery taste that a robust fish, such as grouper, can tolerate. For a more subtle marinade, reduce the pimento paste to one teaspoon (5 mL). Spike with piri-piri sauce. Serve this with Roasted Seasoned Potatoes (page 246).

Rinse the fish under cold running water and pat dry with paper towels. Transfer to a shallow baking dish that will hold the fish in one layer.

TO MAKE THE MARINADE Combine ½ cup (125 mL) wine vinegar, pimento paste, and garlic. Pour the mixture over the fish and turn to coat well. Cover and refrigerate for 3 hours or, if time allows, overnight, turning the fish occasionally. Bring the fish to room temperature 30 minutes before cooking. Drain the marinade from the fish, discarding the marinade, and pat the fish dry with paper towels. Dust with the flour.

In a large skillet, heat 2 Tbsp (30 mL) oil over high heat. Add the fish and brown on both sides. Reduce the heat to medium and cook the fish steaks for 2 to 3 minutes per side, until opaque. With a slotted spatula, transfer the fish to a serving plate and keep warm.

TO MAKE THE SPICY WINE SAUCE In the skillet over medium-high heat, heat 2 Tbsp (30 mL) oil. Add the garlic and cook for 1 minute, until soft. Add the paprika, cumin, bay leaf, wine, wine vinegar, and salt and bring to a boil. Return the fish steaks to the skillet and cook for 2 to 3 minutes, until the fish flakes easily when tested with a fork. Be careful not to overcook or dry out the fish. Season with salt, to taste. Using a slotted spoon, transfer the fish to a serving dish.

Return the pan juices to a boil, stirring to scrape up any browned bits from the bottom of the pan. Simmer until the juices reach the desired consistency. Remove the bay leaf and, if desired, strain the sauce. Stir in the parsley. To serve, pour the sauce over the fish. Garnish with lemon wedges.

MAKES 4 TO 6 SERVINGS

2½ lb (1.25 kg) fish steaks (grouper, cod, or halibut), or fish fillets, about 1 inch (2.5 cm) thick

½ cup (125 mL) red or white wine vinegar, vinho verde, or lemon juice

1 Tbsp (15 mL) pimento paste

2 cloves garlic, minced

2 Tbsp (30 mL) olive oil

1 cup (250 mL) all purpose flour

SPICY WINE SAUCE

2 Tbsp (30 mL) olive oil

2 cloves garlic, minced

1 tsp (5 mL) paprika

½ tsp (2 mL) ground cumin

1 bay leaf

¾ cup (185 mL) dry white wine or vinho verde

1 Tbsp (15 mL) white wine vinegar

Fine salt, to taste

¼ cup (60 mL) chopped fresh parsley

Lemon wedges, for garnish

FISH FILLETS IN BATTER

Filetes de Peixe

MAKES ABOUT 4 SERVINGS

1 lb (500 g) fish fillets

¼ cup (60 mL) lemon juice or
    dry white wine

1 clove garlic, minced

1 bay leaf

¼ tsp (1 mL) coarsely ground
    black pepper

½ tsp (2 mL) fine salt

LIGHT BATTER

3 eggs, separated

½ tsp (2 mL) fine salt

½ cup (125 mL) all-purpose flour

1 tsp (5 mL) baking powder

¼ tsp (1 mL) coarsely ground
    white pepper

Vegetable oil for deep-frying

Lemon wedges, for garnish

This batter tastes good with any type of fish. Try to buy fillets that are similar in size and shape to ensure even cooking. In traditional Portuguese cooking, the fish is simply dusted in flour, egg, and breadcrumbs. In North America, the Portuguese have adopted an English-style crispy batter.

For a flavourful meal, spoon Red Pepper and Olive Relish (page 284) or Parsley Dressing (page 280) over the cooked fillets. Enjoy any leftovers in split fresh buns with a Portuguese-style remoulade sauce (recipe included here) and lots of lettuce.

Rinse the fillets under cold running water and pat dry with paper towels. Transfer the fish to a shallow baking dish.

In a bowl, combine lemon juice, garlic, bay leaf, and pepper. Pour over the fish. Cover and set aside at room temperature for 30 minutes or, if time allows, in the refrigerator for up to 3 hours, turning the fillets occasionally. Drain the fish and pat it dry; discard the marinade. Sprinkle the fish with the salt.

TO MAKE THE LIGHT BATTER Beat the egg whites with the salt until stiff peaks form. In a separate bowl, beat the egg yolks until light. To the yolks, add ¼ cup (60 mL) of the flour and the baking powder and pepper, and just enough egg whites to moisten the batter (about 1 cup/250 mL). Whisk briefly. Fold in the remaining egg whites just until combined.

In a large skillet, heat vegetable oil to a depth of about 1 inch (2.5 cm) over medium-high heat. Place the remaining ¼ cup (60 mL) flour in a dish. Dust the fish in the flour, then dip it in the batter, coating thickly. Cook the fish in batches for about 2 minutes per side, until the edges turn brown and the fish is golden on both sides. Transfer to a plate lined with paper towels and drain well. Garnish with lemon wedges.

REMOULADE SAUCE

To make a remoulade sauce, season the mayonnaise with salt and pepper, to taste, and combine it with the red onion, parsley, pimento paste, hot sauce, and garlic.

MAKES ½ CUP (125 ML)

½ cup (125 mL) mayonnaise

Fine salt and coarsely ground black pepper, to taste

2 Tbsp (30 mL) finely chopped red onion

1 Tbsp (15 mL) finely chopped parsley

½ tsp (2 mL) pimento paste

1 drop hot sauce (approx.)

½ clove garlic, minced

STICKLEBACK IN ONION DRESSING

Cebolada de Chicharro com Molho Cru

MAKES 4 TO 6 SERVINGS

2 lb (1 kg) cleaned stickleback

ONION DRESSING

5 large onions, sliced paper-thin and separated (about 1½ lb/ 750 g)

4 cups (1 L) boiling water (approx.)

¼ cup (60 mL) olive oil

¼ cup (60 mL) red or white wine vinegar

¼ cup (60 mL) chopped fresh parsley

3 cloves garlic, minced

2 tsp (10 mL) ground cumin

1 tsp (5 mL) paprika

2 bay leaves

Fine salt and coarsely ground black pepper, to taste

Vegetable oil for deep-frying

Stickleback are small fish that are very popular with the Portuguese. They are barbecued in the summer and pan-fried all year round. Stickleback are cooked until crispy, and they can be picked up and eaten as a *petisco* (snack). You can substitute smelt for the stickleback or marinate a variety of fish steaks such as grouper or cod in the onion dressing for up to 24 hours (refrigerated) before cooking. (Bring marinated steaks to room temperature about 50 minutes before cooking.)

Serve the stickleback with Corn Cakes (page 306), plain boiled potatoes, or my family favourite, baked sweet potatoes.

TO PREPARE THE FISH Using a sharp knife and working from its tail toward its head, remove the scales from the fish. Cut both sides of the dorsal and anal fins; pull out all of the fins. Rinse the fish under cold running water and pat dry with paper towels. Set aside.

TO MAKE THE ONION DRESSING In a bowl, cover the onions with boiling water. Cover with plastic wrap and let stand for 20 minutes; drain and rinse the onions under cold running water. Drain well and squeeze out the excess liquid with paper towels. Return the onions to the bowl and set aside.

In a separate bowl, combine the oil, wine vinegar, parsley, garlic, cumin, paprika, bay leaves, and salt and pepper. Add the prepared onions and toss to coat well. Set aside.

In a heavy skillet, heat vegetable oil to a depth of about 1 inch (2.5 cm) over medium-high heat. Fry the stickleback, turning once, until golden brown and crispy, 3 to 5 minutes per side. Using a slotted spatula, transfer the cooked fish to a plate lined with paper towels; drain well.

In an 11- × 7-inch (2 L) casserole dish, layer the cooked fish and the onion dressing in 4 alternating layers, finishing with the dressing. Cover and set aside for at least 20 minutes or up to 2 hours for best flavour. Serve at room temperature or, if desired, heat through before serving.

COD WITH SCRAMBLED EGGS AND OLIVES

Bacalhau à Brás

When the Portuguese discovered cod off the coast of the Grand Banks, it became a mainstay of Portuguese cooking. Although an abundance of fish is found in waters closer to home, the salted North American cod remains in high demand. This dish is an impressive and delicious combination of fluffy eggs and cod speckled with olives and parsley. It is usually served for lunch or dinner but also makes a delightful breakfast.

TO PREPARE THE SALT COD Place the cod in a large bowl with enough cold water to cover it completely. Cover the bowl in plastic wrap and refrigerate for 24 to 48 hours or longer, changing the water 2 to 3 times per day, until the fish is spongy in texture and desalted. (Larger pieces of fish may take longer.) Drain and discard the water and pat the fish dry with paper towels. Using a fork or sharp knife, remove the skin and bones from the cod and coarsely shred it; discard the bones and skin. Transfer the cod to a work bowl and set aside.

In a large skillet, heat a 1-inch (2.5 cm) depth of vegetable oil over medium-high heat. Cook the potatoes in batches for about 2 minutes per side, until golden brown. Drain well on a plate lined with paper towels.

Empty the skillet of oil and wipe clean. Add the olive oil and heat over medium-high heat. Add the onion and garlic and cook, stirring occasionally, for 12 minutes, until tender but not browned.

Add the cod, potatoes, and parsley. Carefully stirring so as not to mash the fish, cook for 1 to 2 minutes, until the fish and potatoes are well combined and heated through. Remove from the heat and stir in the olives. Taste the cod and adjust the seasonings with salt, if necessary.

In a bowl, whisk together the eggs. Return the skillet to high heat and slowly pour the eggs into the skillet in a steady stream, whisking the eggs briskly as they land in the pan. Cook for 2 to 3 minutes, until curds have formed but the mixture is still creamy. Remove from the heat, season with pepper, to taste, and serve immediately.

MAKES 4 SERVINGS

1½ lb (750 g) salt cod

1 lb (500g) potatoes (about 3), peeled and finely diced

Vegetable oil for deep-frying

¼ cup (60 mL) olive oil

2 onions, thinly sliced

4 large cloves garlic, minced

¾ cup (185 mL) chopped fresh parsley

12 pimento-stuffed olives, sliced, or large black olives, pitted and diced

4 eggs

Fine salt and coarsely ground black pepper, to taste

COD IN CREAM SAUCE

Bacalhau com Natas

1½ lb (750 g) salt cod

SAUCE

¼ cup (60 mL) butter

¼ cup (60 mL) all-purpose flour

2 cups (500 mL) hot whole milk

½ tsp (2 mL) fine salt

1 tsp (5 mL) finely grated
   lemon zest

4 tsp (20 mL) lemon juice

Pinch freshly grated nutmeg

Pinch coarsely ground black pepper

2 egg yolks, lightly beaten

COD AND POTATOES

1 lb (500 g) potatoes (about 3)

3 Tbsp (45 mL) olive oil

2 large onions, thinly sliced

Fine salt and coarsely ground
   black pepper, to taste

2 hard-boiled eggs, thinly sliced

1 cup (250 mL) double cream
   (see sidebar)

1 Tbsp (15 mL) Dijon mustard

This is an elegant, easy-to-serve dish that, with an early start to soak the cod and make the sauce, is perfect for entertaining or special family dinners. This recipe is from Maria Julia Paim, my husband's aunt, who is an outstanding cook. Manuela Marujo, a family friend, makes a green version of this, with the addition of spinach, which is a refreshing pairing with the rich cream. To green this recipe yourself, steam a bag of chopped spinach until wilted, drain, squeeze all the water out, and add it to the saucepan with the onion and cod, stirring to blend well.

TO PREPARE THE SALT COD Place the cod in a large bowl with enough cold water to cover it completely. Cover the bowl in plastic wrap and refrigerate for 24 to 48 hours or longer, changing the water 2 to 3 times per day, until the fish is spongy in texture and desalted. (Larger pieces of fish may take longer.) Drain and discard the water.

In a saucepan, cover the prepared cod with fresh cold water; bring just to a boil over medium heat. Reduce the heat to low and simmer for 2 to 3 minutes (do not boil). Drain and set aside until cool enough to handle. Remove the bones and skin and, using a fork, finely shred. Set aside.

TO MAKE THE SAUCE In a small saucepan, melt the butter over medium heat; whisk in the flour. Reduce the heat to medium-low and cook, without browning, for about 3 minutes, stirring constantly. Whisk in the hot milk. Increase the heat to medium and bring to a boil; stir in the salt, lemon zest, lemon juice, nutmeg, and pepper. Reduce the heat to medium-low and cook for 5 to 7 minutes, until slightly thickened. Remove the pan from the heat and whisk in the egg yolks. Return the pan to low heat and whisk for 1 minute, blending thoroughly, until the sauce is smooth and creamy. Taste and adjust the seasonings, if needed. Strain, if desired. Cover the surface of the mixture with parchment paper to prevent a skin from forming and set aside.

TO ASSEMBLE THE DISH In another saucepan, cover the potatoes with water; bring to a boil over medium-high heat. Cook for about 20 minutes, just until the potatoes are tender. Set aside until cool enough to handle. When cool, peel the potatoes and cut into ¼-inch (6 mm) slices.

In a large heavy saucepan or deep skillet, heat the olive oil over medium-low heat; cook the onion, covered, for 20 minutes or until tender but not browned, stirring often. Add the cod, season with pepper, to taste, and cook for about 2 minutes, until heated through. Taste and adjust the seasoning with salt, if necessary.

In the bottom of a greased 12-cup (3 L) baking dish (or a dish large enough to hold the cod and potatoes), spoon ¼ cup (60 mL) of the prepared sauce. Top with the fish and onion mixture; cover with half of the remaining sauce. Top with the hard-boiled eggs, followed by the potatoes and the remaining sauce.

In a small bowl, mix the double cream and mustard until smooth; spoon over the potatoes.

Cover and bake in a preheated 350°F (175°C) oven for 20 to 25 minutes, until heated through. Uncover and broil for about 5 minutes, until the top is lightly browned. Remove from the heat, cover, and let rest for 15 minutes before serving.

You can also replace the boiled potatoes in this recipe with crispy-fried julienned potatoes. You can find pre-fried julienned potatoes in Portuguese grocery stores. Look in specialty food stores carrying English imported foods for double cream. Whipping cream is often substituted for the double cream.

TUNA PUDDING IN HOT TOMATO SAUCE

Pudim de Atum

MAKES 6 TO 8 SERVINGS

2 ¼ cups (560 mL) milk

¼ cup (60 mL) butter

8 oz (240 g) day-old French
    or Italian bread, torn into
    large pieces

2 cans light tuna, partially drained
    (7 oz/200 g each)

¼ cup (60 mL) lemon juice

¼ tsp (1 mL) coarsely ground
    black pepper

1 tsp (5 mL) fine salt

2 tsp (10 mL) baking powder

4 eggs, lightly beaten

1 cup (250 mL) Tomato Sauce
    with Port Wine (page 283)

Cayenne pepper, to taste

2 hard-boiled eggs, thinly sliced

¼ cup (60 mL) chopped
    fresh parsley

Tuna, plentiful fished off the Atlantic waters of the nine Azorean islands, frequently appears at mealtimes. In North America, where fresh tuna is not always easily accessible, canned tuna is an excellent substitute.

A fiery tomato sauce splashed on a cream-coloured pudding provides a pleasing contrast and a tangy boost to this dish. If you prefer a less-spicy dish, omit the cayenne pepper. White Sauce (page 278) also pairs nicely with the tuna.

In a saucepan, combine the milk and butter and cook over low heat just until the butter melts. Add the bread, tossing to mix, and set aside for about 20 minutes, until the bread absorbs the milk.

In a food processor, process the tuna until smooth and it forms a ball in the work bowl. In a large bowl, combine the tuna, lemon juice, pepper, salt, and baking powder.

Transfer the bread to the food processor and process until puréed. Add it to the tuna mixture, and add the beaten eggs, and mix until a smooth, light batter is formed. Taste and adjust the seasonings with salt and pepper.

Grease a 9-inch (23 cm) tube pan. Spoon the tuna batter evenly into the pan, patting it down gently with a spoon to remove any air spaces. Place the tube pan in a larger pan; pour in enough hot water to come halfway up the sides of the tube pan.

Bake in a preheated 350°F (175°C) oven for 40 to 50 minutes, until a toothpick inserted into the pudding comes out clean.

Remove the tube pan from the water and set aside for about 10 minutes, until cool enough to handle. Just before serving, run a knife around the edge of the pan and invert the pudding onto a large plate.

Combine the tomato sauce with the cayenne pepper. Drizzle the sauce over the pudding. Garnish with the egg slices and parsley. Serve the remaining sauce on the side. Can be eaten warm, at room temperature, or cold with warm tomato sauce.

TUNA AND VEGETABLE SALAD

Salada de Atum e Vegetais

This hearty no-fuss tuna and vegetable salad is a perfect summer meal when cool, nourishing dinners are in demand. It is a welcome accompaniment to a barbecue or a refreshing one-dish picnic fare. If desired, substitute Oil and Vinegar Dressing (page 54) for the mayonnaise.

Place the potatoes, carrots, and peas in a large bowl.

Break up the tuna with a fork and add it to the vegetables. Add the red onion and one-half of the chopped parsley; stir to combine. Add enough mayonnaise to moisten the mixture and toss to coat. Taste and season with salt and pepper.

Mound the salad in a lettuce-lined serving dish; smooth into an oval shape with the back of a spoon.

Separate the cooked egg whites from the yolks and dice. Garnish the salad with alternate rows of chopped egg whites and yolks. In between, alternate strips of olives and the remaining ¼ cup (60 mL) parsley. If not enjoying immediately, cover and refrigerate for up to 2 days.

MAKES ABOUT 6 SERVINGS

4 cups (1 L) diced cooked potatoes

1 cup (250 mL) diced cooked carrots

1 cup (250 mL) fresh or frozen peas, blanched

2 cans tuna, partially drained (7 oz/200 g each)

1 red onion, finely diced

½ cup (125 mL) chopped fresh parsley or coriander

1 cup (250 mL) mayonnaise mixed with ½ tsp (2 mL) paprika

Fine salt and coarsely ground black pepper, to taste

4 large leaf or Boston lettuce leaves

2 hard-boiled eggs

20 pimento-stuffed olives or large black olives, pitted and diced

BAKED OR BOILED COD DINNER

Bacalhau Cozido ou Assado

2 lb (1 kg) salt cod (approx.)

½ cup (125 mL) olive oil (approx.)

1 cup (250 mL) chopped fresh parsley or coriander

1½ lb (750 g) small potatoes, skin on (about 6 to 8)

2 large carrots or 1 small turnip, peeled and cubed

1 onion, coarsely chopped

6 bay leaves

6 cloves garlic, coarsely chopped + 2 cloves garlic, minced

1 lb (500 g) collard greens or broccoli rabe, rough ends trimmed about ½ inch (1 cm) from base

Fine salt and coarsely ground black pepper, to taste

White wine vinegar, for drizzling

Minced garlic, for garnish

The first time I grilled cod I both undercooked it and dried it out. I have since learned that experienced cooks tightly wrap it in foil with additional oil and cook it over indirect heat. Drizzle warmed garlic oil over the fish and vegetables just before serving to help keep the dinner moist. White wine vinegar, additional finely chopped fresh garlic (for braver taste buds), and salt and pepper lend zip to the adaptable flavour of cod.

TO PREPARE THE SALT COD Place the cod in a large bowl with enough cold water to cover it completely. Cover the bowl in plastic wrap and refrigerate for 24 to 48 hours or longer, changing the water 2 to 3 times per day, until the fish is spongy in texture and desalted. (Larger pieces of fish may take longer.) Drain and discard the water and pat the fish dry with paper towels.

Grill the prepared cod on high (or about 4 inches/10 cm from medium-hot coals), for 2 to 3 minutes per side, until the fish has grill marks on both sides. Transfer the fish to a piece of foil large enough to encase the fish and pour up to 2 to 3 Tbsp (30 to 45 mL) of oil per piece of fish. Sprinkle with a few spoonfuls of chopped parsley and wrap up tightly in the foil. Place the fish packages on a baking pan (in case some of the oil spills out) and finish cooking in a preheated 500°F (260°F) oven for about 15 to 20 minutes, until a knife inserted in the thickest part of the fish is hot to touch. (Alternately, you can boil the cod with the vegetables for roughly the same amount of time as the vegetables, testing the fish and removing when cooked.)

Meanwhile, in a large stockpot, combine the potatoes, carrots, onion, bay leaves, and whole garlic cloves and cover with water. Bring to a boil over medium-high heat. (If you have added the cod to the pot, skim any scum from the top.) Reduce the heat to low and simmer for 12 minutes. When the vegetables (and fish, if added) are almost cooked, add the collards and return to a boil over medium-high heat. Reduce the heat to medium and cook for 3 to 4 minutes, until all the vegetables (and fish) are tender, removing and keeping warm any vegetables that finish cooking early.

TO MAKE THE GARLIC DRESSING In a small saucepan, heat ¼ cup (60 mL) of the oil and the minced garlic over medium-low heat. Cook the garlic until golden, softened, and aromatic, 6 to 8 minutes. Place the small saucepan in a larger pan and pour in enough hot water to come halfway up the sides of the small saucepan (to create a *bain-marie*). Cook, stirring occasionally, over medium heat for 10 to 12 minutes or until the oil and garlic are thoroughly heated. Cover and turn off the heat, leaving the pan in the *bain-marie* until ready to serve (this will keep the dressing warm, and the garlic will continue flavouring the oil).

To serve, use a slotted spoon to carefully remove the vegetables (and the fish, if added) from the liquid and chop the vegetables into bite-sized pieces before transfering to a large serving dish. Arrange the grilled or boiled cod overtop and drizzle with about one-quarter of the garlic oil. Sprinkle with the remaining parsley and salt and pepper, to taste.

(Although the cod pieces are usually served whole with the bones, if desired you can remove them when the cod is cool enough to handle. Use a fork to coarsely shred the cod and then place on the platter.)

Serve the remaining garlic oil at the table, with white wine vinegar and additional minced garlic, if desired.

This dish is very simple and can be prepared and enjoyed any time of the year. When cooking this dish, keep a number of things in mind. Cod is salty so adjust salt, if necessary, only after cooking the cod. Keep an eye on your vegetables throughout simmering and remove and keep warm any that finish cooking early. The general rule is to allow one piece of cod per person; however, the size of cod pieces can vary, and it's hard to determine how much cod you have until it has soaked for a few days and its spongy, soft texture is revealed. Plan for this and err on the side of plenty. If you have leftovers you can always add them to omelettes, pasta, or salad.

COD AND POTATO SOUFFLÉ

Empadão de Bacalhau

MAKES 4 TO 6 SERVINGS

2 lb (1 kg) salt cod (approx.)

3 Tbsp (45 mL) butter

3 Tbsp (45 mL) all-purpose flour

3 cups (750 mL) hot whole milk

1 tsp (5 mL) lemon zest

4 tsp (20 mL) lemon juice

½ tsp (2 mL) freshly grated nutmeg

Pinch coarsely ground
    white pepper

4 eggs, separated

¼ tsp (1 mL) fine salt

Vegetable oil for deep-frying

1½ lb (750 g) potatoes
    (about 4), peeled and cut
    into thick julienne slices

3 Tbsp (45 mL) olive oil

1 large onion, chopped

1 large carrot, chopped

6 cloves garlic, minced

½ cup (125 mL) chopped
    fresh coriander

¼ cup (60 mL) dry breadcrumbs

1 cup (250 mL) shredded
    lettuce, for garnish

1 hard-boiled egg, chopped,
    for garnish

6 black olives, for garnish

I love this simple cod dish passed on by friend and fellow food aficionado Isabel Vieira.

Isabel has prepared it on more than one occasion to grace a luncheon or buffet table. It can be made ahead of time, which makes it easier to cut into squares and gives you more time to socialize with friends and family. As a bonus, it is also tasty served at room temperature or cold the next day.

TO PREPARE THE SALT COD Place the cod in a large bowl with enough cold water to cover it completely. Cover the bowl in plastic wrap and refrigerate for 24 to 48 hours or longer, changing the water 2 to 3 times per day, until the fish is spongy in texture and desalted. (Larger pieces of fish may take longer.) Drain and discard the water and pat the fish dry with paper towels. Using a fork or sharp knife, remove the skin and bones from the cod and coarsely shred it; discard the bones and skin. Transfer the cod to a work bowl and set aside.

In a small saucepan, melt the butter over medium heat; whisk in the flour. Cook, without browning, over medium-low heat for about 3 minutes, stirring constantly. Whisk in the hot milk. Increase the heat to medium and bring to a boil. Stir in the lemon zest, lemon juice, nutmeg, and white pepper. Reduce the heat and cook for 5 to 7 minutes, until slightly thickened. Remove from the heat and whisk in the egg yolks, one at a time. Return to the heat and whisk for 1 minute, mixing well, until the sauce is smooth and creamy. Taste and add salt, if necessary. Strain through a fine-mesh sieve. Cover the surface of the mixture with waxed paper to prevent a skin from forming and set aside.

In a large skillet, heat vegetable oil to a depth of 1 inch (2.5 cm) over medium-high heat; cook the potatoes, in batches, for 3 to 5 minutes or until golden brown. Transfer the potatoes to a dish and set aside.

Empty the skillet and wipe it clean with paper towels. Add the olive oil, onion, carrot, and garlic and cook for 8 to 9 minutes, until the vegetables begin to brown and soften. Add the cod and cook for 2 minutes or until heated through, stirring carefully so as not to mash the cod. Remove from the heat and transfer the mixture to a large mixing bowl. Set aside.

Beat the egg whites until stiff peaks form and set aside.

Add the egg yolk cream sauce to the cod mixture and mix well. In batches, add the cooked potatoes, stirring well after each addition. Fold in the egg whites and coriander. Taste and add salt only if necessary.

Lightly grease an 11- × 7-inch (2 L) baking dish and sprinkle with breadcrumbs. Shake to remove the excess breadcrumbs and pour in the cod and potato mixture.

Bake, uncovered, in a preheated 400°F (200°C) oven for 25 to 30 minutes, until the soufflé is puffed up and golden and a knife inserted in the centre comes out clean. Let cool in the pan for 10 minutes.

To unmould, run a knife around the inside edge of the pan and invert onto a serving plate lined with shredded lettuce. If not serving immediately, cover and refrigerate for up to 2 days.

Serve warm with White Sauce (page 278). Garnish with chopped egg and olives.

COD AND CHEESE TART

Tarte de Bacalhau com Queijo

MAKES 2 PIES

1½ lb (750 g) salt cod (approx.)

2 cups (500 mL) all-purpose flour

¼ tsp (1 mL) fine salt

¼ cup (60 mL) cold butter, slivered

¼ cup (60 mL) cold lard, slivered

1 egg yolk

3 to 4 Tbsp (45 to 60 mL) ice water (approx.)

2 Tbsp (30 mL) olive oil

½ small onion, minced

3 eggs

1 cup (250 mL) whole milk

½ cup (125 mL) grated Edam or Serra da Estrela cheese

¼ cup (60 mL) black olives, pitted, rinsed, and patted dry

¼ cup (60 mL) finely chopped fresh parsley

Fine salt and coarsely ground black pepper, to taste

1 Tbsp (15 mL) cold butter, slivered

Typically, Edam cheese is used in these tarts. I prefer to use Portuguese Serra da Estrela cheese, a semi-soft mild cheese, excellent paired with the cod.

This recipe makes two tarts, which will easily disappear (it is too difficult to soak enough cod just for one tart, and you can freeze one to eat at a later time). You can dress up this dish by serving it with a dollop of White Sauce (page 278).

TO PREPARE THE SALT COD Place the cod in a large bowl with enough cold water to cover it completely. Cover the bowl in plastic wrap and refrigerate for 24 to 48 hours or longer, changing the water 2 to 3 times per day, until the fish is spongy in texture and desalted. (Larger pieces of fish may take longer.) Drain and discard the water.

Transfer the prepared cod to a saucepan and cover with fresh cold water. Bring just to a boil over medium-high heat. Reduce the heat and simmer for about 1 minute (the cod will continue cooking in the oven). Drain and set aside until cool enough to handle. When cool, remove the bones and skin and finely chop. Set aside. (If you have more cod than you need, freeze the remainder for later use.)

TO MAKE THE PIE CRUST In a large bowl, mix together the flour and salt. Using a wooden spoon, gradually beat in the butter and lard until lumps are the size of peas. Add 1 egg yolk and enough ice water, 1 Tbsp (15 mL) at a time (up to 4 Tbsp/60 mL), to make a stiff dough. (Alternatively, in a food processor, combine the flour with the salt. Add the butter and lard and process until lumps are the size of small peas. Add 1 egg yolk and ice water, 1 Tbsp/15 mL at a time—up to 4 Tbsp/60 mL—and process until a dough forms and starts to clump together.)

Using your hands, press the dough together to form 2 discs. Wrap the dough in plastic wrap and refrigerate for at least 30 minutes or until chilled. (Resting the pastry like this will make it easier to work with the dough.)

Grease two 9-inch (23 cm) pie plates almost to the rim. Remove the dough from the refrigerator. Using your fingertips, pat each disc evenly into the bottom and sides of the prepared pie plates.

To prevent a soggy pie crust, blind-bake the crusts: Prick the prepared pie crusts all over with a fork, cover with foil, and fill with beans. Bake for 12 to 15 minutes in a preheated 400°F (200°C) oven then remove the beans and cool the crusts until ready to use.

In a small skillet, heat the oil over medium-high heat. Add the onion and cook for 5 to 6 minutes, stirring often, until softened. Remove from the heat and set aside to cool.

Divide the cod into two equal portions and add to each pie shell, spreading evenly. Sprinkle the onion over the cod.

In a large mixing bowl, combine the whole eggs, milk, cheese, olives, parsley, and salt and pepper. Pour even portions onto each filled pie shell. Dot with 1 Tbsp (15 mL) slivered butter and place in a preheated 350°F (175°F) oven for 30 minutes or until the egg custard is puffy and golden, the eggs are set, and a knife inserted in the centre comes out clean. Let cool in the pan for 5 to 10 minutes before serving.

For a quick and easy variation, substitute cooked shrimp for the salt cod.

COD AND CHICKPEAS

Bacalhau com Grão

MAKES 4 SERVINGS

1½ lb (750 g) salt cod (approx.)

⅓ cup (80 mL) olive oil (approx.)

2 onions, chopped

2 large cloves garlic, minced

1 red bell pepper, seeded, cored, and chopped

1 bay leaf

¾ cup (185 mL) chopped fresh parsley

24 marinated black olives, pitted and chopped

1 cup (250 mL) canned chickpeas or soaked and cooked dried chickpeas

Fine salt and coarsely ground black pepper, to taste

1 lemon, half juiced, half cut into wedges

Colourful and nutritious, this is a versatile one-dish meal that can be easily adapted to allow for a variety of vegetable or legume substitutions. This dish can be eaten warm, typical in winter, or at room temperature in the summer when grilling the cod lends a mild smoky flavour. Most Portuguese are not shy about dressing the cod with olive oil. You may need to do the same. Taste and add more oil, if necessary, to make sure the dish is moist.

TO PREPARE THE SALT COD Place the cod in a large bowl with enough cold water to cover it completely. Cover the bowl in plastic wrap and refrigerate for 24 to 48 hours or longer, changing the water 2 to 3 times per day, until the fish is spongy in texture and desalted. (Larger pieces of fish may take longer.) Drain and discard the water.

In a saucepan, cover the cod with fresh cold water; bring just to a boil over medium heat. Reduce the heat to low and simmer for about 2 to 3 minutes, until partially cooked (do not boil). Drain and set aside until cool enough to handle. When cool, using a fork or sharp knife, remove the skin and bones and, using a fork, finely shred. Discard the bones and skin. Transfer the cod to a work bowl. Set aside.

(Alternately, grill the cod on high, or about 4 inches/10 cm from medium-hot coals, for 2 to 3 minutes per side, carefully turning to get grill marks on both sides. Transfer to a piece of foil, pour 2 Tbsp/30 mL of the oil over the fish, and bake over indirect heat or in a preheated 450°F/230°C oven for 8 to 10 minutes per inch (2.5 cm), until the cod is tender and warmed or a knife inserted in the centre is warm to the touch. Remove from the heat and set aside until cool enough to handle. When cool, remove the skin and bones and coarsely shred. Set aside.)

In a large skillet, heat the 3 Tbsp (45 mL) olive oil over medium heat. Cook the onion, garlic, red pepper, and bay leaf, stirring occasionally, for 8 to 9 minutes, until the vegetables begin to brown and soften. Add the cod, parsley, olives, and chickpeas, stirring carefully (you don't want to mash the cod), and cook for 2 to 3 minutes, until the fish and vegetables are combined and heated through. Taste the cod and add additional olive oil and salt, if necessary. Remove from the heat. Stir in the lemon juice.

Arrange on a large serving platter with lemon wedges alongside. Season with pepper and serve immediately.

If you have time, soak and cook dried chickpeas for exceptional taste and texture. (You can also replace the chickpeas with kidney beans.) Freeze extra chickpeas for use later in the week or month. You can sauté defrosted chickpeas with garlic and onion. Sprinkle with freshly chopped parsley or coriander. Just before serving, add a few drops of olive oil, white wine vinegar, and salt and pepper, to taste. For something different, top with Red Pepper and Olive Relish (page 284).

COD AND APPLES

Bacalhau com Maçãs

MAKES ABOUT 4 SERVINGS

1½ to 2 lb (750 g to 1 kg) salt cod, thicker pieces preferred

7 Tbsp (100 mL) olive oil (approx.)

Fine salt, to taste

Vegetable oil for deep-frying

1½ lb (750 g) potatoes (about 4), peeled and cut lengthwise into batons

2 onions, sliced

6 cloves garlic, minced

2 large apples, peeled, cored, and cut into ½-inch (1 cm) slices

½ cup (125 mL) mayonnaise

2 Tbsp (30 mL) dry breadcrumbs

The sweet flavour in this cod dish comes from the apple, a worthy partner to salt cod's mild taste. Fatima Silva, one of my most avid food contributors, was inspired to make this recipe based on her hometown memories. Far from the sea in the north of Portugal, where Fatima was born, dried cod is a staple. The apples grow everywhere and can be found almost any time of year. Fatima sums it up best when she says that where she came from, cod and apples were meant to be joined in a dish.

The cod used here is a whole bone-in steak. If you do not want to fiddle with the bone at dinnertime, you can use boneless cod or remove the skin and bones from the cod (after soaking) and layer it. Keep in mind that the bone gives the dish more flavour.

TO PREPARE THE SALT COD Place the cod in a large bowl with enough cold water to cover it completely. Cover the bowl in plastic wrap and refrigerate for 24 to 48 hours or longer, changing the water 2 to 3 times per day, until the fish is spongy in texture and desalted. (Larger pieces of fish may take longer.) Drain and discard the water and pat the fish dry with paper towels. The cod is cooked with the bone in and skin on. (If desired, without shredding the cod, carefully remove the bones and cut the fish lengthwise into ½-inch/1 cm fillets. Leave skin on or remove, as desired.)

In a large skillet, heat about 2 Tbsp (30 mL) of the oil over medium-high heat. Add the cod and cook for 1 to 2 minutes per side, until the fish turns golden brown, adding up to 2 Tbsp (30 mL) additional oil, if needed. Using a slotted spoon, transfer the fish to a plate and keep warm. Taste and add salt, if necessary. Set aside.

In a large skillet, heat vegetable oil to a depth of 1 inch (2.5 cm) over medium-high heat. Cook the potatoes, in batches, for 3 to 5 minutes per side or until lightly golden, adding additional oil, if necessary. Transfer to a plate lined with paper towels and drain well; lightly salt.

In a skillet over medium heat, heat 3 Tbsp (45 mL) of the oil and sauté the onion and garlic for 8 to 10 minutes, until evenly browned. Reduce the heat to medium-low and stir often, if necessary, to prevent the garlic from burning. Remove from the heat.

Place half of the onions and garlic in the bottom of greased 11- × 7-inch (2 L) baking dish (or a dish deep and large enough to hold the cod, potatoes, and apples). Closer to the centre of the dish, place half of the apple slices (leaving room for the potatoes to be arranged around the perimeter). Arrange the cod over the apples and top with the remaining onion mixture and apple slices. Arrange the potatoes around the cod and apples. Spoon the mayonnaise over the cod and lightly brush some over the potatoes. Sprinkle breadcrumbs over everything.

Bake in a preheated 425°F (220°C) oven, on the second rack from the top, for about 10 minutes, until heated through and the top is slightly golden. Remove from the oven, taste, and add salt, if necessary. Set aside to rest for 10 minutes and serve.

When I make this dish for my family, who loves apples, I double the apples called for in the recipe. Try it with Fruit Chutney (page 294) on the side.

PEPPERCORN AND GARLIC–CRUSTED TUNA

Atum com Pimenta e Alho

MAKES 1 TO 2 SERVINGS

1 tuna steak, about 1½ inches (4 cm) thick (8 oz/240 g)

1 Tbsp (15 mL) coarsely ground black pepper (approx.)

3 cloves garlic, minced

2 to 3 Tbsp (30 to 45 mL) olive oil

⅓ cup (80 mL) Red Pepper and Olive Relish (page 284)

1 Tbsp (15 mL) raspberry wine vinegar or white wine vinegar

2 Tbsp (30 mL) chopped fresh parsley

Chef José Alves of Via Norte in Toronto has built his reputation on his pan-fried tuna. His secret, he modestly confesses, is using the freshest sushi-grade tuna in the city. Fresh tuna, with its dark, rich colour and meaty texture, is often compared to beef steak.

Watching the chef prepare this dish in his restaurant, I learned two great tips that help me produce similar results. One is to sear the tuna briefly and serve it medium-rare, which results in a flavourful, moist tuna. The other is to take the time to preheat the cast iron pan. Too hot and your garlic-pepper crust will burn; not hot enough and your tuna will lack a golden crust. Follow the careful instructions below for a perfect finish.

Rinse the tuna under cold running water and pat dry. Combine the pepper and the garlic and, using your hands, press an even coating onto both sides of the steak. Set aside for about 15 minutes (longer if time allows).

Heat a large cast iron pan over medium-high heat until it just begins to smoke, about 3 to 4 minutes. (To test when it is hot enough, at different intervals while it is heating, place your hand just above the pan to feel the heat radiating from the pan. It should feel very hot.) Add the oil, coating the pan lightly. Using tongs, immediately place the tuna in the hot pan. Sear for about 1 minute and 15 seconds or until a crispy layer has formed on the bottom of the tuna (be careful not to burn the garlic crust; if your pan or burner gets too hot, adjust the heat and briefly remove the pan from the heat). Carefully flip the tuna and cook for 1 minute and 15 seconds or until a crispy layer has formed on the other side of the tuna. Turn over one final time and cook a further 45 seconds or until desired doneness. Be careful not to overcook the tuna; it should remain pink on the inside. Use the tip of a small knife to check that the inside of the fish is still pink. Transfer the tuna to a cutting board and let it cool briefly, just until cool enough to handle. Using a sharp knife, cut the fish down the middle. Place on a serving plate, the pink meat exposed outwardly.

In the same cast iron pan, add the Red Pepper and Olive Relish with the raspberry wine vinegar and stir to combine. Cook over medium heat for about 1 minute or until the sauce is warmed, stirring to scrape up any browned bits from the bottom of the pan. Pour the sauce over the tuna steak, sprinkle with parsley, and serve immediately.

Chef Alves prepares skate fish in the same manner, searing it first in the same flavourings and finishing it in a hot oven (cooking it up to 10 to 12 minutes further). He adds a few spoonfuls of Red Pepper and Olive Relish (page 284) before serving.

TROUT WRAPPED IN PROSCIUTTO WITH PINE NUT SAUCE

Truta com Presunto em Molho de Pinhões

MAKES ABOUT 2 SERVINGS

1 trout (about 2 to 3 lb/1 to 1.5 kg), cleaned and rinsed

Fine salt and coarsely ground black pepper, to taste

3 to 4 thin slices prosciutto or bacon

¼ cup (60 mL) chopped fresh parsley

2 Tbsp (30 mL) olive oil

¼ cup (60 mL) dry white wine

PINE NUT SAUCE

¼ cup (60 mL) olive oil

1 Tbsp (15 mL) butter

½ cup (125 mL) pine nuts

Trout is a specialty from the north of Portugal where Margarida Rocha, a friend and fellow food aficionado, grew up. The cold water that flowed from the mountains fed the rivers and produced abundant, plump trout. The cold weather also provides perfect frigid temperatures to fatten up the pigs and, in Margarida's opinion, make the best cured meats in the country. Renowned from the north of Portugal, thinly sliced *presunto* (a cured, dried meat interchangeable with prosciutto) imparts a salty and fragrant flavour and is a perfect accompaniment to trout.

Generously grease a baking dish large enough to hold the fish and set aside.

Using a sharp knife, make 3 shallow diagonal cuts about ¼ inch (6 mm) deep along both sides of the trout. Season both sides with salt and pepper. Roll 2 slices of the prosciutto into a cigar and stuff them along with half of the parsley inside the cavity of the fish. Cut the remaining 2 slices of prosciutto into strips and with the remaining parsley tuck into the diagonal cuts.

In a large skillet, heat the oil over high heat until very hot. Add the fish and cook for 2 minutes on each side, until browned on both sides. Add the wine and bring to a boil. Transfer the fish and cooking liquids to the prepared baking dish and loosely cover with foil. Bake in a preheated 450°F (230°C) oven for 10 minutes per 1-inch (2.5 cm) thickness of fish. Once the fish turns opaque, use a lifter to carefully turn the fish over. Sprinkle the fish with pan juices and continue baking until the fish flakes easily when pricked with the tip of a sharp knife or fork.

TO MAKE THE PINE NUT SAUCE Meanwhile, in a small saucepan over medium heat, heat the oil and butter just until the butter is melted. Add the pine nuts and cook until the pine nuts begin to brown, stirring frequently, about 1 to 2 minutes. Place the small saucepan in a larger pan and pour in enough hot water to come halfway up the sides of a small pan (to create a *bain-marie*); set aside until ready to use.

To serve, arrange the fish on a platter, removing and discarding the excess parsley (if desired), and pour the warm pine nut sauce overtop.

When I can't find a whole trout, I use trout fillets. I season the fillets with salt, pepper, and finely chopped parsley, coat them in flour, and wrap them in a piece of thinly sliced prosciutto secured with toothpicks. I then fry the fillets in olive oil. Follow the recipe for browning whole trout, adjusting the time to account for the smaller size of fish. When seasoning the fish with salt, remember that prosciutto is salty and adjust accordingly to taste.

WHOLE EUROPEAN SEA BASS WITH FRESH CORIANDER AND LEMON DRESSING

Robalo com Coentros e Molho de Limão

MAKES 1 TO 2 SERVINGS

½ cup (125 mL) minced garlic

1 cup (250 mL) chopped fresh
    coriander

¾ cup (185 mL) olive oil (approx.)

1 lemon, half cut into thin slices
    and half cut into wedges

1 whole fish, preferably sea bass
    (about 2 to 3 lb/1 to 1.5 kg),
    cleaned and rinsed

Fine salt and coarsely ground
    black pepper, to taste

1 small piri-piri pepper, chopped
    (optional)

One day after work I watched as Cristina Honorato and her husband, Zé, prepared this simple fish quickly and effortlessly. While Zé barbecued the fish, Cristina prepared the spectacular coriander and lemon dressing, which gives the much-loved European sea bass a boost of flavour. Grilled in the summer and broiled in the oven during the colder months, sea bass is frequently prepared in the Honorato household, reminding them of the beautiful coastal village where they were born and now part of a food tradition they enjoy in Canada.

European sea bass is also called Mediterranean sea bass or branzino; ask your fishmonger about it. The sweet and mild-flavoured fish is chock full of healthy omega-3 oils. Sea bream, whole trout, or salmon can be substituted.

In a small bowl, make a paste with ¼ cup (60 mL) of the garlic, ½ cup (125 mL) of the chopped coriander, and 3 Tbsp (45 mL) of the oil. Mix in the lemon slices and set aside.

Using a sharp knife, make 3 shallow diagonal cuts about ¼ inch (6 mm) deep along the meaty sides of the fish; liberally rub the garlic and coriander paste inside the cuts; rub any remaining paste outside and inside of the fish. Rub both sides of the fish with an additional 2 Tbsp (30 mL) of the oil and season with salt and pepper, to taste. If time allows, cover the fish and refrigerate for 2 to 3 hours. Bring to room temperature for 30 minutes before using.

Grill the fish on high (or about 4 inches/10 cm from medium-hot coals) for about 3 minutes on each side, carefully turning to get brown grill marks on both sides. Transfer the fish to indirect heat, brushing occasionally with oil, and cook for 4 to 5 minutes per side or until the fish flakes easily when pricked with the tip of a sharp knife or fork.

Method continues...

WHOLE EUROPEAN SEA BASS WITH
FRESH CORIANDER AND LEMON DRESSING
(continued)

(Alternatively, line a baking dish large enough to hold the fish with parchment paper. Add the fish and pour about 2 Tbsp/30 mL of oil overtop. Place in a preheated 450°F/230°C oven for about 10 minutes per inch/ 2.5 cm thickness of fish. Halfway through cooking, carefully turn the fish over with a lifter and sprinkle with the remaining 2 Tbsp/30 mL oil. Bake until the fish flakes easily when pricked with tip of sharp knife or fork.

TO MAKE THE CORIANDER AND LEMON DRESSING In a small bowl, combine ½ cup (125 mL) oil and the remaining ¼ cup (60 mL) garlic and ½ cup (125 mL) coriander. Mix well and season with salt, pepper, and piri-piri pepper, to taste. Taste and add more oil and coriander, if desired.

Transfer the fish to a serving platter and garnish with lemon wedges. Serve with the dressing alongside.

Here is a tip I learned in a professional kitchen on how to grill fish: Keep the grill clean and wipe it with a wet cloth before cooking. Once you place the fish on the grill, do not turn it over until it has seared and developed a brown bottom crust—it's only at this point that the fish is ready to be turned over.

SARDINE STEW

Caldeirada de Sardinhas

Frugal home-cook Fatima Silva introduced me to sardine stew. Since I've learned that sardines are high in healthy omega-3 fatty acids, I prepare them every chance I get. As a bonus, sardines are low in price and often available in the freezer section of your local grocer. Simple ingredients like coriander, garlic, and sweet tomatoes pair well with the environmentally sustainable fish.

Be sure to season the sardines well with salt—this is an important step that flavours and solidifies the sardines' texture. Although this is a very easy dish to prepare, be careful not to overcook the fish, which could easily happen if you stew the sardines too long in the tasty broth. When Fatima makes it, she sets the finished dish aside for about 20 minutes before serving to allow the fish additional time to take on the fragrant flavours.

White wine vinegar adds a hint of sweetness. Serve it on the side and guests and family can drizzle it on their stew as they like.

Rinse the sardines under cold running water and pat dry with paper towels. Season with the coarse salt, cover loosely, and set aside for 30 minutes to 1 hour. Rinse and pat dry.

In a medium cooking pot, layer half each of the onions, tomatoes, red pepper, and garlic. Top with the sardines. Add the remaining onions, tomatoes, red pepper, and garlic. Top with the coriander and bay leaves. Pour over the oil, wine, and fish stock and season with pepper. Cover tightly with a lid or foil. Bring to boil over medium heat. Reduce the heat to low and simmer, partially covered, for 10 to 12 minutes, shaking occasionally to ensure that the sardines don't stick to the bottom of the pan. Test for doneness while cooking: the fish is done when it is opaque and easily flakes when tested with the point of a sharp knife. Taste the fish and broth and correct the seasoning with salt, if needed. If desired, strain the broth.

To serve, place a slice of cornbread in the bottom of each serving dish and top with 1 or 2 sardines. Spoon over the broth, sprinkle with parsley, and, if desired, drizzle a few drops of oil and white wine vinegar on top.

MAKES 3 TO 4 SERVINGS

1½ lb (750 g) sardines, gutted, heads removed, and scaled

2 tsp (10 mL) coarse salt

2 onions, sliced into ¼-inch (6 mm) rings, separated

2 large tomatoes, peeled and sliced into ¼-inch (6 mm) slices

½ red bell pepper, seeded, cored, and roughly diced

3 cloves garlic, minced

½ cup (125 mL) chopped fresh coriander

2 bay leaves

¼ cup (60 mL) olive oil

½ cup (125 mL) white wine

¼ cup (60 mL) Fish Stock (page 75), vegetable stock, clam juice, or water

Fine salt, to taste

3 or 4 thick slices fresh cornbread

¼ cup (60 mL) finely chopped fresh parsley, for garnish

¼ cup (60 mL) olive oil, for drizzling

White wine vinegar, for drizzling

POULTRY
AND GAME

Aves e Caça

The grilled-chicken industry, better known as *churrasqueira*, is huge in whatever city the Portuguese settle. Rotisserie chicken marinated and brushed with a homemade piri-piri spice blend keeps patrons coming back for more. Few fast-food choices can compete with this tasty take-out chicken that makes a fast and economical meal (especially when last-minute dinner guests drop by).

Each restaurant's spicy marinade recipe is usually a carefully guarded treasure. One chef I got to know said that he rubs his homemade marinade, which contains 25 secret herbs and spices, on his chicken the night before he cooks it. However the chefs prepare their rotisserie or grilled chicken, it is outstanding.

Although my Barbecued Chicken (page 170) has fewer ingredients than rotisserie-style chicken you can buy, it more closely replicates the delicious homestyle versions that I have tasted as a guest in the backyards of friends and family. Every cook has their own secret ingredients, usually influenced by personal preference and what region of Portugal they came from. The basic recipe includes wine or beer and vinegar or lemon juice, and almost always a generous sprinkling of paprika, pimento paste, lots of garlic, and bay leaves.

One secret I did take from Portuguese grill houses is to marinate the chicken as long as possible before grilling—24 hours is ideal. This allows the meat to fully take on the flavours of the marinade and further tenderizes the meat. The idea is to achieve a crispy outer layer and to keep the chicken tender and moist on the inside.

This chapter includes a number of delicious and simple yet lesser-known preparations for the much-loved chicken. Some dishes require marinades that improve the flavour of the meat. Other, more subtle-tasting poultry dishes do not require it. Chicken with Sautéed Mushrooms and Cream Port Sauce (page 188) and Chicken Simmered in Bacon, Moonshine and Herbs (page 190) are two examples of chicken combined with favourite Portuguese spice blends. Chicken cooked in garlic, olive oil, thyme, and port is a theme repeated in hundreds of variations of classic dishes from mainland Portugal.

Drunken Chicken with Port, Mustard, and Sweet Potatoes (page 173), an Azorean dish, has an assertive flavour, and its easy one-pot preparation doesn't require marinating. Most of these dishes are excellent everyday and guest-worthy meals. Chicken in Batter and Lemon Sauce (page 174) and Lemon Chicken in Puff Pastry (page 178) are more time-consuming meals worthy of special occasions.

Duck dishes are Portuguese mainland classics. Duck with Rice and Madeira (page 182) has been updated to include North American cranberries. Roasted and glazed Portuguese-style duck has been simplified in Orange Duck with Herbs in a Tomato Port Sauce (page 194). Individual duck legs are now available at supermarkets and are easily prepared in any of these tasty meals.

Hunting was common when my father-in-law was first married in the Azores over 50 years ago. It was a necessary skill at a time when most people could not afford or find meat at their small local stores. Game, although now easy to purchase at large grocery stores, has remained a favourite of many families. Partridge and quail as well as rabbit are popular in Portuguese cooking and are much loved to this day. Try Rabbit and Chouriço (page 186). You will be sure to include it among your favourites. Wild game pairs nicely with Moonshine Hot Sauce (page 285) or piri-piri sauce. Make sure you have some on hand when you make these dishes.

POULTRY AND GAME

Aves e Caça

BARBECUED CHICKEN

Galinha na Brasa

1 whole chicken (2½ lb/1.25 kg)

¼ cup (60 mL) olive oil

6 large cloves garlic, minced

1 Tbsp (15 mL) paprika

1 tsp (5 mL) piri-piri sauce or
   Tabasco sauce

⅓ cup (80 mL) lemon juice

2 Tbsp (30 mL) finely grated
   lemon zest

½ tsp (2 mL) fine salt

In Portugal, restaurants equipped with large outdoor rotisseries serve perfectly barbecued chicken that bastes itself while it slowly turns over coals. Marinating keeps chicken moist and flavourful and the skin crisp. Serve it with extra piri-piri sauce and french fries for a classic Portuguese meal.

Rinse the chicken under cold running water and pat it dry with paper towels. Using a sharp knife, remove the wing tips from the chicken (and the neck if it's still attached) and trim off the fat and excess skin. Place the chicken in a resealable bag and set in a large bowl.

In a skillet, heat the oil over low heat. Cook the garlic for 3 to 5 minutes, until softened and fragrant. Remove from the heat and let stand for about 20 minutes, until cool.

In a small bowl, combine the oil and garlic with the paprika, piri-piri sauce, and lemon juice and zest. Pour over the chicken; seal the bag and turn to coat well. Refrigerate for 6 hours or overnight, turning several times. Bring to room temperature for 30 minutes before cooking.

Remove the chicken from the marinade, letting the excess drip off; reserve the marinade. Season the chicken with salt. Using butcher's twine, truss the bird so the legs and wings are securely tied to the body.

TO COOK ON A GRILL Insert the rotisserie rod lengthwise through the centre of the bird, checking for balance. Insert the holding forks and tighten to secure the bird. Place a drip pan beneath and slightly in front of the bird to catch any drippings and prevent flare-ups as the bird rotates. Grill on medium-high (or over hot coals), brushing the chicken often with the reserved marinade, for 50 to 60 minutes, until a meat thermometer registers 185°F (85°C). Remove the bird from the skewer and cut into pieces, pouring a little extra marinade from the drip pan overtop.

TO COOK IN THE OVEN Cut the chicken in half, transfer to a roasting pan, and bake in a preheated 350°F (175°C) oven for 40 to 45 minutes, turning halfway through and basting with the reserved marinade and some of the sauce that forms at the bottom of the pan often. Broil the chicken for about 5 minutes per side, until the chicken is golden brown and no longer pink inside.

> If you do not have a rotisserie, this chicken is also delicious grilled on the barbecue. Grill chicken over indirect heat to prevent burning.

CHICKEN IN WINE
AND LEMON SAUCE

Galinha com Molho de Vinho e Limão

MAKES 4 SERVINGS

3 to 4 lb (1.5 to 1.8 kg) chicken
    pieces, bone-in

⅔ cup (160 mL) dry white wine

½ cup (125 mL) lemon juice

4 Tbsp (60 mL) tomato paste

2 Tbsp (30 mL) butter, softened

1 tsp (5 mL) paprika

1 tsp (5 mL) piri-piri sauce or
    Tabasco sauce (optional)

3 cloves garlic, minced

½ tsp (2 mL) fine salt

1 onion, sliced

1 tsp (5 mL) whole allspice

This chicken cooked in a Portuguese lemon sauce is an aromatic dish full of comforting flavour. Serve it with Moonshine Hot Sauce (page 285) and Sautéed Greens and Oranges (page 242).

Rinse the chicken pieces under cold running water and pat dry with paper towels. Arrange the chicken in a single layer in a greased baking dish.

In a small bowl, combine the white wine, lemon juice, tomato paste, butter, paprika, piri-piri sauce, garlic and salt, mixing well. Pour the sauce over the chicken, making sure to coat all the pieces well. Sprinkle with the onion and allspice.

Bake, uncovered, in a preheated 400°F (200°C) oven, turning the meat and drizzling with the pan juices every 15 minutes, for 45 to 50 minutes, until the chicken is cooked and no longer pink inside. Broil for 3 to 5 minutes, until golden brown.

Transfer the chicken to a serving dish. Reserve the onions. Using a spoon, degrease the pan juices and, if desired, strain the sauce. Transfer the sauce to a small saucepan and cook over high heat until reduced to the desired consistency. Taste and adjust the seasonings, if needed.

To serve, top the chicken with the reserved onions and pour the sauce over the meat.

DRUNKEN CHICKEN WITH PORT, MUSTARD, AND SWEET POTATOES

Galinha à Moda da Terceira

In this dish, the delicate sweetness of sweet potatoes is tucked into the bubbling pot of chicken.

Rinse the chicken pieces under cold running water and pat dry with paper towels. In a greased shallow baking dish, arrange the chicken in a single layer and sprinkle with garlic, and salt and pepper. Scatter onions overtop.

In a bowl, combine the whisky, ketchup, port, and mustard. Pour over the chicken.

Bake in a preheated 400°F (200°C) oven for 30 minutes, turning and basting often with the sauce.

In the meantime, in a saucepan, cover the sweet potatoes with water. Bring to a boil over medium-high heat and cook for 15 to 20 minutes, until almost tender. Drain. Add the sweet potatoes to the chicken after it's been baking for 30 minutes and stir to cover with the sauce. Bake for another 10 to 15 minutes or until the chicken is no longer pink inside and the sweet potatoes are tender. Taste and adjust the seasonings with salt and pepper.

Using a slotted spoon, transfer the chicken and sweet potatoes to a serving dish and keep warm. Degrease the pan juices and, if desired, strain the sauce through a fine-mesh sieve. Transfer the sauce to a saucepan and cook over medium-high heat. Simmer until the desired consistency is reached. Taste and adjust the seasonings, if needed. Drizzle the sauce over the chicken and sweet potatoes. Serve immediately.

If you have extra sauce left over, you can use it as a barbecue sauce.

MAKES 6 SERVINGS

3½ lb (1.75 kg) chicken pieces

3 cloves garlic, minced

Pinch each fine salt and coarsely ground black pepper

6 small onions, peeled and quartered, or 15 pearl onions, peeled

½ cup (125 mL) whisky

¼ cup (60 mL) ketchup

¼ cup (60 mL) port

2 Tbsp (30 mL) Dijon mustard

2 sweet potatoes, peeled and cut into 2-inch (5 cm) pieces

CHICKEN IN BATTER AND LEMON SAUCE

Galinha Angolana

MAKES 6 SERVINGS

3 lb (1.5 kg) chicken pieces

3 Tbsp (45 mL) lemon juice (approx.)

1 tsp (5 mL) finely grated lemon zest

¼ tsp (1 mL) coarsely ground black pepper

2 cloves garlic, minced

¼ cup (60 mL) vegetable oil (approx.)

1 Tbsp (15 mL) butter

1 Tbsp (15 mL) lard or shortening

1 large onion, finely chopped

1 tsp (5 mL) salt

5 eggs, separated

2 Tbsp (30 mL) chopped fresh parsley

½ cup (125 mL) cold water

1 Tbsp (15 mL) cornstarch

Fine salt and coarsely ground black pepper, to taste

Lemon slices, for garnish

For an authentic Angolan taste, serve this lemony chicken dish with piri-piri sauce. A side of steamed rice will soak up the delicious sauce. Round out the meal with a mixed green salad.

Rinse the chicken pieces under cold running water and pat dry with paper towels. Transfer the chicken to a resealable bag and set aside in a large bowl.

In a small bowl, combine the lemon juice, lemon zest, pepper, and garlic. Pour the marinade over the chicken and seal the bag; turn to coat well. Refrigerate for at least 3 hours or overnight, turning several times. Bring to room temperature for 30 minutes before using.

In a Dutch oven, heat 2 Tbsp (30 mL) of the oil and the butter and lard over medium heat until the butter and lard melt. Cook the onion for 3 to 5 minutes, until softened. Add the chicken, marinade, and salt; cook, partially covered, until the chicken is almost tender, 10 to 15 minutes. Using a slotted spoon, transfer the chicken pieces to a plate lined with paper towels and drain well. Reserve the pan juices and set aside to cool.

In a bowl, beat the egg whites until soft peaks form. In a large skillet, heat 2 Tbsp (30 mL) of the vegetable oil over high heat. Dip the chicken pieces in the egg whites to coat well and cook, in batches, for 2 to 3 minutes per side, until the chicken is lightly golden and no longer pink inside. Add more oil to the pan, if necessary. Using a slotted spoon, transfer the chicken to a serving dish and keep warm.

Drain and discard all but 1 Tbsp (15 mL) of the fat from the skillet. In a mixing bowl, whip the egg yolks and parsley for about 3 minutes, until pale in colour and thickened. Beat in the reserved cooled pan juices. Combine the water and cornstarch until well blended and add to the egg yolk mixture. Pour into the skillet. Cook over medium heat, whisking constantly, for 3 to 5 minutes, until thickened and smooth. Remove from the heat and adjust the seasonings with salt, pepper, and additional lemon juice, if necessary.

Pour half of the sauce over the chicken; serve the rest in a gravy boat. Arrange a ring of overlapping lemon slices around the chicken and season the chicken with pepper. Serve warm or at room temperature.

CHICKEN AND RICE SALAD

Salada de Galinha e Arroz

MAKES 4 SERVINGS

DRESSING

⅓ cup (80 mL) olive oil

2 Tbsp (30 mL) red or
white wine vinegar

1 Tbsp (15 mL) lemon juice

2 cloves garlic, minced

Fine salt and coarsely ground
black pepper, to taste

SALAD

1⅓ cups (330 mL) cubed
cooked chicken

2 cups (500 mL) cooked short-
or long-grain rice

3 Tbsp (45 mL) finely chopped
red bell pepper

3 Tbsp (45 mL) finely chopped
yellow bell pepper

2 green onions (white and green
parts), finely chopped

¼ cup (60 mL) shredded São Jorge
or sharp cheddar cheese

½ cup (125 mL) chopped tomatoes

⅓ cup (80 mL) frozen or fresh
peas (if using frozen, rinse in a
colander until defrosted)

4 Tbsp (60 mL) chopped fresh
coriander or parsley

Pinch each fine salt and coarsely
ground black pepper

2 large leaf or Boston
lettuce leaves

Tomato wedges, for garnish

Light salads such as this one are an excellent summer meal. You can substitute grilled peppers if you have them on hand and use fresh broad beans (for the peas) when they are in season. For extra flavour, boil the chicken with a sprig of parsley and half an onion; strain and reserve the broth to cook the rice.

TO MAKE THE DRESSING Combine the oil, vinegar, lemon juice, garlic, and salt and pepper; mix well. Set aside.

TO MAKE THE SALAD In a large bowl, add the chicken, rice, red and yellow peppers, green onion, cheese, tomato, peas, 2 Tbsp (30 mL) of the coriander, and salt and pepper and mix gently to combine. (Recipe can be prepared ahead to this point, covered, and refrigerated for several hours or overnight.) Add the prepared dressing and toss lightly until well coated. Taste and adjust seasonings.

To serve, arrange the lettuce leaves on a platter. Top with the chicken salad and garnish with the tomato wedges. Sprinkle with the remaining 2 Tbsp (30 mL) of coriander.

MARINATED GRILLED CHICKEN WITH RED PEPPER AND OLIVE RELISH

Galinha Assada com Pimenta Vermelha e Azeitonas Picadas

I've attended hundreds of Portuguese barbecues since I met my husband and enjoyed a lot of grilled chicken. Not surprisingly, every cook has their own secret ingredients, usually influenced by personal preference and where they came from. The basic recipe usually includes wine or beer, and vinegar or lemon juice, and almost always a sprinkling of paprika, lots of garlic, and bay leaves.

Rinse the chicken under cold running water and pat dry with paper towels. Transfer the chicken to a resealable bag and place in a large bowl. In a small bowl, combine the wine, lemon juice, white wine vinegar, garlic, pimento paste, paprika, bay leaves, and ⅓ cup (80 mL) of the parsley. Pour over the chicken and seal the bag; turn to coat well. Refrigerate for 6 hours or, if time allows, overnight, turning several times. Bring to room temperature for 30 minutes before cooking.

Remove the chicken from the marinade, letting the excess drip off, and season with salt. Reserve the marinade.

Grill the chicken on high (or over medium-hot coals), covered, for 3 to 4 minutes per side or until the chicken is golden brown and no longer pink inside. Brush often with the reserved marinade. Remove from the heat. Using a sharp knife, cut each piece against the grain into thick slices and arrange on a serving dish; cover with foil to keep warm.

In a small frying pan, add the Red Pepper and Olive Relish and the raspberry vinegar and bring to a boil over medium-high heat.

To serve, spoon the sauce over the chicken and garnish with the remaining 3 Tbsp (45 mL) parsley and the olives. Serve warm.

MAKES ABOUT 4 SERVINGS

8 boneless chicken thighs

⅓ cup (80 mL) white wine

3 Tbsp (45 mL) lemon juice

3 Tbsp (45 mL) white wine vinegar

5 cloves garlic, minced

2 tsp (10 mL) pimento paste

1 tsp (5 mL) smoked Spanish paprika

3 bay leaves

½ cup (125 mL) chopped fresh parsley

½ tsp (2 mL) fine salt

½ cup (125 mL) Red Pepper and Olive Relish (page 284)

1 Tbsp (15 mL) raspberry, sherry, or white wine vinegar

4 or 5 black olives, for garnish

LEMON CHICKEN IN PUFF PASTRY

Empadas de Galinha

MAKES 4 SERVINGS

2½ lb (1.25 kg) chicken pieces

2 Tbsp (30 mL) olive oil

¼ cup (60 mL) butter

1 onion, chopped

2 cloves garlic, minced

1½ cups (375 mL) dry white wine

⅓ cup (80 mL) white wine vinegar

¼ tsp (1 mL) whole cloves

2 bay leaves, crumbled

3 Tbsp (45 mL) chopped
   fresh parsley

1 tsp (5 mL) fine salt

Pinch coarsely ground black pepper

½ cup (125 mL) chicken stock

2 Tbsp (30 mL) lemon juice

2 egg yolks, lightly beaten

1 lb (500 g) Puff Pastry (page 313)

1 egg, lightly beaten

This dish can be made as one big pie or as individual sized pastries. Serve the filled pastry over a bed of buttered rice accompanied by a tossed watercress salad. As an alternative, you can do what a Greek friend of mine does and roll the filling in phyllo.

Rinse the chicken pieces under cold running water and pat dry with paper towels.

In a large saucepan, heat the oil and butter over medium heat until the butter is melted. Cook the chicken, in batches, for 2 to 3 minutes per side, until lightly golden. Remove the chicken. Add the onion and garlic to the saucepan and cook, stirring occasionally, for 3 to 5 minutes, until softened. Return the chicken to the saucepan.

Add the wine, vinegar, cloves, bay leaves, parsley, salt, and pepper and bring to a boil over medium-high heat. Reduce the heat to medium-low and simmer gently, partially covered, for 20 minutes or until the chicken is no longer pink inside. Remove the cover for the last 10 minutes of cooking to reduce the sauce slightly. Using a slotted spoon, transfer the chicken to a cutting board and set aside to cool.

Using a fine-mesh sieve, strain the sauce and return it to the saucepan. Add the chicken stock and lemon juice, and bring to a boil over medium heat. Reduce the heat to low. Slowly add the egg yolks, whisking constantly. Cook for about 5 minutes, until slightly thickened. Taste and adjust the seasonings, if necessary.

Remove the skin and bones from the chicken and discard. Using a sharp knife, chop the chicken into bite-sized pieces. Add to the sauce and set aside.

TO MAKE INDIVIDUAL TARTS Grease a 12-cup muffin tin and set aside. Divide the pastry in half and cover one half to keep it from drying out. On a lightly floured surface, roll out the dough to a ¼-inch (6 mm) thickness. Cut out twelve 4-inch (10 cm) circles. Press each circle into each cup and, using a fork, prick the dough all over. Fill each cup to the top with the cooled chicken filling, including the sauce.

Roll out the remaining pastry. Cut out twelve 3-inch (8 cm) circles. Using a fork, prick the circles all over. Loosely place each circle over each of the filled cups. Brush the tops with the lightly beaten egg. (The pastries can be prepared ahead to this stage, covered with plastic wrap, and refrigerated for up to 12 hours.)

Bake on the top rack of a preheated 450°F (230°C) oven for 5 minutes. Reduce the temperature to 400°F (200°C) and cook for another 10 to 15 minutes, until the pastry is golden brown and the filling is bubbling. Remove from the oven and, while still hot, run a knife around the edge of the cups; let stand for only 5 minutes before removing the pastries. (The longer they stay in the tins, the harder they are to remove.) Cool on a wire rack.

TO MAKE ONE LARGE PIE Divide the pastry in half and cover one half to keep it from drying out. On a lightly floured surface, roll out the dough into a 9-inch (23 cm) circle. Place the rolled dough on a greased pie plate and, using a fork, prick all over. Mound the cooled filling evenly in the centre of the circle, leaving a 1-inch (2.5 cm) border of pastry uncovered. Brush the border with a little beaten egg.

Roll out the remaining pastry. Place over the filling, stretching to match the edges. Using your fingers, press the pastry together to seal, then make decorative indentations with the back of a knife. Cut a steam vent in the centre. Score the top of the pastry decoratively and brush with more of the beaten egg.

Bake in a preheated 450°F (230°C) oven for 15 minutes; reduce the temperature to 400°F (200°C) and cook for 15 to 20 minutes longer, until the pastry is golden brown and the filling is bubbling. Cool on a wire rack.

PARTRIDGE SAUTÉED WITH FRESH HERBS

Perdiz com Molho de Ervas

MAKES 4 TO 6 SERVINGS

3 lb (1.5 kg) partridge or chicken pieces or halved Cornish hens

2 cups (500 mL) dry white wine

1 tsp (5 mL) pimento paste (optional)

1 Tbsp (15 mL) + ½ cup (125 mL) olive oil (approx.)

3 cloves garlic, minced

½ tsp (2 mL) paprika

3 sprigs each fresh thyme and rosemary

1 onion, finely chopped

¼ red bell pepper, seeded, cored, and diced

3 Tbsp (45 mL) tomato paste

½ tsp (2 mL) fine salt

1 egg yolk

2 Tbsp (30 mL) lemon juice

Fine salt and coarsely ground black pepper, to taste

In Portugal where hunting is common outside of the cities, flavourful game birds are often stewed, roasted, or grilled. In North America, game birds are not readily available; chicken or rabbit is substituted.

Buttered rice, Sautéed Garlic Rabe Greens (page 261), and grilled red peppers make delicious and colourful accompaniments. Arrange a ring of overlapping vegetables around the outside of the serving platter and place the bird pieces and sauce in the centre.

Rinse the partridge pieces under cold running water and pat dry with paper towels. Transfer to a resealable bag and place in a large bowl. Set aside.

In a small bowl, combine 1 cup (250 mL) white wine, pimento paste, 1 Tbsp (15 mL) oil, garlic, paprika, and 2 sprigs thyme and rosemary. Pour over the partridge and seal the bag; turn to coat well. Refrigerate for 6 hours or overnight, turning several times. Bring to room temperature for 30 minutes before cooking.

Remove the partridge from the marinade, letting the excess drip off; reserve the marinade. Pat the partridge dry with paper towels.

In a large skillet, heat the remaining ½ cup (125 mL) oil over medium-high heat. Cook the partridge pieces, in batches, for 2 to 5 minutes per side, until browned; add more oil to the pan, if necessary. Transfer the partridge to a serving plate and keep warm.

Drain and discard all but 2 Tbsp (30 mL) of the oil from the skillet. Add the onion and bell pepper; cook over medium heat, stirring constantly, for 3 to 5 minutes, just until the vegetables are softened and golden brown. Stir in the tomato paste, ½ tsp (2 mL) salt, remaining 1 cup (250 mL) wine, and the remaining sprigs of thyme and rosemary. Return the partridge to the pan and add the reserved marinade and the salt. Bring to a boil. Reduce the heat and simmer, uncovered and stirring frequently, for about 20 minutes, until the partridge is tender and no longer pink inside and the sauce is thickened. (If desired, the recipe can be prepared ahead to this point; make the final preparations when everyone is seated for dinner.)

Using a spoon, degrease the pan juices. Remove the skillet from the heat and set aside to cool for 5 to 10 minutes. Beat the egg yolk with the lemon juice and whisk into the pan with the partridge and sauce until well combined. Cover and set aside for 10 minutes. Season with salt and pepper. Transfer the partridge to a serving platter and pour half of the sauce overtop; serve the remaining sauce separately. Serve immediately.

DUCK WITH RICE AND MADEIRA

Arroz de Pato

MAKES 4 SERVINGS

1 whole duck (4 lb/1.8 kg)

16 cups (4 L) cold water

4 oz (120 g) lean bacon

4 oz (120 g) chouriço, unchopped

2 onions, chopped

1 carrot, chopped

1 stalk celery, chopped

3 cloves garlic

8 sprigs fresh parsley

3 bay leaves

10 whole black peppercorns, crushed

2 tsp (10 mL) paprika

1 tsp (5 mL) fine salt

¼ cup (60 mL) Madeira

3 Tbsp (45 mL) lemon juice

1 cup (250 mL) long-grain rice

Chopped fresh parsley, for garnish

Lemon wedges, for garnish

Golden-glazed duck is a familiar dish in the north of Portugal. The duck is brushed with savoury Madeira sauce during a final bake, giving it a deeper colour and crispy skin.

Place the duck in a stockpot; add the water and bring to a boil over medium-high heat. Skim off any scum from the surface. Add the bacon, chouriço, onion, carrot, celery, garlic, parsley, bay leaves, peppercorns, paprika, and ½ tsp (2 mL) salt. Reduce the heat to medium-low, partially cover, and simmer for 50 to 60 minutes, until the meat is tender. Skim off any scum from the surface.

Transfer the duck to a large bowl; reserve the stock. Using kitchen shears, cut the duck into 6 to 8 pieces, reserving the neck to add back to the stock. Shred ¼ cup (60 mL) of the duck. Using a slotted spoon, remove the chouriço and bacon from the pot and cut into thick pieces. Set all meat aside and keep warm.

Return the neck to the stock and continue simmering over medium heat, uncovered, for 30 minutes, until the stock is reduced by one-third. Using a spoon, degrease the pan juices, and strain the stock through a fine-mesh sieve; reserve.

TO MAKE THE SAUCE In a small saucepan, add 4 cups (1 L) of the reserved stock and the Madeira and cook over high heat until reduced by half. Taste and adjust the seasonings, if needed. Keep warm and set aside.

TO PRECOOK THE RICE In a large saucepan, add 2½ cups (625 mL) of the stock (the stock near the bottom of the stockpot is the most flavourful), lemon juice, remaining ½ tsp (2 mL) salt, and the reserved ¼ cup (60 mL) shredded duck. Bring to a boil over medium heat. Add the rice and cook, partially covered, for 15 minutes or until almost cooked.

Set the oven rack in the second position from the top. In a greased baking dish or ovenproof clay dish, mound the rice and its liquid. Arrange the pieces of duck evenly over the top and scatter over the reserved chouriço and bacon. Brush with ¼ cup (60 mL) of the sauce.

Bake in a preheated 400°F (200°C) oven for 15 to 20 minutes, until the duck is golden brown and the rice is tender. Brush with additional sauce if the pieces look dry. (If the duck is browning too quickly, cover it loosely with foil.)

Garnish with the parsley and lemon wedges and serve with the remaining sauce spooned overtop.

Alternatively, creative cooks substitute orange juice for the lemon juice and tuck in fresh orange and dried cranberries to bake with the rice and duck for a North American twist on this traditional entrée.

QUAIL IN CREAM SAUCE

Codornizes com Molho de Natas

MAKES 4 SERVINGS

8 quail

3 cloves garlic, minced

1 Tbsp (15 mL) olive oil

1 Tbsp (15 mL) paprika

½ tsp (2 mL) coarsely ground
 black pepper

2 tsp (10 mL) piri-piri sauce or
 Tabasco sauce

2 cups (500 mL) dry white wine
 (approx.)

1 onion, chopped

4 bay leaves

¼ cup (60 mL) vegetable oil

¼ cup (60 mL) whipping cream

Fine salt and coarsely ground
 black pepper, to taste

½ cup (125 mL) chopped fresh
 parsley (approx.)

Keep the quail covered in the oven until ready to enjoy, as they cool down quickly. The quail can also be baked or barbecued instead of fried. The marinade is a classic that can be used for a wide variety of light meals featuring rabbit, chicken, and veal. Serve this dish with mashed potatoes or sweet potatoes and steamed green vegetables.

Using a sharp knife, remove the neck and blood clots from the quail and trim off the fat and excess skin or any remaining feathers. Rinse the quail under cold running water and pat dry with paper towels. Set aside.

In a small bowl, combine the garlic, olive oil, paprika, pepper, piri-piri sauce, and wine.

In the bottom of a large shallow bowl, place half of the quail. Top with half of the onions and half of the bay leaves. Add the remaining quail, onion, and bay leaves. Pour the prepared marinade overtop (the marinade should completely cover the quail; top up with more wine, if necessary). Cover and refrigerate for 6 hours or overnight. Bring to room temperature for 30 minutes before cooking.

Remove the quails from the marinade, letting the excess drip off; reserve the marinade. Pat the quails dry using paper towels.

In a large skillet, heat the vegetable oil over medium-high heat. Cook the quail, in batches, for 8 to 10 minutes per side, until tender and no longer pink inside. Using a slotted spoon, transfer the quail to a serving dish and keep warm.

TO MAKE THE SAUCE Drain the fat from the skillet. Strain the marinade through a fine sieve and pour into the skillet. Bring to a boil over medium-high heat; simmer gently for 3 to 4 minutes, stirring constantly, until reduced by one-third. Add the cream; reduce the heat to low and simmer for 2 to 3 minutes, until the sauce begins to thicken. Season with salt and pepper, if necessary.

To serve, arrange the quail on a serving plate; top with half of the sauce and sprinkle with parsley. Serve the extra sauce in a warm gravy boat.

RABBIT AND CHOURIÇO

Coelho com Chouriço

MAKES 6 SERVINGS

3 to 4 lb (1.5 to 1.8 kg)
    rabbit pieces

8 oz (240 g) chouriço, cut into
    1-inch (2.5 cm) pieces

12 large cloves garlic, minced

1 onion, sliced

1 Tbsp (15 mL) tomato paste

2 tsp (10 mL) piri-piri sauce or
    Tabasco sauce

2 tsp (10 mL) paprika

Pinch coarsely ground black pepper

Pinch ground anise seed

Pinch dried red chili flakes

1½ cups (375 mL) red wine
    (approx.)

1½ cups (375 mL) beer (approx.)

1 tsp (5 mL) fine salt

Vegetable oil for deep-frying

Fine salt and coarsely ground
    black pepper, to taste

At a feast I attended in a small Azorean village, the meal consisted of rabbit and limpets, and was served with cornbread. (If there is no refrigeration, limpets can be safely consumed with 24 hours of being caught.) It was a simple meal that reminded me that life existed without grocery stores.

Rinse the rabbit pieces under cold running water and pat dry with paper towels. Transfer the rabbit and chouriço to a resealable bag and place in a large bowl. In a small bowl, combine the garlic, onion, tomato paste, piri-piri sauce, paprika, pepper, ground anise seed, and chili flakes. Pour over the rabbit and turn to coat. Add enough wine and beer to cover the rabbit. Seal the bag and refrigerate for 6 hours or overnight, turning several times. Bring to room temperature for 30 minutes before cooking.

Remove the chouriço from the marinade and set aside. Transfer the rabbit and marinade to a large Dutch oven and add the salt. Bring to a boil over high heat. Reduce the heat to medium and simmer, uncovered, for 20 minutes (the rabbit will not be fully cooked yet). Remove the rabbit from the cooked marinade, letting the excess drip off; reserve the marinade. Pat the rabbit pieces dry with paper towels.

In a large skillet, heat the vegetable oil to a depth of 1 inch (2.5 cm) over high heat; brown the chouriço for 2 to 3 minutes and remove to a serving platter; in the same oil, cook the rabbit, in batches, for 2 to 3 minutes per side, until golden brown and no longer pink inside. Add more oil, if necessary. (The rabbit and chouriço can also be barbecued.) With a slotted spoon, transfer the rabbit to a plate lined with paper towels and drain well. Add the rabbit to the chouriço and keep warm.

TO MAKE THE SAUCE Strain the cooked marinade through a fine-mesh sieve and bring to a boil in a saucepan over medium-high heat. Cook, uncovered, until the marinade is the desired consistency. Taste and adjust the seasonings with salt and pepper.

To serve, drizzle half of the sauce over the meat. Serve the remaining sauce alongside.

Serve this dish with Collard Greens, Cornbread, and Garlic Stir-Fry (page 269) or Sautéed Garlic Rabe Greens (page 261). Barbecuing instead of deep-frying the rabbit adds a fragrant, smoky aroma and taste.

CHICKEN WITH SAUTÉED MUSHROOMS AND CREAM PORT SAUCE

Frango com Cogumelos Salteados

MAKES 3 TO 4 SERVINGS

2½ lb (1.25 kg) chicken legs, thighs attached (about 4)

2 cloves garlic, minced

1 tsp (5 mL) fine salt

3 to 4 sprigs fresh thyme, chopped

¼ cup (60 mL) all-purpose flour

3 Tbsp (45 mL) olive oil

3 Tbsp (45 mL) butter

2 shallots, minced

1 lb (500 g) mushrooms (such as oyster, shiitake, and portobello caps), thinly sliced

¼ cup (60 mL) dry white wine

¼ cup (60 mL) chicken broth

3 Tbsp (45 mL) port

2 tsp (10 mL) Dijon mustard

3 Tbsp (45 mL) whipping cream

Fine salt and coarsely ground pepper, to taste

¼ cup (60 mL) chopped fresh coriander

Alexandra Faria, reporter and photographer for a Portuguese newspaper, is a creative and skilled cook and baker. I learned this about six months after I met her. She did all she could to generate interest in this book by writing a story in the newspaper and introducing me to fellow food aficionados. Imagine my surprise when I learned that the single mother who seemed to work around the clock had time in her busy life to cook! She gave me many personal recipes that she had collected from her grandmother. This recipe, like some of her other favourites, is laced with port.

I double the amount of mushrooms called for in her recipe, using the varieties that I readily find at my local grocer's, such as cremini, shiitake, and portobello. Combined with port, the mushrooms lend a woodsy, rich boost of flavour to the chicken.

Rinse the chicken under cold running water and pat it dry with paper towels. Using a sharp knife, separate the chicken thighs from the legs and transfer them both to a resealable bag. Combine the garlic, salt, and thyme, and rub into the skin, tucking some under the skin. Refrigerate for 4 hours or, if time allows, overnight. Bring the chicken to room temperature for 30 minutes before using.

Place the flour in a shallow bowl. Dredge the chicken in the flour, shaking off the excess flour, and set aside; discard the remaining flour.

In a heavy, large skillet over medium heat, heat 2 Tbsp (30 mL) oil and 2 Tbsp (30 mL) butter until the butter has melted. Cook the chicken for about 4 minutes on each side, until browned. Reserve the pan juices. Transfer the chicken to a baking sheet or ovenproof pan and bake for 10 to 15 minutes in a preheated 425°F (220°C) oven, until the chicken is tender and no longer pink inside. Transfer the chicken to a platter and keep warm.

Drain and discard all but 1 Tbsp (15 mL) of the pan juices from the skillet. Add the remaining 1 Tbsp (15 mL) oil and 1 Tbsp (15 mL) butter and heat over high heat. When the butter has melted, add the shallots and cook for about 2 minutes, until softened. Add the mushrooms and cook until golden and softened, 3 to 5 minutes. Add the white wine and bring to a boil over medium-high heat. Simmer until the wine sauce is reduced by one-third and clings to the mushrooms.

In a small bowl, combine the chicken stock, port, and mustard and whisk to combine. Pour over the mushrooms and increase the heat to medium-high. Bring to a boil and cook for 2 to 3 minutes, until the sauce has thickened and reduced by one-third. Add the cream, whisk to combine, and cook for 1 minute or until the sauce is well blended and heated through. Return the chicken and pan drippings to the pan, turning the pieces to coat with the sauce, and cook until the chicken is warmed through, 2 to 3 minutes. Taste and adjust the seasonings with salt and pepper. Sprinkle coriander overtop and serve.

CHICKEN SIMMERED WITH BACON, MOONSHINE, AND HERBS

Frango na Pucara

MAKES ABOUT 4 SERVINGS

1 chicken, cut into 8 pieces
(3 to 3¼ lb/1.5 to 1.6 kg)

4 cloves garlic, minced

¼ cup (60 mL) finely chopped
fresh parsley + ¼ cup (60 mL)
parsley leaves

1 Tbsp (15 mL) chopped
fresh thyme

1 cup (250 mL) all-purpose flour

2 Tbsp (30 mL) paprika

1½ tsp (7 mL) fine salt (approx.)

½ tsp (2 mL) coarsely ground
black pepper (approx.)

4 Tbsp (60 mL) olive oil

1 Tbsp (15 mL) butter

4 oz (120 g) thinly sliced
prosciutto, chopped

2 slices bacon, roughly chopped

6 shallots, quartered

2 red bell peppers, seeded, cored,
and sliced into wide strips

1 Tbsp (15 mL) Dijon mustard

1 cup (250 mL) canned tomatoes,
roughly chopped in juice

½ cup (125 mL) dry white wine

½ cup (125 mL) port

2 Tbsp (30 mL) Aguardente
or whisky

3 bay leaves

2 to 3 sprigs each fresh rosemary,
thyme, and oregano

Fine salt and coarsely ground
pepper, to taste

Irene Faria, a family friend, remembers the first time she had chicken in a clay pot: it was in a restaurant in Ourem, Portugal, when she was a young teen. She makes a similar version with her stepson, Adam. Irene makes sure there is always a supply of chicken, bacon, and potatoes on hand to make this family favourite whenever they feel like having some. Creamy mashed potatoes, made Portuguese-style with a hint of grated nutmeg and lots of butter and milk, is a perfect accompaniment to the chicken—it soaks up the flavourful juices from the simmered chicken. This recipe is inspired by Irene and Adam's dish.

Wash the chicken under cold running water and pat dry with paper towels. Make a paste with the ¼ cup (60 mL) chopped parsley and 1 Tbsp (15 mL) chopped thyme. Rub the paste all over the chicken, cover, and refrigerate for 4 hours or, if time allows, overnight. Bring to room temperature 30 minutes before cooking.

In a large bowl, whisk together the flour, 1 Tbsp (15 mL) paprika, salt, and pepper. Dredge the chicken pieces in the seasoned flour, shaking out the excess flour; discard the remaining flour. In a heavy large skillet, heat 2 Tbsp (30 mL) of the oil over medium heat. Add the chicken, skin side down, and cook for about 4 minutes per side, until browned. Transfer the chicken to a large ovenproof dish and arrange in a single layer.

Discard all but 1 Tbsp (15 mL) of the chicken fat in the skillet. Add the remaining 2 Tbsp (30 mL) of oil and the butter. When the butter has melted, add the prosciutto, bacon, shallots, and red peppers. Cook for 6 minutes, stirring occasionally. Spoon over the chicken.

To the same skillet, add the mustard and cook over medium heat for 1 minute, stirring to scrape up any brown bits from the bottom of the pan. Add the tomatoes, white wine, port, Aguardente, and the remaining 1 Tbsp (15 mL) paprika. Bring to a boil over medium-high heat, stir well, and cook for about 2 minutes or until thickened. Pour the sauce over the chicken. Scatter the ¼ cup (60 mL) parsley leaves as well as the bay leaves and sprigs of rosemary, thyme, and oregano over the chicken. Cover and transfer to a preheated 350°F (175°C) oven. Bake the chicken until tender, about 45 minutes. Discard the bay leaves and herb sprigs. Using tongs, transfer the chicken and vegetables to a platter.

Degrease the sauce in the pan, scrape up any brown bits, and pour the sauce into a small saucepan. Bring to a simmer over medium-high heat and cook, whisking often, until the sauce thickens to the desired consistency. Adjust the seasonings with salt and pepper.

Spoon the sauce over the chicken and serve.

SENHOR JOSÉ'S STUFFED CHICKEN THIGHS

Recheio do Senhor José para Pernas de Galinha

MAKES ABOUT 4 SERVINGS

4 Tbsp (60 mL) olive oil

¼ cup (60 mL) finely chopped farinheira sausage (about 1 oz/30 g)

¼ cup (60 mL) finely chopped chouriço (about 1 oz/30 g)

1 leek, white part only, finely chopped

¼ cup (60 mL) finely chopped bacon (about 1 oz/30 g)

⅓ cup (80 mL) chopped fresh parsley

8 chicken thighs, deboned, skin-on

½ cup (125 mL) finely chopped onion

4 cloves garlic, minced

½ cup (125 mL) dry white wine

Farinheira sausage was created during the Portuguese Inquisition. Jewish–Portuguese citizens made a lookalike of the famous Portuguese pork sausage, chouriço. Instead of pork, they used flour and spices and shaped them into sausages that they hung in their windows—a sign to everyone who walked by that the homeowners were Christian and therefore there was no reason to contact the Inquisition for further investigation.

Fairinheira sausage became a fast favourite that is still much loved and used in soups or fried up and served as an appetizer. If you don't have a local Portuguese butcher who sells farinheira sausage, increase the amount of chouriço and bacon called for in this recipe instead.

Senhor José, the butcher at a grocery store in Toronto, prepares a chicken leg stuffed with farinheira and chouriço sausages for his patrons to throw in the oven or saucepan. Inspired by Senhor José, I created this lighter version with more vegetables and less meat.

In a skillet over medium heat, heat 2 Tbsp (30 mL) of the oil until hot. Add the sausages, leek, and bacon and cook, stirring occasionally, for about 6 minutes, until the leek and meat have browned. Set aside until cool enough to handle.

Skim all but about 1 Tbsp (15 mL) of the fat from the frying pan. Transfer the sausage and leek mixture to a bowl and add the parsley and 1 Tbsp (15 mL) of the oil; mix to combine. (Alternatively, process in a food processor just until combined.) Set aside.

Place the chicken between 2 sheets of parchment paper. Using either the flat edge of a cleaver or the bottom of skillet, flatten the chicken to a ½-inch (1 cm) thickness. Remove the chicken from the parchment paper. Discard the parchment paper. Lie the chicken flat, skin side down, and spread about ½ Tbsp (7 mL) of the sausage mixture on top. Roll up the chicken and secure with baking twine or toothpicks (ensure that the skin is on the outside of the roll); tuck the chicken in place. Repeat with all of the remaining chicken.

In a skillet large enough to hold all of the chicken, heat the remaining 1 Tbsp (15 mL) of oil over medium-high heat. Add the chicken rolls and cook about 4 minutes, turning to brown on all sides. Transfer the chicken to a baking sheet and set aside.

In the same skillet, add the onion and garlic and cook for 4 to 5 minutes over medium heat, until browned. Add the wine and cook for 2 minutes, stirring to loosen any brown bits from the bottom of the pan. Pour the wine sauce over the prepared chicken and bake for about 10 minutes in a preheated 350°F (175°C) oven, until the chicken is tender (depending on your oven, the chicken may cook in less time; the filling is already cooked). Transfer the chicken, seam side down, to a serving dish and cover with foil to keep warm.

Using a spoon, degrease any fat from the baking sheet. Transfer the onion and juices to a food processor and purée. Pour into a gravy boat and serve the sauce alongside the meat.

Remove the string or toothpicks from the chicken rolls, slice diagonally into thirds, and serve.

ORANGE DUCK WITH HERBS IN A TOMATO PORT SAUCE

Pato com Laranja e Molho de Tomate e Vinho do Porto

MAKES ABOUT 4 SERVINGS

2 cups (500 mL) dry white wine

¾ cup (185 mL) fresh orange juice

1 tsp (5 mL) finely grated
    orange zest

1 onion, sliced

8 cloves garlic, minced

2 sprigs fresh rosemary

2 bay leaves

4 duck legs (about ½ to 1 lb/
    250 to 500 g each)

½ cup (125 mL) tomato sauce, or
    peeled, seeded, and chopped
    tomatoes with juices

½ cup (125 mL) port

2 oranges, sliced

Fine salt and coarsely ground
    black pepper, to taste

2 Tbsp (30 mL) chopped
    fresh parsley

If you are cooking for less-traditional Portuguese tastes, this twist on the classic dish Duck with Rice and Madeira (page 182) is sure to please. Marinating duck legs for two days in orange and herbs infuses a fruity kick that pairs perfectly with the gamey, rich flavour of duck.

Individual frozen duck legs can be found at select grocery stores, making duck a dish that can easily appear at your dinner table. Chopped collards, sautéed in a few pieces of garlic and a healthy helping of olive oil, and baked sweet potatoes are two perfect accompaniments to this dish.

TO MARINATE THE DUCK In a resealable bag, combine 1½ cups (375 mL) wine, ¼ cup (60 mL) orange juice, orange zest, half of the onion and garlic, and the rosemary and bay leaves. Add the duck legs, turning to coat. Cover and refrigerate overnight or for up to 2 days, turning several times. Bring to room temperature for 30 minutes before cooking.

In a small saucepan, add the remaining ½ cup (125 mL) of orange juice and cook over high heat for 1 to 2 minutes, until reduced to about ¼ cup (60 mL).

In a large, ovenproof dish, arrange the duck legs in a single layer and pour the marinade over the duck. Top with an additional ½ cup (125 mL) of the wine, the remaining onion and garlic, and the tomato sauce, port, reduced orange juice, and orange slices, and season with salt and pepper, to taste. Bake, loosely covered with foil, in a preheated 450°F (230°C) oven for about 1 hour and 20 minutes, basting every 30 minutes (check for doneness during the last 20 minutes of cook time; the duck legs are ready when they are tender and no longer pink inside). Uncover for the last few minutes of cooking to brown the meat.

Arrange the cooked orange slices on a serving platter and place the duck overtop. Set aside and keep warm.

Using a spoon, degrease the pan juices, and strain through a fine-mesh sieve into a small saucepan. Cook over high heat until the desired consistency is reached. (Reserve the onion pieces and serve alongside the duck, if desired; they are extra-sweet from the delicious duck and marinade.)

To serve, drizzle some of the sauce over the duck and sprinkle with parsley. Serve the remaining sauce in a gravy boat.

If you are lucky enough to have leftovers, try this great recipe the following day: Prepare long-grain rice using leftover roasted duck bones, parsley, reserved drippings, chicken broth, and slivers of chouriço. Serve the rice sandwiched between warmed and shredded leftover duck pieces. Your friends and family won't know they are getting leftovers.

BEEF, LAMB AND PORK

Carne de Vaca, Borrego e Porco

The Portuguese make good-tasting beef, lamb, and pork dishes. This is always a surprise given their talent with fish and seafood. The favourite sirloin steak appears just as frequently as sardines at Portuguese barbecues. The steak is usually rubbed in a tasty combination of garlic, black pepper, bay leaf, and salt to heighten the flavours before grilling. During the winter months, inexpensive cuts of beef marinated and slow-cooked in onion and wine melt in your mouth in dishes such as the comforting Marinated Roast Beef (page 202).

Beef, Sausages, and Vegetables in Broth (page 206), a classic Portuguese dish, combines beef, pork, sausages, bacon, vegetables, and spices and is cooked slowly in a flavourful broth. A cross between a New England dinner and a boiled choucroute feast, this *cozido* is celebrated among all Portuguese and can be found bubbling in pots in Portugal, the Azores, Cape Verde, and frequently in Toronto, with slight regional differences. In Cape Verde, for example, they add cornmeal to the broth near the end of cooking. However you prepare *cozido*, it's an excellent dish to serve at a winter gathering—just make sure you have extra chouriço, a favourite that quickly disappears.

One food aficionado who was determined to teach me about all Portuguese cooking insisted on making me her *cozido* even though I insisted I had many recipes for the famous dish. The feast that followed could have fed an army; luckily we enjoyed the leftovers in *roupa velha*, which translated means "old clothes," for days. These "old clothes" recipes are simple preparations for the bits of meat, vegetables, and broth that no one can bear to throw out, leftovers renewed in other meals. Often *roupa velha* include variations of soups or, more typically, the meat and vegetables tossed together with eggs and fresh greens to make a yummy omelette-style meal. The possibilities are endless.

Baby lamb or goat, a northern speciality known as *chanfana*, is marinated for days in well-guarded family recipes and slow-cooked for amazing results. Requiring minimal preparation, this hearty dish simmers in the oven for a melt-in-your-mouth tender roast that has soaked up all the delicious flavourings.

Pork also appears frequently in the Portuguese diet. One of my favourite pork gems is a recipe for Portuguese Pulled Pork (page 222). Cooked slowly over a number of hours, pork shoulder (also known as Boston butt) makes for fork-tender and flavourful results at little expense. Marinating enhances the flavour of the meat, although a simple spice blend of pimento paste and garlic is sufficient seasoning for the roast. Pork shoulder is also used in a number of other more classical dishes, such as Lemon and Garlic Pork Cubes (page 218).

Thinly sliced, the same pork cut is used to make *bifanas*—a Portuguese fast-food sandwich. Pork slices are briefly sautéed in onions and garlic with a splash of wine and Worcestershire sauce (known as *molho inglês*), drizzled with pan juices and a dab of mustard and piri-piri sauce, and served in crusty buns.

While collecting recipes, I frequently encountered dishes that contained lesser-known parts of pork, beef, and even chicken. Ingredients such as pork ears, beef tongue, and chicken blood are reminiscent of farming communities where every part of an animal is used. Those who grew up on farms in Portugal frequently prepared and savoured crispy-fried marinated pork ears and rice stews made with fried chicken-blood. I was surprised with the moist and tender results of Melt-in-Your-Mouth Tongue Stew (page 229). Although a little more work is required to seek out and prepare tongue, the results are well worth the effort. Once ignored or just thrown out, these types of ingredients are now being used in North America as part of the "nose to tail" trend, in which every part of the animal is used. As a bonus, these are protein choices that are also economical.

In this chapter you'll also find well-known Portuguese classics such as Pork and Clams Alentejo-Style (page 220), Pine Nut–Crusted Rosemary and Garlic Lamb Ribs (page 214), and easy-to-make Veal Scaloppini in Madeira Sauce (page 225) that are sure to become family favourites.

BEEF, LAMB, AND PORK

Carne de Vaca, Borrego e Porco

MARINATED ROAST BEEF

Alcatra

MAKES 8 SERVINGS

MARINADE

2 Tbsp (30 mL) tomato paste

1 tsp (5 mL) coarsely ground
black pepper (approx.)

2 Tbsp (30 mL) paprika (approx.)

3½ cups (875 mL) dry white wine,
red wine, beer, or a mixture
of beer and wine (approx.)

ROAST BEEF

6 lb (2.7 kg) beef shank,
neck roast, T-bone, rib roast,
round roast, or blade roast, cut
into steaks 3 inches (8 cm) thick

12 cloves garlic, minced

8 oz (240 oz) lean bacon,
cut into 1-inch (2.5 cm) pieces

4 onions, chopped

2 Tbsp (30 mL) lard

12 whole allspice berries

8 bay leaves, crumbled

1 Tbsp (15 mL) butter

2 Tbsp (30 mL) olive oil

2 tsp (10 mL) fine salt

Fine salt and coarsely ground
black pepper, to taste

"Anything I can do to help, I will," Maria Pereira offered when she heard that I was preparing a Portuguese cookbook. Maria, now deceased, was a major contributor to my first book 20 years ago, and her passion for the food comes through in all that she shared with me.

This dish is a specialty of Maria's native home, Terceira, one of the nine Azorean islands. When times were hard, the dish was prepared only on special occasions, such as religious feasts or weddings. When Maria prepared this dish for me, I was with her large extended family shortly after watching a procession from Our Land of Angels Church celebrating the Feast of the Holy Spirit.

This roast beef is typically enjoyed with sweet bread and boiled sweet potatoes. It's excellent accompanied by Sautéed Garlic Rabe Greens (page 261) and steamed rice (to catch the flavourful sauce).

TO MAKE THE MARINADE In a large bowl, combine the tomato paste, pepper, paprika, and wine and mix well. Set aside.

In a large, shallow bowl, combine the beef and garlic, using your hands to rub the garlic into the beef. Divide the beef into 2 equal portions and set aside.

In a separate bowl, combine the bacon and onions; divide into 3 equal portions and set aside.

Rub the inside of an *alguidar* or baking dish with the lard. Layer one-third of the bacon and onion mixture in the bottom of the dish. Arrange half of the beef on top. Add enough marinade to just cover the meat. Add another one-third of the bacon and onions. Top with the remaining beef. Scatter the allspice and bay leaves evenly overtop. Add the remaining bacon and onions and top with enough marinade to cover the meat. Dot with butter and drizzle with oil. Reserve the leftover marinade for basting. Cover and refrigerate for 24 to 48 hours.

Cook, uncovered, in a preheated 400°F (200°C) oven for 11 to 14 minutes per 1 lb (500 g) for rare or medium-rare, respectively (or until a cooking thermometer pushed into the centre of the roast reads 140°F/60°C to 150°F/65°C). Turn the top layer (beef, onion, and bacon pieces) after about 15 minutes or when the top of the beef is brown. Midway through cooking, remove the baking dish from the oven and transfer the top layer of meat to a plate. Transfer the bottom layer of beef and bacon pieces to a separate plate. Return the browned top layer of meat to the bottom of the baking dish. Top with the other portion of beef and bacon and season with salt. If the marinade does not cover the top of the meat, add the reserved marinade or more wine. Return the baking dish to the oven and continue cooking until the meat is tender and evenly browned. If the meat is browning too quickly, cover with foil. Remove from the oven and keep warm.

TO MAKE THE SAUCE Degrease the pan juices and strain through a fine-mesh sieve into a small saucepan. Bring the juices to a boil over medium-high heat and cook until reduced to the desired consistency. Taste and adjust the seasonings with salt and pepper.

Slice the meat thinly and serve with spoonfuls of sauce overtop.

For the best results, use a few different cuts of beef, with or without bones.

SIRLOIN STEAK WITH EGG AND SHRIMP

Bife com Ovo "à Cavalo"

MAKES 1 SERVING

7 oz (200 g) sirloin steak or striploin, about ¾ inch (2 cm) thick

5 Tbsp (75 mL) olive oil

4 cloves garlic, smashed

Fine salt and coarsely ground black pepper, to taste

1 Tbsp (15 mL) butter

⅓ cup (80 mL) + 1 Tbsp (15 mL) dry white wine (approx.)

Dash piri-piri sauce or Tabasco sauce

2 large shrimp, peeled and deveined

1 egg

1 tsp (5 mL) chopped fresh parsley

1 Tbsp (15 mL) Worcestershire sauce

1 lemon wedge, for garnish

Most Portuguese restaurants have their own *bife a casa* or "beef house specialty." Some slide a slice of ham and an egg on a steak and crown it with homemade potato chips. Others top steak and egg with scampi or crab. Try making this version below your house specialty. Garlic lovers can mince and rub half the garlic into the steak and set it aside at room temperature for 30 minutes before cooking. Serve the steak with Roasted Seasoned Potatoes (page 246) and a mixed salad.

Using a sharp knife, trim the excess fat from the steak. Rinse and pat dry with paper towels.

Heat a large cast iron pan over low heat and add 2 Tbsp (30 mL) of the oil; add half of the garlic and cook for 5 to 7 minutes, until the oil is fragrant and the garlic is golden brown. Using a slotted spoon, transfer the garlic to a small bowl and set aside. Increase the heat to medium-high and heat just until it begins to smoke. Add another 2 Tbsp (30 mL) of the oil, and sear the steak for 1 to 2 minutes per side. Reduce the heat to medium and cook, turning once, for 5 to 8 minutes or to desired doneness (if desired, you can finish cooking the steak in a hot oven). Using a slotted spatula, transfer the steak to a serving dish and season with salt and pepper; keep warm. Wipe the pan clean of oil.

In the same skillet, add the remaining 1 Tbsp (15 mL) oil and 2 cloves garlic, the reserved cooked garlic, and the butter, ⅓ cup (80 mL) wine, and piri-piri sauce. When the butter has melted, add the shrimp and cook over medium-high heat for 1 to 2 minutes, until pink and firm when pierced with a fork. Transfer the shrimp to a plate and keep warm. Reserve the skillet and pan juices, including the garlic.

In a small bowl, break the egg and gently slide onto a small skillet. Cook for 3 to 4 minutes, until the egg yolk is covered with an opaque film and the egg white is set. Gently slide the egg onto the steak; arrange the shrimp on either side of the egg.

In the reserved skillet, add the Worcestershire and 1 Tbsp (15 mL) white wine to the pan juices and simmer over medium-high heat. Stir to scrape up any brown bits from the bottom of the pan and cook until the liquid is reduced by about half. Discard the garlic.

To serve, pour the sauce over the steak. Sprinkle with parsley. Serve with a lemon wedge alongside.

BEEF, SAUSAGES, AND VEGETABLES IN BROTH

Cozido à Portuguesa

MAKES 6 TO 8 SERVINGS

2 lb (1 kg) flank steak, quartered

1 lb (500 g) pork ribs,
   back preferred

8 oz (240 g) pork hock, chopped
   into 1-inch (2.5 cm) pieces

1 lb (500 g) morcela

1 lb (500 g) chouriço, unchopped

8 oz (240 g) salpicão

8 oz (240 g) lean bacon,
   in one piece

12 cups (3 L) water

1 tsp (5 mL) fine salt

½ tsp (2 mL) whole black
   peppercorns, crushed

3 onions, coarsely chopped

4 cloves garlic, coarsely chopped

10 sprigs fresh mint or parsley

3 bay leaves

½ tsp (2 mL) whole cloves

3 sweet potatoes, peeled and
   cut into large cubes

½ small turnip, peeled and cut
   into large cubes

½ cabbage, cut into thick wedges

2 carrots, thickly sliced

1 bunch collard greens, trimmed
   and roughly chopped

Fine salt, to taste

½ cup (125 mL) chopped fresh
   parsley, for garnish

Cozido is a Portuguese favourite made in generous quantities—enough for family *and* friends. It is traditionally served on religious or festive occasions. Somewhat similar to the boiled New England dinner, cozido combines simmering flavours of smoky bacon and chouriço with the sweet cinnamon taste of morcela sausage. The aromatic broth tastes even better the next day, and you can use any bits of leftover meat and vegetables to make a rice dish. Whole cloves are an Azorean accent.

In a large stockpot, place flank steak, ribs, pork hock, the three sausages, and bacon and cover with the water. Bring to a boil over medium-high heat. Skim off any skum from the surface. Add the salt, peppercorns, onions, garlic, mint, bay leaves, and cloves. Reduce the heat to medium-low, cover, and simmer for about 1 hour, transferring the sausages to a serving dish after 40 minutes or when cooked (keep sausages warm). Test the remaining meat during the balance of the cooking time and transfer to the serving dish with the sausages when cooked. Continue to skim off any skum during cooking. Drain off the fat.

Add all of the vegetables to the stockpot (if the broth has reduced too much, add enough water to cover the vegetables). Season with salt, to taste. Cook, covered, over medium-low heat for about 20 minutes, until the vegetables are tender when pierced with a fork. Use a slotted spoon to remove the vegetables from the pot as they become cooked and place them with the reserved meat. Using a fine-mesh sieve, strain the broth and set aside.

Method continues . . .

BEEF, SAUSAGES, AND VEGETABLES IN BROTH
(continued)

Cut the meat and vegetables into serving-sized pieces. Drizzle 1 cup (250 mL) of the broth over the vegetables and meat to moisten. Garnish with parsley. Serve with steamed rice and salad.

Traditionally, pig's ears and snout are included in this dish; they are marinated in wine, garlic, and bay leaves for 24 to 48 hours beforehand. I eliminated them in this recipe.

There are numerous variations on the beloved cozido. Ana Sanca, a friend and poet, prepares a West African–style cozido called *cachupa*. The only differences are the addition of hominy and lima beans for some of the potatoes and turnip. Everyone looks forward to thickened pieces of cachupa the next day, which is pan-fried and enjoyed for breakfast.

SKEWERED BEEF

Espetada à Moda da Madeira

In Madeira the beef is skewered on a bay-leaf branch, which adds an additional layer of flavour to the beef as it cooks over coals. Nine to eleven pounds (four or five kilograms) of beef are cooked all at once and the branch is brought to the table. If you have fresh bay leaves, thread them alternately with the meat onto the skewers. For a complete meal, grill tomatoes, onion, and zucchini along with the beef.

In a resealable bag placed in a large bowl, combine the beef, 18 crumbled bay leaves, garlic, oil, and pepper. Seal the bag and turn to coat well. Refrigerate for at least 8 hours or overnight, turning several times. Bring to room temperature for 30 minutes before cooking.

Remove the beef from the marinade, season with salt, and thread onto wooden or metal skewers (soak wooden skewers in water for 2 hours before using to prevent burning).

Grill the beef on medium (or 4 to 6 inches/10 to 15 cm from medium-hot coals) for 3 to 4 minutes per side, until browned and cooked to desired doneness. Sprinkle with the remaining 2 crumbled bay leaves. Serve the meat with crusty buns and piri-piri sauce, if desired.

MAKES 2 SERVINGS

1 lb (500 g) beef striploin or tenderloin cut into 1-inch (2.5 cm) cubes

20 bay leaves (fresh if available), crumbled

3 cloves garlic, minced

2 tsp (10 mL) olive oil

¼ tsp (1 mL) coarsely ground black pepper

½ tsp (2 mL) fine salt

LEG OF LAMB STUFFED WITH MINT AND PARSLEY

Perna de Borrego Recheada

MAKES 6 TO 8 SERVINGS

4 oz (120 g) chouriço or salpicão

¼ cup (60 mL) chopped fresh parsley

¼ cup (60 mL) chopped fresh mint

3 Tbsp (45 mL) olive oil

1 Tbsp (15 mL) white wine vinegar

1 Tbsp (15 mL) lemon juice

¼ cup (60 mL) onion, chopped

3 cloves garlic, minced

1 tsp (5 mL) paprika

½ tsp (2 mL) fine salt

¼ tsp (1 mL) coarsely ground black pepper

1 leg of lamb, boned and butterflied (about 5 to 6 lb/ 2.2 to 2.7 kg)

1 cup (250 mL) vinho verde (approx.)

Fine salt and coarsely ground black pepper, to taste

½ cup (125 mL) chopped fresh mint, for garnish

In Portugal's farming communities in the northern provinces, lamb is on the table as much as fish is in the south. The light-bodied, acidic vinho verde (green wine) used in this recipe balances nicely with the full-bodied flavours of lamb and chouriço. Serve the remaining wine with this dish.

Have your butcher debone the lamb for quicker preparation. Allow two thick slices per person, and serve with Roasted Seasoned Potatoes (page 246) and a Mixed Green Salad (page 240).

Using a sharp knife, remove the skin of the chouriço and slice it into small pieces. Remove and discard any fat. Transfer the chouriço to a food processor and process for a few seconds, until the consistency of fine ground beef. Add the parsley, mint, oil, vinegar, lemon juice, onion, garlic, paprika, salt, and pepper and pulse just until blended. (Alternatively, mix the ingredients in a bowl until well combined.) Set aside.

Trim and discard the excess fat from the lamb; place the lamb in a shallow baking dish. Open the meat flat like a book. Reserve 1 Tbsp (15 mL) of the stuffing and spread the remainder over the lamb to within 1 inch (2.5 cm) of the edges. Starting at the narrow end, roll up the lamb jelly-roll-style into a sausage-shaped roast. Secure with baker's twine in 1-inch (2.5 cm) intervals. Cover the lamb and refrigerate overnight. Bring to room temperate for 30 minutes before cooking.

Place the lamb on a greased rack set in a baking pan. Pour the wine over the lamb. Roast in a preheated 450°F (230°C) oven, uncovered, for 20 minutes. Reduce the heat to 325°F (160°C). Continue to roast, turning and basting often with the pan juices, for about 70 minutes (18 to 20 minutes per pound/500 g), until a meat thermometer inserted into the centre of the roast registers 140°F (60°C) for rare, 160°F (71°C) for medium, or 170°F (77°C) for well done. Cover the lamb with foil and set aside for 10 minutes before slicing.

Using a fine-mesh sieve, strain the pan juices into a saucepan and spoon off the excess fat. Add the reserved stuffing and bring to a boil over medium-high heat. Boil for 2 to 3 minutes, until reduced by about half. (If less than about ½ cup/125 mL of juices remain in the pan, add more wine, to taste.) Taste and adjust the seasonings with salt and pepper.

Pour the sauce over the lamb before serving. Garnish with fresh mint.

SAUTÉED LAMB'S LIVER PORTUGUESE-STYLE

Iscas de Borrego Fritas

MAKES 2 TO 3 SERVINGS

1 lb (500 g) baby beef liver

1 lb (500 g) lamb's liver

1 cup (250 mL) dry white wine

¼ cup (60 mL) + 2 Tbsp (30 mL) white wine vinegar

2 Tbsp (30 mL) lemon juice

2 large cloves garlic, minced

1 bay leaf

2 Tbsp (30 mL) olive oil

Fine salt and coarsely ground black pepper, to taste

¼ cup (60 mL) pickled peppers, finely chopped

A large order of *iscas de borrego* frito is prepared at a Portuguese club in Toronto, Casa do Alentejo, for the Saturday regulars who spend the evening enjoying home cooking, folk music, and dancing. The liver, prepared earlier in the day and left marinating in a delicious wine sauce all afternoon, is infused with a subtle Portuguese flavour. Serve this dish with baked potatoes, corn-bread slices, and olives. If you cannot find lamb's liver, double the amount of baby beef liver.

Rinse the liver under cold running water and pat dry with paper towels.

In a large resealable bag, combine ¾ cup (185 mL) white wine, ¼ cup (60 mL) vinegar, lemon juice, garlic, and bay leaf. Add the liver to the marinade, turning to coat well. Cover and refrigerate for 2 hours or overnight. Bring to room temperature for 30 minutes before cooking.

Remove the liver from the marinade and wipe dry with paper towels; discard the marinade. In a skillet, heat the oil over medium-high heat. Add the liver and cook for about 2 minutes per side, until the liver is light pink inside. Season with salt and pepper. Add the remaining ¼ cup (60 mL) white wine and 2 Tbsp (30 mL) vinegar; bring just to a boil. Transfer the liver to a serving plate. Simmer the pan juices, stirring to scrape up any brown bits from the bottom of the pan, until thickened to the desired consistency.

To serve, drizzle the pan juices and sprinkle pickled peppers over the liver.

LAMB IN WINE AND GARLIC

Chanfana

In the north of Portugal, almost everyone has a guarded family recipe for *chanfana*, irresistible golden-glazed lamb steeped in its own savoury juices. The secret to this dish is marinating and slow-simmering the lamb in wine and garlic. The longer you marinate the meat (three days if time allows), the stronger the flavour. Serve the lamb with Rice and Broccoli Rabe with Onion and Garlic Oil (page 260) or Collard Greens, Cornbread, and Garlic Stir-Fry (page 269).

Using a sharp knife, trim the excess fat from the lamb. Rinse under cold running water and pat dry with paper towels. Transfer to a resealable bag and place in a large bowl. Set aside.

In a bowl, combine 3 cups (750 mL) wine, oil, garlic, bay leaves and herbs. Pour over the lamb. If necessary, add more wine to cover the lamb. Seal the bag and turn to coat well. Refrigerate for up to 2 days (or 3 days if you have the time). Bring to room temperature for 30 minutes before cooking.

Pour the lamb and marinade into a clay baking dish (use a regular baking dish if you do not have a clay one). Add the chouriço, salt, hot pepper, and black pepper; stir to combine. Top with the onion and tomatoes. If necessary, add more wine to cover the lamb.

Cover and bake in a preheated 325°F (160°C) oven, turning twice, for 45 to 60 minutes, until the lamb is almost tender. If the wine has reduced, add more wine to cover the lamb. Uncover, increase the heat to 375°F (190°C), and bake for about 30 minutes, turning often, until all the pieces are browned and the lamb is tender. Transfer the lamb to a serving platter; reserve the cooking juices.

TO MAKE THE SAUCE Pour off the fat and strain the meat juices through a fine-mesh sieve. Bring to a boil in a saucepan over medium-high heat and simmer gently until reduced by one-third. Taste and adjust the seasonings with salt and pepper.

Pour the sauce over the meat, garnish with mint, and serve.

MAKES ABOUT 6 SERVINGS

- 2 lb (1 kg) lamb or goat shoulder, with a few bones, cut into 3 or 4 pieces
- 3 to 5 cups (750 mL to 1.25 L) dry rosé or white wine
- 3 Tbsp (45 mL) olive oil
- 1 head of garlic, minced (about 12 cloves)
- 4 bay leaves
- 4 to 5 sprigs each fresh thyme, rosemary and parsley
- 2 to 3 slices chouriço, prosciutto, or lean bacon
- 1 Tbsp (15 mL) fine salt
- ½ hot red chili pepper, chopped (optional)
- ¼ tsp (1 mL) coarsely ground black pepper
- 1 onion, sliced
- 1 cup (250 mL) tomatoes, peeled, seeded, and chopped
- ½ cup (125 mL) chopped fresh mint, for garnish

PINE NUT–CRUSTED ROSEMARY AND GARLIC RACK OF LAMB

Costeletas de Borrego com Pinhões e Alho

MAKES 2 TO 3 SERVINGS

1 rack of lamb (2 lb/1 kg)

⅓ cup (80 mL) chopped fresh rosemary

5 cloves garlic, minced

1 tsp (5 mL) fine salt

⅓ cup (80 mL) pine nuts

¼ cup (60 mL) dried breadcrumbs

Coarsely ground black pepper, to taste

½ cup (125 mL) Dijon mustard

Vegetable oil for frying

This rack of lamb, inspired by Chef José Alves, owner of Via Norte in Toronto, is a hit among his patrons who enjoy familiar ingredients with a North American twist. Alves, a Portuguese-trained chef, has spent 30 years honing his skills and making palate-pleasing food. Easy to prepare, this dish delivers, combining the much-loved lamb with pine nuts, rosemary, and an abundance of aromatic garlic. Prepare most of the dish up to 24 hours ahead of time and roast just before serving.

Have the butcher trim the rack French-style and crack the backbone between each rib to facilitate carving.

TO PREPARE THE LAMB Using a sharp knife, score the fat on the lamb and separate the ribs in portions of 2 to 3 ribs each. Trim the fat and flesh, exposing the rib bones (your butcher can prepare French-trimmed ribs to this point if you ask). Rinse the lamb under cold running water and pat dry with paper towels.

Place the ribs in a resealable bag. In a small bowl, combine the rosemary, garlic, and 1 tsp (5 mL) salt. Rub all over the ribs and seal the bag. Cover and refrigerate overnight. Bring to room temperature for 30 minutes before cooking.

TO PREPARE THE PINE NUTS Spread the pine nuts in a single layer on a baking sheet. Bake in a preheated 350°F (175°C) oven, shaking the baking sheet occasionally, for 5 to 8 minutes, until browned. Set aside to cool. When cool, transfer to a food processor or blender and process until finely ground.

Method continues . . .

PINE NUT-CRUSTED ROSEMARY AND GARLIC LAMB RIBS

(continued)

In a bowl or resealable bag large enough to fit the ribs, combine the bread-crumbs and pine nuts and season with pepper, to taste. Set aside.

Using a brush, lightly coat the ribs with Dijon mustard. Place the ribs in the pine nut mixture and turn and shake to coat all over.

In a large skillet over medium-high heat, heat 3 Tbsp (45 mL) oil until hot. Add the ribs to the pan and cook, in batches, until golden brown, about 2 minutes per side (add more oil to the skillet, if needed). Brown the remaining ribs and transfer to a baking sheet lined with parchment paper.

Roast in a preheated 425°F (220°C) oven for 5 to 7 minutes per side, until the meat is pinkish-grey when tested with a knife in the thickest part or a meat thermometer reads 140°F (60°C) for medium-rare. Let the lamb rest at least 8 minutes before serving. Serve with Baked Sweet Potatoes in Madeira (page 243) and a Mixed Green Salad (page 240).

LEMON AND GARLIC PORK CUBES

Torresmos/Rojões

2 lb (1 kg) boneless pork loin, cut into large 2-inch (5 cm) cubes

1¼ cups (310 mL) dry white wine

¼ cup (60 mL) white wine vinegar

¼ cup (60 mL) lemon juice

1 large head garlic, minced

6 bay leaves, crumbled

¾ tsp (3 mL) pimento paste

½ tsp (2 mL) paprika

¼ tsp (1 mL) whole black peppercorns, crushed

¼ tsp (1 mL) whole cloves

¼ tsp (1 mL) piri-piri sauce or Tabasco sauce

6 Tbsp (90 mL) lard (approx.)

Fine salt and coarsely ground black pepper, to taste

Called *torresmos* in the Azores and *rojões* in mainland Portugal, this dish is traditionally eaten during *Domingo Gordo* (Fat Sunday). The feast ends the day before Ash Wednesday, which marks Lent and 40 days of leaner eating. As an excuse to eat pork for the last time until Easter, large batches of torresmos are prepared. In the Azores, this dish is traditionally served with baked sweet potatoes or taro root and cornbread. In the north of Portugal, steamed chestnuts are sautéed with the pork pieces.

Fattier pork pieces make these cubes more juicy, but if you do not want the extra fat, use leaner meat and barbecue or broil, basting often with the marinade.

Rinse the pork under cold running water and pat dry with paper towels. Transfer to a resealable bag and place in a large bowl. In a bowl, combine 1 cup (250 mL) wine, wine vinegar, lemon juice, garlic, bay leaves, ½ tsp (2 mL) pimento paste, ¼ tsp (1 mL) paprika, peppercorns, cloves, and piri-piri sauce. Pour over the pork and seal the bag; turn to coat well. Refrigerate for at least 8 hours or overnight, turning several times. Bring to room temperature for 30 minutes before cooking.

Remove the pork from the marinade, letting the excess drip off. (If barbecuing, reserve and strain the marinade; otherwise discard.) Pat the pork dry with paper towels.

In a skillet, heat the lard over medium-high heat until melted. Cook the pork, in batches, for about 2 minutes per side, until golden brown. (If barbecuing, grill the pork on medium or 4 to 6 inches/10 to 15 cm from medium-hot coals, brushing occasionally with the reserved marinade, for 3 to 4 minutes per side, until brown.) Transfer the pork to a plate and keep warm.

Drain all the fat from the skillet and pour in the remaining ¼ cup (60 mL) wine, ¼ tsp (1 mL) pimento paste, ¼ tsp (1 mL) paprika, and salt and pepper. Bring to a boil over medium-high heat, stirring to scrape up any brown bits from the bottom of the pan. Add the pork pieces, reduce the heat to low, cover, and cook for 1 to 2 minutes, until the pork juices run clear. Transfer the pork to a serving dish. Using a spoon, degrease the pan juices and drizzle the sauce over the pork.

Dress up these tender chunks of marinated pork by threading on bamboo skewers with onion, red and yellow pepper slices, and cherry tomatoes before grilling.

Pimento paste adds a hint of Azorean flavouring to the pork in this dish. The same marinade and sauce used in this recipe is used to make *bifanas*, a traditional Portuguese fast-food snack. To make bifanas at home, briefly sauté paper-thin pork cutlets and place in crusty buns; drizzle with the pan juices and top with mustard and Pickled Peppers (page 221).

PORK AND CLAMS ALENTEJO-STYLE

Carne de Porco à Alentejana

MAKES 6 SERVINGS

2 lb (1 kg) pork tenderloin,
    cut into 2-inch (5 cm) cubes

4 tsp (20 mL) paprika (optional)

1 tsp (5 mL) cumin

4 cloves garlic, minced

¼ hot red chili pepper,
    chopped (optional)

¼ tsp (1 mL) whole cloves

3 bay leaves

1¼ cups (325 mL) white wine
    (approx.)

½ cup (125 mL) vegetable oil
    (approx.)

1½ lb (750 g) potatoes (about 4),
    peeled and cut into 1-inch
    (2.5 cm) cubes

Fine salt, to taste

2 Tbsp (30 mL) olive oil (approx.)

1 onion, chopped

2 lb (1 kg) Manila clams

¼ cup (60 mL) chopped fresh
    coriander, for garnish

½ cup (125 mL) Pickled Peppers
    or mixed pickled vegetables
    (see facing page and sidebar),
    finely chopped, for garnish

1 lemon cut into wedges,
    for garnish

A specialty of the southern Portuguese province of Alentejo, this dish is a perfect combination for the Portuguese, who enjoy both seafood and pork.

Most of the meal can be made ahead and reheated, with the clams tossed in just before serving, for an elegant one-dish dinner.

Rinse the pork cubes under cold running water and pat dry with paper towels. Place the pork in a resealable bag placed in a large bowl. In a small bowl, combine 1 tsp (5 mL) paprika (if using), cumin, garlic, chili pepper (if using), whole cloves, bay leaves, and 1 cup (250 mL) wine. Pour over the pork cubes and seal the bag, turning to coat well. Refrigerate overnight or for up to 2 days, turning periodically. Bring to room temperature for 30 minutes before cooking.

In a large skillet, heat the vegetable oil over medium-high heat; cook the potatoes, in batches, adding more oil if necessary, for 4 to 5 minutes, until golden and cooked through. Using a slotted spoon, transfer the potatoes to a plate, sprinkle with salt, and keep warm. Drain the oil from the pan.

Remove the pork from the marinade, letting the excess drip off; discard the marinade and pat the pork dry with paper towels.

Add the olive oil to the skillet. Add the cubed pork and cook over medium-high heat, in batches if necessary, for about 2 minutes per side, until browned. Transfer to a plate and keep warm. Add onion and more oil, if necessary, and cook over medium heat, stirring occasionally, for 8 to 10 minutes, until softened. Add 1 Tbsp (15 mL) paprika and 2 Tbsp (30 mL) wine and stir to scrape up any brown bits from the bottom of the pan. Return the pork to the pan, add salt, to taste, and up to 2 Tbsp (30 mL) wine if the sauce has dried up. Stir and remove from the heat; set aside.

Meanwhile, scrub the clams with a stiff brush under cold running water to remove any surface sand and grit. Discard any clams that are not tightly closed.

Return the pan to the heat and add the prepared clams. Increase the heat to high, cover, and bring to a boil. Cook until the clams open, 5 to 7 minutes (reduce the heat to medium if the sauce is sticking). Discard any clams that do not open. Check the pork for doneness; the juices should run clear when pierced with a fork.

Using a slotted spoon, transfer the pork and clams to a serving dish. Add the fried potatoes to the pork and clams. Garnish with coriander, pickled vegetables, and lemon wedges.

Drain the fat from the pan juices and spoon the juices over the dish.

PICKLED PEPPERS

Using a sharp knife, core, seed, and cut peppers into ¼-inch (6 mm) strips. Stuff vegetables into a 4-cup (1 L) sterilized preserving jar.

In a large pot, bring vinegar, water, salt, and peppercorns to a boil over medium-high heat. Boil for 1 minute. Pour hot liquid over the peppers in the jar, leaving ½ inch (1 cm) of head space.

PROCESS IN A HOT-WATER CANNER Place the filled jar in the bottom of a canning pot filled with boiling water (water should cover the jar by 1 inch/ 2.5 cm). Cover the pot and bring to a full boil; boil for 5 minutes. Carefully remove the jar and allow it to cool completely, about 3 to 4 hours or overnight. Check the seal: the lid of the jar should be depressed. Store in a cool, dark place. Once opened, refrigerate and consume within 2 weeks.

Another favourite pickle combines julienned celery, sweet peppers, pickling cucumbers, carrots, and piri-piri peppers, with cauliflower florets and whole pearl onions. It is made in the same manner with the addition of two whole peeled cloves and one clove minced garlic.

MAKES 4 CUPS (1 L)

PICKLED PEPPERS

5 sweet banana peppers
   (red and yellow)
1 cup (250 mL) white vinegar
2 cups (500 mL) water
1 tsp (5 mL) coarse salt
4 whole black peppercorns

PORTUGUESE PULLED PORK

Cachaço

MAKES 6 TO 8 SERVINGS

1 boneless or bone-in pork butt
   roast or boneless pork roast, fat
   intact (3 to 4 lb/1.5 to 1.8 kg)

½ cup (125 mL) chopped fresh
   parsley

10 cloves garlic, minced

1 Tbsp (15 mL) paprika

¼ cup (60 mL) Red Pepper Pimento
   Paste Seasoning (page 286)

6 hot chili peppers, stemmed,
   seeded, and chopped

8 Tbsp (120 mL) olive oil

1 cup (250 mL) beer or white wine

¼ cup (60 mL) port

½ cup (125 mL) white wine vinegar

4 bay leaves, crumbled

Fine salt and coarsely ground
   black pepper, to taste

½ cup (125 mL) tomato sauce

1 cup (250 mL) chicken or
   vegetable stock

1 Tbsp (15 mL) lard

3 large onions, 1 quartered +
   2 thinly sliced

6 to 8 crusty buns, split in half

Pickled Peppers (page 221)

Pimento Mayonnaise

piri-piri sauce

Cachaço is the Portuguese name for pork shoulder, also known as Boston butt. It is nicely marbled with fat and collagen. Smeared with a combination of Portuguese seasonings and cooked slowly over a number of hours, this cachaço dish is fork-tender and flavourful.

Homemade Red Pepper Pimento Paste Seasoning (page 286) lends a sweet finish to the pork that the fermented variety lacks. If you are using store-bought pimento, use only two tablespoons (30 mL) of pimento paste rather than the one-quarter cup (60 mL) called for in the recipe, and reduce the amount of salt accordingly (pimento paste is salty).

If you can, use Portuguese-flavoured lard for this dish. You can find it in Portuguese grocery stores or make your own by mixing the drippings from roasted chouriço with regular lard.

Rinse the pork under cold running water and pat dry with paper towels. Using a sharp knife, make deep holes in the roast to allow the marinade to penetrate the meat. Set aside.

TO MAKE THE MARINADE In a food processor, process the parsley, garlic, paprika, pimento paste, and chili pepper until combined; in a steady stream, add 4 Tbsp (60 mL) of the oil and process to a smooth paste. In a resealable bag placed in a large bowl, combine the pork with the spice paste, using your hands to force some of the sauce into the holes. Add the beer (or wine), port, vinegar, and bay leaves. Seal the bag and turn to coat. Refrigerate for at least 8 hours or overnight, turning several times.

Remove the pork from the marinade, brushing off the spices and any excess marinade; reserve the marinade. Pat the pork dry with paper towels. Season the roast with salt and pepper and set aside, covered, at room temperature for at least 1 hour before using.

In a large skillet, heat 2 Tbsp (30 mL) of the oil until hot. Add the pork and cook for 8 minutes, turning to sear all sides. Transfer the pork to a roasting pan or baking dish and set aside.

In the same skillet, stir in the tomato sauce, chicken stock, and reserved marinade; bring to a boil over high heat and simmer for 1 minute, stirring to scrape up any brown bits from the bottom of the pan. Remove from the heat and pour the cooked marinade over the roast. Dot the roast with the lard and add the quartered onion. Cover tightly. Transfer the roasting pan to a preheated 325°F (160°C) oven and baste every 45 minutes with the pan juices. Roast until the meat is very tender, about 2½ to 3 hours (the roast is done when a knife inserted in the thickest part easily penetrates the meat or a meat thermometer reads 195°F/91°C). Cover the roast and set aside for at least 30 minutes before using to allow the flavours to develop.

Meanwhile, in a large Dutch oven or skillet, add the remaining 2 Tbsp (30 mL) oil and heat over medium-low heat. Add the sliced onions and cook, stirring often, for 15 to 20 minutes until tender but not browned. Remove the pot from the heat and set aside.

Once the roast has cooled, transfer it to a cutting board or serving dish, reserving the pan juices. Using 2 forks, shred the meat. Transfer the shredded meat to a serving platter, cover, and keep warm.

Using a spoon, degrease the pan juices, and strain through a fine-mesh sieve. Pour into a saucepan and cook over high heat until reduced by half (about 4 to 5 minutes). Season with salt and pepper, to taste.

Method continues . . .

Spoon one-third of the sauce over the pork, mixing evenly. Serve the remaining sauce alongside in a gravy boat.

To serve, pile the pork in the crusty buns and drizzle with sauce (if desired). Top with the sautéed onions, pickled hot peppers, pimento mayonnaise (below), and piri-piri sauce.

PIMENTO MAYONNAISE

Dress up your sandwiches Portuguese-style by slathering them with this spicy mayonnaise.

Combine ½ cup (125 mL) mayonnaise with 2 tsp (10 mL) of hot pimento paste (or to taste). Store any unused portion in the fridge for up to 1 week.

Ana Vieira, home cook and family friend, introduced me to Portuguese-style pulled pork. Ana says that the seasonings she uses can vary; sometimes she adds cumin and orange juice to the marinade.

If time allows, cook the pork shoulder earlier in the day, allowing plenty of time for the meat to cool and the pan drippings to be refrigerated, which allows the grease to come to the surface and solidify, making it easier to discard.

VEAL SCALOPPINI IN MADEIRA SAUCE

Escalopes de Vitela com Molho Madeira

An elegant and easy entrée, these veal cutlets are flattened until extra thin and then cooked in a generous portion of Madeira. This is perfect to create tender morsels of meat in a sweet-tasting sauce. Top with sautéed mushrooms and serve over steamed rice.

Place the veal between 2 sheets of waxed paper. Using either the flat edge of a cleaver or the bottom of skillet, flatten the veal to a ⅛-inch (3 mm) thickness.

In a shallow dish, add the flour and season with salt and pepper. Dredge the veal lightly in the seasoned flour; discard the remaining flour.

In a large skillet, heat the butter and oil over medium-high heat. Cook the veal, in batches, for about 2 to 3 minutes per side, just until cooked through and the edges are browned (adding more butter and oil to the pan, if necessary). Transfer the veal to a dish and keep warm.

To the same skillet, add boiling water, Madeira, and 2 Tbsp (30 mL) parsley. Bring to a boil over medium-high heat, stirring to scrape up any brown bits from the bottom of the pan. Reduce the heat to medium-low, add the veal, and cook, covered, for 2 to 3 minutes, until the meat is warmed through, turning once to coat with the sauce. Season with salt and pepper.

To serve, transfer the veal and sauce to a serving platter and top with 2 Tbsp (30 mL) parsley.

MAKES 4 TO 6 SERVINGS

1½ lb (750 g) thinly sliced veal or veal scaloppini

½ cup (125 mL) all-purpose flour

¼ tsp (1 mL) fine salt

Pinch coarsely ground black pepper

1 Tbsp (15 mL) butter (approx.)

1 Tbsp (15 mL) vegetable oil (approx.)

⅓ cup (80 mL) boiling water

⅓ cup (80 mL) Madeira

Fine salt and coarsely ground black pepper, to taste

¼ cup (60 mL) chopped fresh parsley

VEAL AND VEGETABLE ROLLS

Rolos de Carne e Vegetais

MAKES 16 TO 24 APPETIZER SERVINGS OR 4 TO 6 MAIN-COURSE SERVINGS

1½ lb (750 g) thinly sliced veal or veal scaloppini

2 cloves garlic, minced

Pinch dried red chili flakes

¼ cup (60 mL) finely chopped fresh parsley

Fine salt and coarsely ground black pepper, to taste

4 eggs

1 large carrot

4 oz (120 g) chouriço; or Black Forest ham, cut into matchsticks

¼ cup (60 mL) grated São Jorge, Parmesan, or cheddar cheese (approx.)

1 cup (250 mL) all-purpose flour

¼ cup (60 mL) olive oil (approx.)

FOR APPETIZER

1 cup (250 mL) Tomato Sauce with Port Wine (page 283)

FOR MAIN COURSE

2 cloves garlic, minced

2 Tbsp (30 mL) port

Palmira Almeida, a friend who works at the Portuguese consulate in Toronto, makes these addictive, compact, and colourful rolls using thinly sliced veal. Small yet packed with flavour, they are sliced into pinwheels—perfectly sized for popping in your mouth. You can also leave them whole to serve as a main meal.

Place the veal between 2 sheets of waxed paper. Using either the flat edge of a cleaver or the bottom of a skillet, flatten the veal to a ⅛-inch (3 mm) thickness.

In a large bowl, combine the veal, garlic, chili pepper, 1 Tbsp of the (15 mL) chopped parsley, and about 1 tsp (5 mL) salt; cover and refrigerate for an hour or, if time allows, overnight. Bring to room temperature for 20 minutes before cooking.

In a large deep saucepan, place 4 eggs in a single layer; pour in enough cold water to come at least 1 inch (2.5 cm) above the eggs. Cover and bring to a boil over high heat. As soon as the water boils, turn off the heat; let stand, covered, for 20 minutes on the burner. Drain and run cold water over the eggs for 2 minutes. Peel off the shells. Using a sharp knife, slice each egg in half lengthwise. Gently remove the yolk halves and finely dice; set aside in a bowl. Finely dice the egg whites and set aside in a separate bowl.

Peel and julienne the carrot. In a saucepan, steam or boil the carrot until almost tender, about 5 minutes. Drain and set aside to cool.

Using a sharp knife, remove the skin of the chouriço and slice into small pieces. Remove and discard any fat. Transfer the chouriço to a food processor and process for a few seconds or until the consistency of fine ground beef. Set aside. (If using ham, there is no need to process.)

Scrape off and discard any excess garlic or spices from the veal. Lay the veal out flat on a work surface. Using about 1 to 2 tsp (5 to 10 mL) of each, in the following order, place a layer of cooked egg whites, top with the cooked egg yolks, followed by 2 Tbsp (30 mL) parsley. Top with a light sprinkling of cheese. Use your hands to evenly distribute each filling, leaving ¼-inch (6 mm) border on all sides, before adding the next filling overtop. Mound the carrot and chouriço in the centre. Add an additional sprinkling of parsley at the end, if desired.

Holding the veal firmly, carefully roll to form sausages. Use 3 to 4 toothpicks to hold the filling securely in place. Using the same method, roll the remainder of the veal and filling. Set aside.

In a shallow dish, combine the flour, salt and pepper, to taste, and the remaining 1 Tbsp (15 mL) parsley. Dredge the veal lightly in the seasoned flour; discard the remaining flour.

In a large skillet, heat the oil over medium-high heat. Cook the rolls, in batches, for 2 to 3 minutes, turning until the meat browns evenly (be careful not to overcook them; the filling is already cooked). Set aside and keep warm.

TO SERVE AS AN APPETIZER Transfer the baked rolls to a plate, cover, and refrigerate about 30 minutes to allow the filling to set. (If refrigerating longer than 30 minutes before serving, wrap each roll in foil until ready to use.)

Carefully remove the toothpicks. Using a sharp knife, carefully cut the rolls into 1-inch (2.5 cm) slices and place on an ovenproof serving platter, filling face up (be careful not to spill the filling). Warm the rolls in a preheated 350°F (175°C) oven for about 15 minutes or until heated through. Drizzle with some of the tomato sauce and sprinkle with parsley just before serving. Serve the remaining tomato sauce on the side, for dipping.

Method continues . . .

VEAL AND VEGETABLE ROLLS

(continued)

TO SERVE AS A MAIN COURSE To the same skillet, add more oil, if necessary, and the garlic; cook over medium heat until softened, about 4 minutes. Add the tomato sauce and port; bring to a boil, stirring to scrape up any brown bits from the bottom of the pan. Reduce the heat to medium and cook for 6 to 8 minutes, to allow the flavours to blend. Reduce the heat to medium-low and return the prepared rolls to the pan. Cook for 2 to 3 minutes or until the meat is warmed through, turning once to coat with the sauce. Season with salt and pepper. Transfer the rolls to a platter, remove the toothpicks, and pour the sauce overtop. Sprinkle with parsley just before serving.

This dish lends itself to creative substitutions, depending on your taste and what you have on hand. Sautéed or roasted red peppers and any number of seasonal fresh herbs can be used in place of the carrots or parsley. Turkey or chicken can be substituted for the veal, and cheddar or Parmesan can be substituted for São Jorge cheese.

MELT-IN-YOUR-MOUTH TONGUE STEW

Deliciosa Lingua Guisada

Many Portuguese dishes, like this one, began in farming communities where every part of an animal was used, better known today as the "nose to tail" trend. Fatima, friend and fellow food lover raised in a small town in the north of Portugal, was brought up on dishes like this one that used tongue to produce moist and tender stew. As a bonus, tongue, in addition to hearts, lungs, and feet, are economical protein choices.

TO PREPARE THE VEAL TONGUE Using a sharp knife, starting at the tip end, slit the underside of the tongue; peel off the white skin. Remove any gristle from the large end and trim the tongue neatly. Chop the tongue into 2-inch (5 cm) pieces; set aside.

In a large skillet, heat the oil over medium-high heat. Add the onion and garlic and cook, stirring occasionally, for about 6 minutes, until softened. Add the bay leaves and cook for about 5 minutes, until the vegetables begin to brown. Add the chopped tongue and turn to coat. Add 2 cups (500 mL) of the chicken stock, 1½ cups (375 mL) of the tomato sauce, and salt; stir well. Bring to a boil over medium-high heat. Partially cover and reduce the heat to medium; simmer for 40 to 50 minutes, until the meat is tender. If the liquids dry up, add up to ½ cup (125 mL) each of chicken stock and tomato sauce. Using the tip of a sharp knife, test for doneness (the knife should easily pierce the meat). Transfer the cooked tongue to a plate and keep warm.

Using a spoon, degrease the remaining sauce and cook over high heat until reduced by half. Transfer the sauce to a food processor and purée until smooth. Return the tongue to the pan with the sauce. Taste and adjust the seasonings with salt and pepper. Add the parsley and coriander and toss.

Serve the meat and sauce in small bowls with plenty of sliced cornbread for dipping and piri-piri sauce, if desired.

MAKES ABOUT 4 SERVINGS

1 large veal tongue
  (approx. 3½ lb/1.75 kg)

2 Tbsp (30 mL) olive oil

1 large onion, diced

4 cloves garlic, finely chopped

3 bay leaves

2½ cups (625 mL) chicken stock

2 cups (500 mL) Tomato Sauce
  with Port Wine (page 283)

1 tsp (5 mL) fine salt

Fine salt and coarsely ground
  black pepper, to taste

¼ cup (60 mL) chopped
  fresh parsley

2 Tbsp (30 mL) chopped
  fresh coriander

Cornbread slices (about 6 to 8)

Piri-piri sauce

TRIPE AND BEANS PORTO-STYLE

Tripas à Moda do Porto

MAKES 6 TO 8 SERVINGS

3 cups (750 mL) dried
    white kidney beans

1 lb (500 g) honeycomb tripe

2 tsp (10 mL) fine salt

1 lemon, halved

1 chicken breast, halved, bone in

1 veal chop, cut into 3 pieces

1 small pork ribs, cut into
    4 pieces, back preferred

4 oz (120 g) chouriço, cut into
    1-inch (2.5 cm) slices

3 bay leaves

4 sprigs fresh parsley

12 oz (360 g) pork hock,
    cut into pieces

¼ cup (60 mL) olive oil

3 onions, chopped

10 cloves garlic, minced

2 carrots, cut into 1-inch
    (2.5 cm) slices

1 Tbsp (15 mL) ground cumin

2 tsp (10 mL) paprika

¼ tsp (1 mL) dried red chili flakes

¼ tsp (1 mL) coarsely ground
    black pepper

Fine salt and coarsely ground
    black pepper, to taste

Ground cumin, for garnish

Tripe and beans can be found bubbling in almost every stewing pot in Porto, the beautiful city of northern Portugal. The simple combination of beans, tripe, meat, cumin, and paprika produces an aromatic sauce that will become a classic in your home, too.

Serve this as a main dish with steamed rice and cornbread. Traditionally, extra ground cumin is served on the side so diners can season to their preference.

Rinse the beans under cold running water, discarding any shrivelled or off-coloured ones. Transfer the beans to a bowl and cover with cold water; set aside, covered, to soak overnight. (Alternatively, transfer the beans to a large saucepan, cover the beans with water, and boil for 2 minutes over medium-high heat. Remove from the heat and let stand, covered, for 1 hour.)

Rinse the tripe under cold running water and pat dry with paper towels. Sprinkle the tripe with 1 tsp (5 mL) salt; rub with half a lemon. Using a sharp knife, cut the tripe into 1-inch (2.5 cm) pieces and set aside.

In a large bowl, combine the chicken breast, veal chop, pork ribs, chouriço slices, 1 bay leaf, and 2 sprigs parsley. Squeeze the remaining half a lemon over the meat, turning to coat well. Cover and set aside for 30 minutes.

Pat the meat dry with paper towels and set aside.

Place the soaked beans in a strainer and rinse under cold running water. Transfer the beans to a large saucepan or Dutch oven and add the pork hock and tripe. Cover with 9 cups (2.25 L) of water. Bring to a boil over medium-high heat. Reduce the heat to medium-low and cook, partially covered and barely simmering, stirring occasionally, for 40 to 45 minutes, until the beans are almost tender. Skim off any scum and foam.

Meanwhile, in a large heavy saucepan or Dutch oven, heat the oil over medium-high heat. Add the marinated chicken breast, veal chop, pork rib, and chouriço and cook for 4 minutes per side or until browned all over. Add the onion and garlic and cook for 3 to 5 minutes, until softened. Stir in the carrots, cumin, paprika, chili flakes, black pepper, and the remaining 2 bay leaves. Cook for 1 minute, stirring to loosen any brown bits from the bottom of the pan. Add ½ cup (125 mL) water, cover, and simmer for 5 minutes. Add the remaining 1 tsp (5 mL) salt and 1½ cups (375 mL) water. Cook for 20 to 30 minutes, until the meat is tender. Using a slotted spoon, transfer the meat to a serving dish and set aside.

Add the onion and garlic mixture and the remaining parsley to the beans and tripe and reduce the heat to low. Cover and simmer, stirring occasionally, for about 15 to 20 minutes, until the beans, pork hock, and tripe are tender. Add an additional 1 cup (250 mL) of water if the mixture dries up too quickly. Return the meat to the saucepan and heat through. Taste and adjust the seasonings with salt and pepper. (The recipe can be prepared ahead to this point, covered, and refrigerated for several hours or overnight for the best flavour. Heat through before serving.)

To serve, remove the bay leaves and parsley and mound the meat and beans in the centre of a serving platter. Sprinkle with additional cumin.

BEANS AND PORK HOCK IN BEER

Feijoada Deliciosa

MAKES 6 SERVINGS

1 cup (250 mL) dried
   white kidney beans

1 carrot

1 Tbsp (15 mL) butter

2 Tbsp (30 mL) olive oil

2 onions, chopped

2 cloves garlic, minced

4 oz (120 g) lean bacon, diced

4 oz (120 g) chouriço, diced

1 cup (250 mL) chicken stock

¼ cup (60 mL) tomato paste

1 bottle beer (12 oz/355 mL)
   (approx.)

½ hot red chili pepper, seeded
   and chopped, or 1 tsp (5 mL)
   dried red chili flakes

1½ lb (750 g) pork hock,
   cut into 6 pieces

Fine salt and coarsely ground
   black pepper, to taste

Many variations of this beans and pork recipe can be found in most Azorean kitchens. Most include beer. Feel free to experiment in your kitchen.

This dish makes a lot of sauce and is delicious served over steamed rice. To make this dish in a hurry, use canned beans instead of the dried variety.

Rinse the beans under cold running water, discarding any shrivelled or off-coloured ones. Transfer the beans to a bowl and cover with cold water; set aside, covered, to soak overnight. (Alternatively, transfer the beans to a large saucepan, cover the beans with water, and boil for 2 minutes over medium-high heat. Remove from the heat and let stand, covered, for 1 hour.) Place the beans in a strainer and rinse under cold running water.

In a Dutch oven, combine the beans with 6 cups (1.5 L) water. Bring to a boil over medium-high heat. Reduce the heat to medium-low and gently simmer for 50 minutes, until almost tender.

Peel and cut the carrot in half lengthwise, then cut diagonally into 1-inch (2.5 cm) pieces.

In a large saucepan, heat the butter with the oil over medium heat; add the carrot and onion and cook, stirring often, for 3 to 5 minutes, until the onion is softened. Add the garlic, bacon, and chouriço. Simmer, partially covered, for about 5 minutes, until the vegetables, bacon, and chouriço are golden brown. Pour off the fat from the skillet and discard.

In a small bowl, mix ½ cup (125 mL) of the chicken stock and the tomato paste. Add to the saucepan with ½ cup (125 mL) of the beer and the chili pepper, stirring to scrape up any brown bits from the bottom of the pan. Simmer for 3 minutes, until the sauce is thickened. Add the pork hock and the remaining beer. Bring to a boil over medium-high heat; reduce the heat to low. Partially cover and simmer, stirring occasionally, for about 1 hour, until the pork is almost cooked.

Add the soaked beans, partially cover, and cook, barely simmering, for about 20 minutes, stirring occasionally, until the beans are tender and the pork falls off the bones. If you want to make a generous sauce and also need to prevent the beans from sticking to the pot, add equal amounts of water and beer (up to about ½ cup/125 mL each) and stir. Season with salt and pepper. (The dish can be prepared to this point and set aside for a few hours. The flavours improve with time. Add up to ½ cup/125 mL of chicken stock before serving.)

Serve with Mixed Green Salad (page 240) and Sautéed Greens and Oranges (page 242).

VEGETABLES AND RICE

Legumes e Pratos de Arroz

Simple and tasty vegetable side dishes often make an appearance at the dinner table alongside the beautiful main meal. Although vegetables are much loved, they are not always celebrated as much as main entrées. Driven to learn more about Portuguese vegetable dishes, I watched closely and discovered some gems.

I learned that a variety of greens, collard greens (*couves*) in particular, is regularly found at the Portuguese dinner table. I often saw home cooks toss steamed greens in a healthy helping of olive oil and garlic. Coarsely chopped collard greens can also be sautéed in a blend of nicely browned onion, garlic, and bacon, which is then further cooked in a few spoonfuls of chicken stock until the greens are perfectly tender. The dish is finished with a hint of white wine vinegar.

Most people consider such dishes peasant food, not particularly noteworthy, but I knew these simple sides would pair nicely with the dishes in this book. Azorean Broad Beans (page 258) and Greens, Potatoes, and Eggs in Garlic Oil and White Wine Vinegar (page 262) are simple yet tasty ways to bring more vegetables to our tables.

Most of these dishes can be paired with mains or can stand alone with or without the addition of crusty bread or a fried egg or two. For a hearty meal, try Green Beans Stewed in Tomato Sauce (page 241) or Baked Sweet Potatoes in Madeira (page 243). Grilled Pineapple and Vegetables with Fresh Mint (page 264) and Sautéed Greens and Oranges (page 242) will give your table an exotic flavour boost. There are vegetable dishes in the appetizers chapter too: Green Beans in Light Batter (page 52) accompany Cod Croquettes (page 44) and a glass of wine or beer. Dip them in piri-piri sauce or pimento mayonnaise for a spicy treat.

Potato combinations are endless, and it is not at all unusual to see both a potato and rice side dish on a dinner plate. (Maybe it's hard to choose between the two.) Baked Potatoes with Pimento and Garlic (page 244) and Potatoes and Chouriço (page 247) are excellent examples of special dishes with an Azorean flair. Roasted Seasoned Potatoes (page 246) is a classic side dish that can easily feed a crowd. If desired, throw in a few pieces of chicken while cooking to feed the meat lovers at your table.

The secret to preparing vegetables begins at the market. Purchase the freshest seasonal vegetables you can find. If possible, purchase vegetables the same day you intend to use them. Having vegetables sit in the refrigerator often produces wilted vegetables that yield less-than-desirable results. Root vegetables can be bought ahead and stored for longer periods in a dark, cool place. Be sure to taste and season vegetables as you cook; I sometimes forget to salt vegetable dishes until the end. Keep in mind that accompaniments such as chouriço and bacon may contain enough salt to season the vegetables as well.

Do not confuse vegetables' secondary position at the dinner table with a lack of importance or pride. More than one cook has told me that guests rave over Portuguese-style mashed potatoes: boiled potatoes, butter, milk, and sautéed garlic with its cooking oil mashed with the bottom of a wine bottle to get just the right texture. Another described her roasted new potatoes, baked in the oven or barbecued in the summer and then smashed to bring out their fluffy centres before being tossed in garlic oil and seasoned with a sprinkling of salt and pepper (pictured on page 56).

Green salads are traditionally brought to the table with slices of onions, tomatoes, green peppers, olives, and oil and vinegar for guests to serve themselves. Creative chefs, wishing to cater to modern palates, will dress up a bed of greens or Mixed Green Salad (page 240) with presunto-wrapped fresh figs and slivers of São Jorge cheese. Main-meal salads are excellent additions to the Portuguese diet. Often beans, rice, and tuna are paired with bits of onions, olives, and parsley to make some extraordinary meals.

Portuguese home cooks typically use long-grain rice in side dishes and short-grain rice in stews. Arborio rice is a relatively new addition to Portuguese kitchens for risotto-style dishes and stews. Most rice dishes are enjoyed as a main meal, with bits of meat or fish, tomatoes, and beans added along with aromatics. It takes a little practice and attention to prepare risottos. I discovered some tricks watching the preparation of hundreds of risotto dishes. Follow some of these tips to make the rice dishes in this chapter.

VEGETABLES AND RICE
Legumes e Pratos de Arroz

MIXED GREEN SALAD

Salada Mista

MAKES 4 SERVINGS

1 head romaine lettuce

1 head watercress

2 tomatoes, sliced

1 red onion, thinly sliced

DRESSING

⅓ cup (80 mL) olive oil

1 clove garlic, minced

2 Tbsp (30 mL) white wine,
    red wine, or balsamic vinegar

1 tsp (5 mL) Dijon mustard

Fine salt and coarsely ground
    black pepper, to taste

10 black olives, for garnish

This basic green salad traditionally includes green tomatoes and olives, and oil and vinegar are usually provided on the side so you can serve yourself. In North American kitchens, the basic salad is inspired by new flavours, of different vinegars and Dijon mustard, as reflected in this recipe.

Tear the lettuce into bite-sized pieces. Trim the stem ends of the watercress and discard.

In a large salad bowl, combine the lettuce, watercress, tomatoes, and red onion. (If not eating immediately, cover and refrigerate for up to 4 hours.)

TO MAKE THE DRESSING In a small bowl, whisk together the oil, garlic, vinegar, and Dijon. Season with salt and pepper.

To serve, toss the salad with just enough dressing to coat. Garnish with olives.

For a magnificent starter injected with favourite Portuguese ingredients, Chef José Alves of Via Norte in Toronto adds fresh figs wrapped in prosciutto to this salad and tops it with slivers of shaved São Jorge cheese.

GREEN BEANS STEWED IN TOMATO SAUCE

Feijão Verde Guisado com Tomate

Most early Portuguese immigrants ate only the familiar potatoes, sweet potatoes, and taro root, but that all changed as they discovered the vegetables available year round in North American markets, such as Brussels sprouts and green beans. The allspice gives this dish an Azorean flavour.

In a large saucepan, heat the oil over medium heat. Add the bacon, chouriço, onion, and garlic and cook for about 6 to 8 minutes, until the bacon and vegetables are softened and begin to brown.

Add the tomatoes, breaking them up with a fork, and stir in the green beans, allspice, bay leaf, and salt and pepper. Cover and bring to a boil over medium-high heat; reduce the heat to medium-low and simmer, covered, just until the green beans are tender, about 10 minutes, stirring occasionally. Using a slotted spoon, transfer the green beans and chouriço from the sauce to a serving bowl, arranging the chouriço in a circle around the green beans; set aside and keep warm.

Increase the heat to medium-high. Cook the remaining tomato sauce, partially covered, stirring frequently, until reduced by one-third and thickened. Remove the bay leaf and allspice and discard. If desired, transfer the sauce to a food processor and purée. Pour the sauce over the green beans.

Garnish with the black olives and hard-boiled egg and serve immediately.

MAKES 4 TO 6 SERVINGS

1 Tbsp (15 mL) olive oil

2 slices lean bacon, chopped

4 oz (120 g) chouriço, cut into ¼-inch (6 mm) slices

1 small onion, chopped

1 clove garlic, minced

2 cups (500 mL) peeled, seeded, and crushed tomatoes

6 cups (1.5 L) green beans (about 2 lb/1 kg), cut into 1-inch (2.5 cm) pieces

4 whole allspice

1 bay leaf

Fine salt and coarsely ground black pepper, to taste

½ cup (125 mL) chopped black olives (optional), for garnish

1 hard-boiled egg, finely chopped (optional), for garnish

SAUTÉED GREENS AND ORANGES

Couve à Mineiro

MAKES 4 TO 6 SERVINGS

10 oz (300 g) collard greens
   (about 1 bunch)
1 large orange
3 Tbsp (45 mL) olive oil
1 onion, finely chopped
3 large cloves garlic, minced
Fine salt, to taste

This dish got its name from miners who packed collard greens and fruit in their lunch buckets. Brazilians often eat *couves* with bananas instead of the oranges.

Bring a large saucepan of salted water to a boil over medium-high heat.

Meanwhile, rinse the collard greens and trim off the coarse stems. Roll up the leaves tightly and, using a sharp knife, cut on the diagonal into ½-inch (1 cm) slices. Add to the boiling water and boil, uncovered, until tender and bright green, about 4 to 6 minutes. Drain. (This step can be completed up to 30 minutes before serving, keeping the greens covered until final assembly.)

Meanwhile, peel the orange; cut away the pith and membrane and separate into sections or cut crosswise into thin slices. Set aside.

In a large skillet, heat the oil over medium-high heat. Cook the onion and garlic, stirring occasionally, for 3 to 5 minutes, until softened. Add the prepared collards and toss quickly to coat well. Cook just until heated through. Season with salt, to taste.

Transfer to a serving plate, top with orange slices, and serve.

BAKED SWEET POTATOES IN MADEIRA

Batata Doce Assada com Madeira

Madeira lends a decadent sweetness to this favourite Portuguese side dish.

Bring a large saucepan of water to a boil over medium-high heat. Add the sweet potatoes and cook until the potatoes are almost tender, 25 to 30 minutes. Drain and set aside until cool enough to handle. Peel the potatoes and cut into ¼-inch (6 mm) slices.

In a small bowl, combine the 1 Tbsp (15 mL) melted butter with the breadcrumbs and parsley; set aside.

In a lightly greased 8-cup (2 L) baking dish, layer the potatoes, seasoning each layer with salt and pepper. Dot with 1 Tbsp (15 mL) butter. In a bowl, combine the Madeira and stock and pour over the sweet potatoes. Sprinkle the sweet potatoes with the parsley-breadcrumb mixture.

Bake in a preheated 350°F (175°C) oven, uncovered, for 15 to 20 minutes, until tender.

MAKES 4 SERVINGS

2½ lb (1.25 kg) sweet potatoes (about 3 large)

1 Tbsp (15 mL) butter, melted and cooled

3 Tbsp (45 mL) dry breadcrumbs

2 Tbsp (30 mL) chopped fresh parsley

Fine salt and coarsely ground black pepper, to taste

1 Tbsp (15 mL) butter

¼ cup (60 mL) Madeira

¼ cup (60 mL) chicken stock or water

BAKED POTATOES WITH PIMENTO AND GARLIC

Batatas Apimentadas

MAKES 6 TO 8 SERVINGS

2 lb (1 kg) small new potatoes (about 12)

3 Tbsp (45 mL) pimento paste

2 Tbsp (30 mL) olive oil

2 cloves garlic, minced

12 black olives, for garnish

3 to 4 sprigs fresh parsley, for garnish

Steamed potatoes stuffed with pimento paste are served piping hot at many bars and bullfight arenas on the Azorean islands of Terceira and São Miguel, where they are often accompanied by spicy broad beans, boiled eggs, and fresh live limpets. These spectacular-looking and-tasting crispy potatoes can be served as a snack or a side dish with piri-piri sauce.

Bring a large cooking pot of water to a boil over medium-high heat. Add the potatoes, return to a boil, and boil for 7 minutes.

Meanwhile, in a small bowl, blend the pimento paste, oil, and garlic.

Drain the potatoes and cut a slit into each one with a sharp knife. Place cut side up on a baking sheet lined with greased foil. Brush with half of the pimento mixture. Bake in a preheated 425°F (220°C) oven for 15 to 20 minutes, until the potatoes are tender. Brush the potatoes with the remaining sauce and broil for 3 to 5 minutes, until golden brown.

Pile the potatoes on a serving platter and garnish with olives and a few sprigs of parsley. Serve immediately.

ROASTED SEASONED POTATOES

Batatas no Forno com Tomate

2½ lb (1.25 kg) baking
  potatoes (about 5)

1½ cups (375 mL) peeled,
  seeded, and chopped
  tomatoes or tomato sauce

1 cup (250 mL) dry white wine

½ cup (125 mL) chicken stock

2 cloves garlic, minced

2 bay leaves

1 onion, sliced

2 Tbsp (30 mL) butter

2 tsp (10 mL) paprika

½ tsp (2 mL) fine salt

Coarsely ground black
  pepper, to taste

3 Tbsp (45 mL) olive oil

To add a boost of flavour to these crisp-skinned potatoes, add one-quarter cup (60 mL) of the pan juices from an accompanying dish (such as Portuguese Pulled Pork, page 222) and use it to replace half of the stock in the recipe below. For a hint of chouriço flavouring, I sometimes substitute smoked Spanish paprika for the regular paprika.

Peel the potatoes; cut each in half lengthwise and cut each half into 4 wedges. Arrange the potatoes in a single layer on a greased rack over a foil-lined baking sheet.

Combine the tomatoes, wine, chicken stock, garlic, and bay leaves. Pour over the potatoes, scatter the onions overtop, and dot with butter. Season with 1 tsp (5 mL) paprika, ¼ tsp (1 mL) salt, and pepper, to taste.

Cover with foil and bake in a preheated 400°F (200°C) oven for about 35 minutes or until the potatoes are tender when pierced with a fork.

Increase the heat to 425°F (220°C), uncover, and bake for 5 to 10 minutes, until the potatoes are golden brown. If the potatoes are drying out, add up to 2 Tbsp (30 mL) water. Turn the potatoes over, brush with the oil, and season with the remaining 1 tsp (5 mL) paprika, ¼ tsp (1 mL) salt, and pepper, to taste. Cook for 5 more minutes.

Remove the bay leaves and serve.

These potatoes are excellent made ahead a few hours and covered until ready to eat. Just before serving, pan-fry them in a few drops of olive oil to return the potatoes to their crispy finish.

POTATOES AND CHOURIÇO

Batatas no Forno com Chouriço

This zingy Azorean combination of spicy Portuguese sausage and potatoes can be served as a main meal as well as a side dish. If serving as a *petiscos* (snack), have plenty of crusty buns or cornbread on hand to soak up the delicious juices. You can use hot chouriço, if you like, or serve with piri-piri sauce and adjust the spice to suit your taste.

In a large saucepan, cover the potatoes with water. Bring to a boil over medium-high heat and boil for 5 minutes. Drain. Line the bottom of an 11- × 7-inch (2 L) baking dish with a single layer of the potatoes and chouriço.

Using a mortar and pestle or a small bowl and the back of a spoon, combine the garlic, paprika, tomato paste, cinnamon, allspice, cumin, and salt until paste-like. Brush the paste evenly over the chouriço and potatoes. Scatter the onion over top. Dot with the butter and pour the wine overtop.

Cover and bake in a preheated 400°F (200°C) oven for 40 minutes, turning the potatoes and chouriço and basting twice. Uncover and bake for 10 to 15 minutes, until the potatoes are tender when pierced with fork. Taste and adjust the seasonings with salt, if necessary. Serve with a crisp Mixed Green Salad (page 240).

MAKES 4 TO 6 SERVINGS

2 lb (1 kg) small new potatoes (about 12), peeled

1 lb (500 g) chouriço, cut into ½-inch (1 cm) slices

2 cloves garlic, minced

1 tsp (5 mL) paprika

1 Tbsp (15 mL) tomato paste

Pinch ground cinnamon

Pinch ground allspice

Pinch ground cumin

¼ tsp (1 mL) fine salt

1 onion, finely chopped

2 Tbsp (30 mL) butter

1 cup (250 mL) dry white wine or beer (approx.)

BEAN AND CHOURIÇO SALAD

Salada de Feijão Frade

1 cup (250 mL) dried black-
   eyed beans (also called
   black-eyed peas)

3 cups (750 mL) water

12 pimento-stuffed olives

12 large black olives, pitted

1 red onion, finely chopped

8 oz (240 g) chouriço

1 hard-boiled egg, for garnish

½ cup (125 mL) chopped fresh
   parsley, for garnish

DRESSING

⅓ cup (80 mL) olive oil

3 Tbsp (45 mL) wine vinegar

1 clove garlic, minced

½ cup (125 mL) chopped fresh
   parsley or coriander

Fine salt and coarsely ground
   black pepper, to taste

Beans are as much a Portuguese staple as rice and fish. They play a major role in classic dishes such as Tripe and Beans Porto-Style (page 230) and dozens of *feijoadas* (bean stews). Their nutritional value and long shelf-life are appealing factors.

Although canned beans are used to save time, nothing compares to the texture and taste of freshly cooked beans in this fresh-tasting salad.

Instead of the chouriço you can use shredded cod or a can of tuna, partially drained. Other popular substitutes for the beans are potatoes or chickpeas. The salad is best set aside for a few hours before serving to allow all the flavours to blend. If refrigerated, bring to room temperature before serving.

Rinse the beans under cold running water, discarding any shrivelled or off-coloured ones. In a bowl, cover the beans with cold water and soak overnight. (Alternatively, in a large saucepan, cover the beans with water and boil for 2 minutes over medium-high heat. Remove from the heat and let stand, covered, for 1 hour.)

Place the beans in a strainer and rinse under cold running water. Transfer to a heavy saucepan and cover with water. Bring to a boil over medium-high heat. Reduce the heat to medium-low; cover and simmer, stirring occasionally, for 50 minutes to 1 hour, just until the beans are tender. Drain and refresh under cold water; drain again. Transfer to a salad bowl and toss with the olives and onion. (The recipe can be prepared ahead to this point, covered, and set aside in the refrigerator for up to 24 hours before using.)

TO MAKE THE DRESSING In a small bowl, whisk together the oil, vinegar, garlic, parsley, and salt and pepper, to taste. Pour half of the dressing over the bean mixture to infuse the flavours while still warm.

Prick the chouriço a few times with a fork. Grill the chouriço on medium (or 4 to 6 inches/10 to 15 cm from medium-hot coals) for about 20 minutes, turning often, until the sausage is evenly browned and warmed through, and the liquid runs clear. (Alternatively, pan-fry or warm in a preheated 375°F/190°C oven.) Slice the chouriço into rounds and drain on paper towels. Add the chouriço to the bean mixture and toss with the remaining dressing. Taste and adjust the seasonings with salt and pepper, if necessary.

Separate the egg white and the egg yolk and finely chop.

To serve, decorate the salad with alternating lines of egg yolk, egg white, and parsley to create yellow, white, and green stripes.

CHESTNUTS

Castanhas Cozidas ou Assadas

As soon as the first chestnuts arrive each fall, many families stock up for weekend snacks of boiled and roasted chestnuts. Sometimes a first taste of the year's homemade wine accompanies the chestnut feast.

Boiling the chestnuts produces a softer filling, while baking results in a crisper chestnut.

Using a sharp knife, score a cross on the flat side of each chestnut. In a large saucepan, add the chestnuts and enough water to cover them. Cover and bring to a boil over medium-high heat. Reduce the heat to medium and simmer for 20 to 30 minutes, until tender. (Alternatively, place the chestnuts on a baking sheet and bake in a preheated 400°F/200°C oven, shaking the sheet occasionally, for 30 minutes, until tender.)

Sprinkle with salt and serve warm.

MAKES 4 SERVINGS

1 lb (500 g) fresh chestnuts

1 tsp (5 mL) coarse salt (or to taste)

CLAMS AND RICE

Arroz de Amêijoas

MAKES 6 SERVINGS

2 Tbsp (30 mL) butter

1 onion, finely chopped

2 cloves garlic, minced

3 Tbsp (45 mL) pimento paste

¼ cup (60 mL) chopped
  fresh parsley

1 can clams, undrained
  (5½ oz/156 mL)

1¼ cups (310 mL) short-grain rice

1¼ cups (310 mL) tomato purée

Fine salt, to taste

For a special occasion, spoon the hot cooked rice into a lightly greased ring mould and turn out onto a platter just before serving. If you are serving this rice with fish, use a fish-shaped mould and decorate with olives for the eyes and parsley sprigs for the fins. You can substitute chopped shrimp or crab for the clams, if desired.

In a large heavy saucepan or Dutch oven, melt the butter over medium-high heat. Cook the onion and garlic, stirring occasionally, for 2 to 3 minutes, until tender. Stir in the pimento paste and parsley; cook for 1 minute, until fragrant. Drain the clams, reserving the liquid. Add the clams to the saucepan. Measure the clam juice and top up with enough water to measure 1¼ cups (310 mL) liquid; add to the pan. Add the rice and tomato purée and bring to a boil over high heat. Simmer for 2 to 3 minutes to blend the flavours, stirring constantly. Reduce the heat to low; cover tightly, and simmer for 20 minutes, until the rice is tender and all the liquid is absorbed. Season with salt, if necessary. Fluff the rice with a fork.

Transfer the rice to a bowl and serve immediately.

To make a tomato purée, use canned crushed tomatoes or seed and drain plum tomatoes, then purée in a food processor or food mill.

To add a boost of flavour, substitute fish stock or bottled clam juice for the water called for in the recipe.

RICE IN BEER

Arroz de Cerveja

Serve this rice as a side dish or dress it up with a medley of vegetables, fish, or chouriço for a satisfying one-dish meal.

Long-grain rice, which cooks up drier and fluffier, is used in this dish. Pimento paste adds an assertive Azorean flavour and colour.

In a bowl, combine ¼ cup (60 mL) of the fish stock with the saffron threads and set aside.

In a saucepan, heat the oil over medium-high heat. Add the onion and cook, stirring often, for 3 to 5 minutes, until softened. Add the garlic and cook for 1 minute. Add the remaining 1 cup (250 mL) fish stock, beer, pimento paste, piri-piri sauce, bay leaf, and salt. Bring to a boil over high heat. Simmer for 2 to 3 minutes, stirring constantly.

Add the reserved fish stock with saffron and the rice to the saucepan and return to a boil. Reduce the heat to low. Cover and simmer for 25 minutes, until the rice is tender and all the liquid is absorbed. Fluff with a fork.

Transfer to a bowl and serve.

MAKES 4 TO 6 SERVINGS

1¼ cups (310 mL) Fish Stock (page 75)

¼ tsp (1 mL) saffron (about 4 to 6 threads)

2 Tbsp (30 mL) olive oil

1 onion, finely chopped

2 cloves garlic, minced

1¼ cups (310 mL) beer

1 Tbsp (15 mL) pimento paste (optional)

Dash piri-piri sauce or Tabasco sauce (optional)

1 bay leaf

¼ tsp (1 mL) fine salt

1¼ cups (310 mL) long-grain rice

CORIANDER RICE

Arroz com Coentros

MAKES 4 SIDE-DISH SERVINGS

5 cups (1.25 L) chicken, seafood, or vegetable stock

2 Tbsp (30 mL) olive oil

1 Tbsp (15 mL) butter

½ cup (125 mL) onion, finely chopped

3 cloves garlic, minced

1 cup (250 mL) arborio rice

½ tsp (2 mL) fine salt

1 bay leaf

2 cups (500 mL) chopped fresh coriander (approx.)

Many dishes have been created by chefs using ingredients encountered abroad and brought to the table with the Portuguese palate in mind. This dish is no exception. Arborio, not a rice typically used in Portuguese kitchens, is combined with an abundance of coriander to make this spectacular green side dish.

Most Portuguese rice dishes tend to be hearty meals. Whole chicken, beef, and seafood with bits of chouriço are tossed into the rice pot to round out and further flavour the meal. Coriander rice can similarly be turned into a full meal with the addition of sautéed garlic shrimp, an excellent pairing with the intensely flavoured rice. If serving with shrimp, add about 1 Tbsp (15 mL) of grated lemon zest overtop the finished dish.

In a medium saucepan, add the stock and bring to a simmer over medium heat. Reduce the heat to medium-low and keep it warm or set it aside and bring it to a simmer just before using.

In a large saucepan, heat the oil and butter over medium heat until the butter has melted. Cook the onion and garlic for 5 to 6 minutes, until softened and golden brown. Add the rice and cook over medium-high heat for 2 to 3 minutes further. Run a spoon over the bottom of the pan occasionally to ensure that the rice does not stick, and lower the heat, if necessary. The rice should be hot, white in the centre, and opaque around the edges (do not brown). Add about ¼ to ½ cup (60 to 125 mL) of hot stock or just enough to cover the rice. Add the salt and bay leaf and cook until the rice absorbs the stock, 3 to 5 minutes or as needed. Continue adding up to ¼ to ½ cup (60 to 125 mL) of stock at a time, up to about 4 cups (1 L) of stock in total, cooking for 2 to 3 minutes or as needed between additions to allow the rice to cook and absorb each addition of stock. The rice should be at a low simmer in between additions of hot stock; adjust the heat as necessary. When the rice becomes somewhat thickened and starts sticking to the bottom of the pot, it is time to add more stock. Test for doneness while cooking (the rice should be cooked until al dente, softened with some resistance to the grain). Cook for between 12 to 15 minutes in total. Add the coriander during the last 3 minutes of cooking. Just before serving, add an additional ¼ to ½ cup (60 to 125 mL) stock over the rice. The rice should be moist but not overly so.

Serve immediately (the rice absorbs the liquid quickly and will continue to cook).

It takes a little practice and attention to prepare risotto. Some of the tricks I discovered include heating the stock on low heat and keeping it close at hand while making the rice. Stir the rice infrequently and allow the rice and liquids to cook in between stock additions. Taste the rice and remove it from the heat when the rice still has a bit of bite remaining.

MONKFISH RICE

Arroz de Tamboril

MAKES ABOUT 6 CUPS (1.5 L)

MONKFISH STOCK

1 large monkfish, cut into bite-
    sized pieces (3 lb/1.5 kg)

8 to 12 extra-large tiger shrimp,
    in shells

A variety of fish bones
    (about 2 to 3 lb/1 to 1.5 kg)

24 cups (6 L) cold water

1 large onion, quartered

2 cloves garlic, crushed

12 whole black peppercorns,
    crushed

½ cup (125 mL) beer

2 bay leaves

If you can, simplify your life and make the fish stock the day before making this recipe. If you don't have time to make your own fish stock, you can purchase store-bought fish stock or substitute half clam juice and half water, chicken stock or vegetable stock for the same quantity called for in the recipe.

Chef Luisa loves cooking and usually has about four or five cauldrons simmering at one time at a grill house in Toronto. Her easy-going and professional nature shines through in the fast-paced kitchen. In addition to the popular grilled and rotisserie chicken, she usually has two or more traditional Portuguese dishes stewing in pots. A few visits to this busy kitchen with the talented staff reveals why this place is so popular: the delicious rice, beans, and roasted chicken.

Monkfish Rice was one of the dishes she prepared during one of my visits. The following recipe is loosely based on what I saw in Luisa's kitchen.

MONKFISH STOCK

Rinse the monkfish, shrimp, and fish bones under cold running water and pat dry with paper towels. Using kitchen shears, cut each shrimp shell along the back. Pull out the intestinal vein. Remove the legs but leave the shell and tail on each shrimp. Rinse under cold running water and pat dry with paper towels.

Place the monkfish, shrimp, and fish bones in a large stockpot and cover with water. Bring to a boil over medium-high heat. Skim off any scum from the surface. Reduce the heat and add the onion, garlic, peppercorns, beer, and bay leaves. Return to a boil, reduce the heat to medium-low, and simmer for 10 to 12 minutes, until the fish is cooked. Using a slotted spoon, transfer the fish and shrimp to a bowl. Peel the shrimp and return the shrimp shells to the stockpot; reserve the fish and shrimp for the rice.

Cook the stock for 80 minutes, occasionally skimming any scum from the surface. Taste and adjust the seasonings with salt, if necessary (you should be left with about 6 cups/1.5 L). Carefully strain the stock through a cheesecloth set over a fine-mesh strainer into a bowl; discard the solids. If you will not be using the stock immediately, transfer it to an airtight container and refrigerate for up to 1 week or freeze for a few months.

MONKFISH RICE

In a medium-sized pot, add the stock and saffron and bring to a low boil over medium heat. Reduce the heat to low and keep warm, or set aside and bring to a simmer just before using.

In a large saucepan, heat the oil and butter over medium heat until the butter has melted. Cook the onion and garlic for 5 to 6 minutes, until softened and golden brown. Add the red pepper and cook, stirring occasionally, for 4 minutes or until beginning to brown. Add the rice and cook over medium-high heat for 2 to 3 minutes; run a spoon over the bottom of the pan occasionally to ensure that the rice does not stick, and lower the heat, if necessary. The rice should be white in the centre and opaque around the edges (do not brown).

Add about ¼ to ½ cup (60 to 125 mL) of hot stock or just enough to cover the rice. Add salt and the bay leaf and cook until the rice absorbs the stock, 3 to 5 minutes or as needed. When the rice begins to thicken and stick to the bottom of pot, add the tomatoes and cook until the rice absorbs the liquid, 2 to 3 minutes. Continue adding ¼ to ½ cup (60 to 125 mL) of stock at a time, up to about 4 cups (1 L) of stock in total, cooking for about 2 to 3 minutes between additions to allow the rice to absorb each addition of stock. The rice should be at a low simmer; adjust the heat as necessary. Add each addition when the rice becomes somewhat thickened and starts sticking to the bottom of the pot. The rice should be cooked until *al dente*, softened with some resistance to the grain, between 12 to 15 minutes in total.

Add the reserved monkfish and shrimp to the pan for the last 2 to 3 minutes of cooking. Taste and adjust the seasonings with salt and pepper. Add parsley and continue cooking until the rice is almost tender and the seafood is heated through. Add about ½ cup (125 mL) or more stock just before serving. The rice should be moist but not overly so. Serve immediately. (The rice absorbs the liquid quickly and will continue to cook.)

MONKFISH RICE

6 cups (1.5 L) Monkfish Stock (facing page)

½ tsp (2 mL) saffron threads (about 8 to 12 threads)

3 Tbsp (45 mL) olive oil

3 Tbsp (45 mL) butter

1 large onion, finely chopped

5 cloves garlic, crushed

2 Tbsp (30 mL) finely chopped red bell pepper

1 cup (250 mL) arborio rice

Pinch fine salt

1 bay leaf

½ cup (125 mL) peeled, seeded, and chopped tomatoes with juices or tomato sauce

Monkfish and shrimp reserved from Monkfish Stock

Coarsely ground black pepper, to taste

¼ cup (60 mL) chopped fresh parsley or coriander

AZOREAN BROAD BEANS

Favas à Moda dos Açores

MAKES ABOUT 4 SERVINGS

3 Tbsp (45 mL) olive oil

6 oz (180 g) chouriço or lean bacon, sliced into 3 to 4 pieces

2 onions, finely chopped

4 cloves garlic, minced

1 bay leaf

1½ cups (375 mL) tomato sauce or peeled, seeded, and chopped tomatoes

1 cup (250 mL) chicken stock (approx.)

1 tsp (5 mL) pimento paste

½ tsp (2 mL) paprika

3 cups (750 mL) broad beans, shelled, peeled, and rinsed

Fine salt and coarsely ground black pepper, to taste

Piri-piri sauce, to taste

¼ cup (60 mL) chopped fresh mint, for garnish

The traditional combination of meat, broad beans, and vegetables make for an easy and filling one-pot meal. Azoreans prefer a robust tomato sauce. The continental version calls for the substitution of one or two chopped tomatoes and additional stock in place of the tomato sauce. Raquel Gonçalves, a family friend, created this entrée based on her memories of the much-loved beans she had tasted on a visit to the Azores.

In a large heavy saucepan or Dutch oven, heat the oil over medium-high heat. Add the chouriço and cook to brown the meat and render the fat, 8 to10 minutes. Transfer the chouriço to a cutting board, cool, and chop; set aside.

Discard all but 3 Tbsp (45 mL) of the fat in the pan. Add the chopped onion and cook over medium-high heat, stirring often, until lightly browned on the edges, 5 to 6 minutes. Stir to scrape up any brown bits at the bottom of the pan. Add the garlic and bay leaf and cook about 2 minutes, until the vegetables are evenly browned. Reduce the heat, if necessary, and stir often to prevent the garlic from burning.

Add the tomato sauce, ½ cup (125 mL) chicken stock, pimento paste, and paprika and bring to a boil. Reduce the heat to medium and cook for 10 to 12 minutes or until the sauce thickens and the flavours blend. Add the broad beans and prepared chouriço and bring to a boil. Reduce the heat to low and cook, partially covered, for 8 to 10 minutes, until the beans are softened (for less time if fresh beans are used). Stir or shake the pan occasionally to prevent the mixture from sticking to the bottom of the pan. If the sauce gets too dry, add up to ½ cup (125 mL) additional chicken stock. Taste and adjust the seasonings with salt and pepper. Remove and discard the bay leaf. Add piri-piri sauce, to taste.

Serve immediately or set aside for a few hours to allow the flavours to blend further. Top with chopped mint just before serving.

Broad beans are plentiful in the spring, grown in home gardens or available in supermarkets. Since broad beans can also be purchased frozen, this dish can be prepared all year round.

When purchasing frozen broad beans, parboil them for about 90 seconds and then plunge them in ice water. Using a sharp knife, remove the outer brown skin and discard. Once the skin is removed, the bean will have an appetizing bright green colour and a tender, less-bitter taste. If the beans are fresh, parboil them for 30 seconds and use a sharp knife to shell and peel them.

RICE AND BROCCOLI RABE WITH ONION AND GARLIC OIL

Arroz e Grelos

MAKES 4 SERVINGS

6 Tbsp (90 mL) olive oil

1 onion, finely chopped

4 cloves garlic, minced

1 tsp (5 mL) fine salt

1 cup (250 mL) parboiled rice

½ small head broccoli rabe
(1 lb/500 g), rough ends
trimmed and cut into
2-inch (5 cm) pieces

Fine salt and coarsely ground
black pepper, to taste

The basic ingredients in this recipe are easily found in any farmhouse near the town of Fatima, Portugal, where Irene Alves, a family friend, grew up: rice, broccoli rabe, onion, and oil. Combined, they make for a very simple, delicious, and quick side dish. Every Portuguese family seems to have a version of this rice dish in their repertoire of favourites.

In a small saucepan, heat the oil over medium-low heat. Cook the onion and garlic until golden, softened, and aromatic, 6 to 8 minutes. Set aside.

Fill a medium saucepan two-thirds full of water, cover, and bring to a boil over medium-high heat. Add the salt and rice. Cover and return to a boil. Once boiling, uncover and reduce the heat to medium; cook for about 10 minutes, until the rice is almost cooked (the rice should still be slightly chewy). Add the broccoli rabe and cook a further 3 to 5 minutes, until it's tender.

Drain the water and transfer the mixture to a serving dish (it may be somewhat watery). Add half of the onion and garlic oil and stir to combine. Top with the remaining oil. Taste and adjust the seasonings with salt and pepper.

Serve immediately.

For a variation on this homestyle rice dish, substitute one whole head of garlic for the greens.

SAUTÉED GARLIC RABE GREENS

Grelos com Alho

The garlicky taste of these sautéed broccoli rabe greens makes for a side dish that pairs perfectly with many of the earthy homestyle dishes in this cookbook. Greens are plentiful in most farming communities making it a regular at dinner tables in Portugal. Top steamed greens with Sardines in a Golden Batter (page 59) and a drizzle of Red Pepper Pimento Paste Seasoning (page 286) and extra olive oil, to taste.

In a large pot, combine the water, salt, and broccoli rabe. Bring to a boil and simmer for 4 minutes or just until bright green and tender. Drain and set aside until cool enough to handle. When cool, squeeze out as much water as possible from the greens and dry on kitchen towels to remove any additional water. Set aside.

In a frying pan or Dutch oven large enough to accommodate all of the greens, heat the oil over medium-low heat. Cook the garlic until golden, softened, and aromatic, 6 to 8 minutes. Add the rabe and toss until evenly coated. Sprinkle with chili flakes (if using) and continue to cook until warmed through, about 3 minutes. Add salt and pepper, to taste, and serve.

I like to cook the greens in advance and toss them in ice water to stop the cooking. I drain and dry them as much as possible and store them in the refrigerator until dinnertime, when I can easily sauté them in garlic oil just before serving. This also prevents the greens from becoming mushy.

MAKES ABOUT 6 SERVINGS

8 cups (2 L) water

2 tsp (10 mL) fine salt

2 heads broccoli rabe, rough ends trimmed about ½ inch (1 cm) from base (1 lb/500g each)

½ cup (125 mL) olive oil

1 head garlic, minced

¼ tsp (1 mL) dried red chili flakes (optional)

Fine salt and coarsely ground black pepper, to taste

GREENS, POTATOES, AND EGGS IN GARLIC OIL AND WHITE WINE VINEGAR

Esparregado de Espinafres

MAKES 2 TO 4 SERVINGS

8 cups (2 L) water

1 tsp (5 mL) fine salt

1 large head broccoli rabe, rough ends trimmed about ½ inch (1 cm) from base

1 large potato

2 eggs

¼ cup (60 mL) olive oil

6 to 8 cloves garlic, minced

Fine salt and coarsely ground pepper, to taste

4 to 6 Tbsp (60 to 90 mL) white wine vinegar or cider vinegar

These vibrant, fresh, sautéed green vegetables perked up with white wine vinegar make a memorable vegetarian dish. Palmira, a friend who works at the Portuguese Consulate in Toronto, learned to make this dish from her father, who wanted to use up all the vegetables that might otherwise go to waste on the family farm.

Esparregado is a classic Portuguese side dish of creamed spinach. Palmira's heartier version includes broccoli rabe, potatoes, and eggs. Prepare the greens, potatoes, and eggs earlier in the day and put a satisfying one-dish meal together closer to dinnertime in a matter of minutes.

In a large saucepan or Dutch oven, combine the water and salt. Bring to a boil over medium-high heat and add the broccoli rabe. Return the water to a boil and simmer for about 4 minutes, just until the rabe is bright green and tender. Drain and set aside to cool slightly. When cool enough to handle, squeeze out as much water as possible from the greens and dry on kitchen towels to remove any excess water. Using a sharp knife, chop finely. Transfer to a large bowl and set aside.

In a saucepan, cover the potato with water. Bring to a boil over medium-high heat and boil for 5 to 10 minutes. Drain and set aside until cool enough to handle. When cool, roughly dice and place in the bowl with the greens.

In a large deep saucepan, place the eggs in a single layer. Pour in enough cold water to come at least 1 inch (2.5 cm) above the eggs. Cover and bring to a boil over high heat. As soon as the water comes to a boil, remove the pan from the heat. Let stand, covered, for 20 minutes. Drain under cold running water for 2 minutes. Peel the eggs. Chop and add to the potato and broccoli rabe.

Using a fork, mix all of the chopped ingredients together—the mixture should not be mashed (it should retain some rough texture).

In a large frying pan or Dutch oven, heat the oil over medium-low heat. Sauté the garlic until golden, softened, and aromatic, 6 to 8 minutes. Stir frequently. Add the broccoli rabe mixture and toss to coat evenly; cook until warmed through, about 3 minutes. Add salt and pepper, to taste. Remove from the heat and add vinegar, to taste. Serve warm over cornbread toast.

Substitute any number of your favourite greens for the broccoli rabe; simply adjust the cooking time to suit the greens you are using. It is best to chop the vegetables and eggs for this dish by hand. A food processor will overwork the ingredients and most likely result in a mash or purée.

GRILLED PINEAPPLE AND VEGETABLES WITH FRESH MINT

Ananás Grelhado com Vegetais e Hortelã

MAKES ABOUT 4 SERVINGS

1 cup (250 mL) olive oil

3 garlic cloves, minced

2 Tbsp (30 mL) chopped
   fresh thyme

½ cup (125 mL) vegetable oil for
   brushing grill (approx.)

½ pineapple, cored and peeled,
   cut lengthwise into ¾-inch
   (2 cm) quarter-moon slices

1 onion, cut crosswise into
   ¾-inch (2 cm) slices

1 red bell pepper, seeded, cored,
   and halved

½ cup (125 mL) chopped
   fresh mint

Fine salt and coarsely ground
   black pepper, to taste

Grilled seafood makes for a hearty appetizer that is best savoured at a gathering of friends and family. It is perfect with sides of marinated olives, cornbread, and Portuguese white wine. Have the additional garlic oil on hand for dipping the bread, and serve with piri-piri sauce or Red Pepper and Olive Relish (page 284). When making this dish, grill squid and shrimp right next to the pineapple and vegetables.

In a small saucepan, heat the oil over medium-low heat. Cook the garlic until golden, softened, and aromatic, 6 to 8 minutes. Remove from the heat and let cool. Cover and set aside for 1 hour to allow the flavours to develop. Using a fine-mesh sieve, strain into a bottle or jar; discard the garlic. Add the thyme and stir. (At this stage the oil can be covered and refrigerated for up to 1 week. Bring to room temperature for 1 hour before using.)

Grill the pineapple on a greased grill set to high (or 4 inches/10 cm from medium-hot coals) until grill marks appear, about 2 to 3 minutes per side. Set aside and keep warm while preparing the vegetables.

Grill the onion until grill marks appear, about 2 minutes per side, basting frequently with the garlic-infused oil. Move the onion to indirect heat and cook 3 to 4 minutes further, until softened. Set aside and keep warm.

Grill the red pepper over direct heat for 2 to 3 minutes per side or until blackened in parts. Plunge into ice water and set aside for about 5 minutes. Using a sharp knife, scrape off the skin. Slice the peppers into ½-inch (1 cm) strips and set aside.

In a large skillet, heat 3 Tbsp (45 mL) garlic-infused oil over medium-high heat. Add the grilled pineapple and vegetables and toss to combine; cook for 1 to 2 minutes or until the oil coats all of the vegetables and fruit and everything is warmed through.

Place the vegetables in a serving dish. Toss with mint, and salt and pepper to taste, and serve.

This dish lends itself well to substitution. You can use zucchini or partially cooked carrots or squash for the red pepper. Make the herb-infused garlic olive oil in advance and let it rest for an hour before using.

The leftover garlic oil can be used in Greens, Potatoes, and Eggs (page 262), Collard Greens, Cornbread, and Garlic Stir-Fry (page 269), and Rice and Broccoli Rabe (page 260). It can also be used to add a dash of flavour to fried fish fillets, chicken breast, and rice.

CUMIN, TOMATO, AND CHOURIÇO BEANS

Feijão e Chouriço em Tomatada com Cominho

MAKES ABOUT 5 CUPS (1.25 L)

CUMIN-SCENTED BEANS

2 cups (500 mL) white beans, rinsed, picked over and irregular beans removed

1 large onion, kept whole

3 cloves garlic, smashed

2 bay leaves

1 Tbsp (15 mL) ground cumin

Beans are a large part of the Portuguese diet. Keep a reserve of these cumin-scented beans in the fall and winter months to add to soups and rice dishes, or to use as a base for shellfish stew.

Two recipes are presented here: The Cumin-Scented Beans are used to make Cumin, Tomato, and Chouriço Beans. If you prefer to use canned beans, skip the precooking step.

CUMIN-SCENTED BEANS

In a large saucepan, cover the beans with water and boil for 2 minutes over medium-high heat. Remove from the heat and let stand, covered, for 1 hour. Drain the soaking water and rinse the beans under cold running water. Return the beans to the saucepan and add enough fresh water to cover the beans by 4 inches (10 cm). Add the onion, garlic, bay leaves, and cumin. Cover and bring to a boil. Reduce the heat to low and, with the lid slightly ajar, gently simmer for 50 to 60 minutes, stirring occasionally. Check for doneness by tasting: you want the beans to be soft in the middle and almost fully cooked (they will not cook for long in the recipe for Cumin, Tomato, and Chouriço Beans). Drain the beans and set aside; discard the onion, garlic, and bay leaves.

If not using immediately, the beans can be cooled and stored in the refrigerator for up to 5 days or frozen for up to 3 months. To freeze, drain the cooled beans and spread them in an even layer on a baking sheet. Place the whole pan in the freezer for anywhere from 5 to 15 minutes. Transfer the frozen beans to an airtight container or resealable bag and store in the freezer.

If making Cumin, Tomato, and Chouriço Beans from frozen or refrigerated beans, place them directly into the cumin tomato sauce; you don't need to thaw or bring to room temperature first.

CUMIN, TOMATO, AND CHOURIÇO BEANS

Heat the oil in large heavy saucepan or Dutch oven over medium-high heat. Add the onion and garlic and cook for 3 to 5 minutes, until softened. Add the chouriço and bacon; cook for 6 to 8 minutes, until fragrant and the meat and vegetables have softened. Add the white wine and cook for 2 to 3 minutes, until reduced by half. Add 1 cup (250 mL) of the tomato sauce, ½ cup (125 mL) of the chicken broth, and the 1 Tbsp (15 mL) cumin and bay leaves. Mix well and cook at a low boil over medium-low heat for 6 to 8 minutes, until the sauce thickens slightly and is aromatic (lower the heat if the mixture begins to burn or dries too quickly).

Increase the heat to medium and add the reserved cooked beans; stir well. (To make a generous sauce and prevent the beans from sticking to the pot, add an additional ¼ cup/60 mL broth and ¼ cup/60 mL tomato sauce, or more if necessary.) When the mixture returns to a boil, reduce the heat to low and cook until heated through and the beans are tender, 8 to 10 minutes, stirring occasionally. Continue adding more stock and tomato sauce if the beans dry too quickly. Add the parsley and stir. Taste and adjust the seasonings with salt and white pepper. (The dish can be prepared ahead to this point, covered, and refrigerated for several hours or overnight. Heat through before serving. You may need to add additional tomato sauce and broth if the beans stick to the bottom of the pot and are too thick.)

Serve sprinkled with additional cumin. This dish goes well with steamed rice and Sautéed Garlic Rabe Greens (page 261).

If time allows, make the Cumin-Scented Beans using dried beans; it will yield a more flavourful dish at a fraction of the cost. Soaking and cooking the beans ahead of time produces beans that retain their shape and endure further cooking.

CUMIN, TOMATO, AND CHOURIÇO BEANS

3 Tbsp (45 mL) olive oil

1 large onion, finely chopped

5 cloves garlic, finely minced

4 oz (120 g) chouriço, diced

2 oz (60 g) bacon, diced

½ cup (125 mL) dry white wine

2 cups (500 mL) tomato sauce or canned chopped tomatoes with juice (approx.)

1½ cups (375 mL) chicken broth (approx.)

1 Tbsp (15 mL) ground cumin + 1 to 2 Tbsp (15 to 30 mL) more for serving

2 bay leaves

5 cups (1.25 L) Cumin-Scented Beans (facing page)

½ cup (125 mL) finely chopped fresh parsley

Pinch each fine salt and coarsely ground white pepper

ORANGE-INFUSED MASHED SWEET POTATOES

Batata Doce à Moda do Pico

MAKES ABOUT 4 SERVINGS

2½ lb (1.25 kg) sweet potatoes (about 3), peeled and cut into 2-inch (5 cm) chunks

2 Tbsp (30 mL) butter

1 Tbsp (15 mL) orange zest

½ tsp (2 mL) fine salt

¼ cup (60 mL) orange juice

2 Tbsp (30 mL) whole milk

Fine salt and coarsely ground black pepper, to taste

2 Tbsp (30 mL) finely chopped fresh parsley

On a recent trip to the island of Pico, I was inspired by a memorable sweet-potato side dish. Orange juice and peel provide a simple flavour-enhancing boost to the much-loved sweet-potato mash.

In a large saucepan, cover the potatoes with water and bring to a boil over medium-high heat. Reduce the heat and simmer until the potatoes are tender when pierced with the tip of a knife, 15 to 20 minutes. Drain.

Transfer to a mixing bowl and stir in the butter, orange zest, salt, and half of the orange juice and milk. Using a potato masher, mash until smooth. If necessary to reach the desired consistency, stir in the remaining orange juice and milk. Taste and adjust the seasonings with salt and pepper. Serve with parsley sprinkled overtop.

CRISPY CINNAMON SWEET POTATOES

Here's another tasty spin on sweet potatoes that I learned in a professional kitchen: Sprinkle ground cinnamon onto thick slices of unpeeled, cooked sweet potatoes. Fry them in a hot oiled saucepan until the edges are browned and crispy. Serve warm.

COLLARD GREENS, CORNBREAD, AND GARLIC STIR-FRY

Migas

Migas means "crumbs" and is a very clever and delicious way the Portuguese have devised to use up day-old cornbread and collard greens. The first time I tasted migas I was delighted and surprised with its full, garlicky flavour. I thought I had a very unique recipe. I quickly learned there are hundreds of migas recipes, each one a little different than the next. Some add romano beans, chouriço, eggs, pine nuts, and just about anything else that pairs nicely with day-old cornbread. There are also sweet migas.

Irene, a family friend, made steamed migas to accompany her ribs and fried fish (which is typical) when I was a guest in her kitchen. It reminds her of her childhood, growing up on a farm in central Portugal, where there was always an abundance of collards, garlic, olive oil, and cornbread.

I have since learned of a stir-fried version, served up crispy and crunchy; it is equally delicious. I prefer the crispy version as the main meal and the boiled version as a side dish. Both recipes are included here. Serve with fried eggs and Mixed Green Salad (page 240).

Break the cornbread into large crumbs with some bite-sized pieces and place in a large bowl. Set aside.

In a large pot, combine the water, salt, and collard greens. Bring to a boil and simmer for 5 to 7 minutes, until bright green and tender; if you are making boiled migas, reserve 1 cup (250 mL) of the cooking water. Drain the collards and set aside until cool enough to handle. When cool, squeeze out as much water as possible from the collards. Dry on kitchen towels to remove any excess water. Set aside.

Method continues . . .

MAKES 4 TO 6 SERVINGS

3 cups (750 mL) crumbled
    day-old cornbread

5 cups (1.25 L) water

1 tsp (5 mL) fine salt

3 cups (750 mL) finely shredded
    collard greens (approx.)

½ cup (125 mL) olive oil

10 cloves garlic, smashed

Fine salt and coarsely ground
    black pepper, to taste

COLLARD GREENS, CORNBREAD, AND GARLIC STIR-FRY
(continued)

TO MAKE BOILED MIGAS In a small saucepan, heat the oil over medium-low heat. Cook the garlic until golden, softened, and aromatic, 6 to 8 minutes; remove from the heat. Spoon the heated garlic oil 1 Tbsp (15 mL) at a time (up to 2 Tbsp/30 mL total, just enough to moisten and season the bread) over the prepared cornbread and mix well. Add the prepared collards and mix thoroughly. If the mixture seems dry, add more of the reserved cooking water and garlic oil (up to 2 Tbsp/30 mL of each) and mix until combined (the mixture should be wet but not soggy). Taste and adjust the seasonings with salt and pepper. Serve with the remaining garlic oil.

TO MAKE STIR-FRIED MIGAS In a saucepan large enough to fit the bread and collards, heat the oil over medium-low heat. Cook the garlic until golden, softened, and aromatic, 6 to 8 minutes. Transfer half of the oil and garlic to a bowl and reserve. Heat the remaining oil in the saucepan over medium heat. Add the prepared collards to the pan and toss to coat well; cook for 1 to 2 minutes, until warmed through. Transfer the collards to a bowl and set aside, covered, to keep warm. Add 2 Tbsp (30 mL) of the reserved garlic oil to the saucepan. Add the cornbread and toss to combine; cook for 2 to 3 minutes, until the cornbread is well coated and begins to toast and turn golden brown; adjust the heat as necessary. Return the collards to the pan and stir well to combine, 1 to 2 minutes. Add an additional 1 to 2 Tbsp (15 to 30 mL) of garlic oil, to taste, 1 Tbsp (15 mL) at a time, to coat the collards (the collards and bread should be lightly coated in oil). Taste and adjust the seasonings with salt and pepper. Serve immediately with the remaining garlic oil.

SAUCES AND SWEET SPREADS

Molhos

Sauces are a favourite of mine. A wide range of flavourful combinations can transform simple ingredients into special dishes. I like to think of the handful of recipes that follow as a cook's special arsenal of ingredients that elevate some very good meals to memorable ones. If I have minimal time or energy to make a meal and I didn't get around to marinating my fish, chicken, or meat, I can depend on my sauces to make me look like a star. Any one of the splendid sauces in this chapter can be made in a hurry. If you are catering to less-daring taste buds, you can serve the sauces on the side for those who might want to dribble just a little spoonful onto their meal.

Many of these sauces can also be prepared ahead and set aside in the refrigerator for when you get home from work or whenever you are ready to prepare a meal. With these sauces and a few easy steps (for example, breading chicken breasts, frying an egg, making toast, or opening a can of chickpeas), a meal full of flavour can be ready in a matter of minutes.

Add a dash of Azorean flavour by spooning Sautéed Onion Sauce (page 279) or Four Pepper Sauce (page 281) over baked or fried fish or roasted chicken pieces. Parsley Dressing (page 280) will dress up any fried fish. Both the dressing and the onion sauce are easily made with ingredients that can be found all year round. For special occasions, make White Sauce (page 278) to serve with baked, boiled, or barbecued cod (although the Portuguese tend to prefer a dressing of olive oil and garlic over their fish). I like to follow my Brazilian friend Angelita's example and add generous spoonfuls of Red Pepper and Olive Relish (page 284) onto boiled sweet potatoes, chouriço, or warmed cornbread.

Most Portuguese dishes can be sinfully simple. The sauces, many of Azorean or African origin, add a dash of exotic spice to the everyday. Piri-piri sauce lends a splash of heat for those who like spicy foods. Comforting soups that are usually enjoyed with a spoonful of oil, cornbread croutons, coriander, or mint can be transformed with a drizzle of Parsley Dressing or Lemon Piri-Piri Sauce (page 282).

Although a little more time-consuming than most, Red Pepper Pimento Paste Seasoning (page 286) is another gem with a variety of uses and worth making ahead. Pimento paste is an all-purpose seasoning used liberally in Azorean cooking and primarily in marinades.

Pimento paste (in addition to paprika) is what makes prepared foods at Azorean take-out counters red. The flavour of homemade pimento paste cannot be matched by the store-bought variety. I love to add a few tablespoons of pimento paste when I cook meat or fish for a sweetness that is a nice foil to the acidic wines, vinegars, or lemon juice that flavour many main dishes. I also like to add a spoonful or two to mayonnaise. Pimento Mayonnaise (page 224) is a delicious addition to Portuguese sandwiches. Spread some on split sandwich rolls and top with any leftover Marinated Grilled Chicken (page 177) or Fish Fillets in Batter (page 138). Pile on shredded lettuce and finely chopped red onions or Pickled Peppers (page 221) for a spectacular treat. The possibilities that pimento paste brings to your culinary repertoire are endless.

I like to double or triple Tomato Sauce with Port Wine (page 283) and freeze whatever I don't need in one-cup (250 mL) measures so that I have enough to dress up a variety of dishes. Pour some onto Roasted Seasoned Potatoes (page 246), Seafood Stew (page 91), or Cumin-Scented Beans (page 266) instead of chopped fresh tomatoes for a depth of flavour.

Celebrate Portuguese food by experimenting with the sauces in this chapter and bring something different to the plates of your friends and family. In fact, throw caution to the wind and add these versatile sauces to *any* meal. Most people will be delighted by what they taste.

SAUCES AND SWEET SPREADS
Molhos

WHITE SAUCE

Molho Branco

MAKES ABOUT 1 CUP (250 ML)

2 Tbsp (30 mL) butter

2 Tbsp (30 mL) all-purpose flour

1 cup (250 mL) hot whole milk

¼ tsp (1 mL) fine salt

1 tsp (5 mL) finely grated
lemon zest

4 tsp (20 mL) lemon juice

Pinch freshly grated nutmeg

Pinch coarsely ground white
pepper

1 egg yolk, lightly beaten

Creamy white sauce adds an elegant touch to simple dishes. Dress up baked or fried fish and Green Onion and Parsley Mini-Omelettes (page 34) to make everyday meals special enough for company.

The sauce is actually light yellow in colour; for a whiter sauce, omit the egg yolk. Finely chopped parsley or green onions can also be mixed in or a drop or two of hot sauce added.

In a small saucepan, melt the butter over medium heat; whisk in the flour. Reduce the heat to medium-low and cook, stirring constantly to prevent browning, for about 3 minutes. Whisk in the hot milk. Bring to a boil over medium heat; stir in the salt, lemon zest, lemon juice, nutmeg, and white pepper. Reduce the heat to medium-low and cook for 5 to 7 minutes, until slightly thickened.

Remove the pan from the heat and whisk in the egg yolk. Return to the heat and whisk for 1 minute, blending thoroughly, until the sauce is smooth and creamy. Taste and adjust the seasonings with salt and white pepper. Strain using a fine-mesh sieve, if desired. Cover the surface of the sauce with waxed paper to prevent a skin from forming until ready to use.

SAUTÉED ONION SAUCE

Cebolada

This full-bodied Azorean sauce perks up grilled fish, chicken, pork, or liver.

While you are making the sauce, pan-fry or broil the meat. Then place the meat in a shallow dish, spread the onion sauce overtop, cover tightly with foil, and let stand in a warm oven for 30 minutes to allow the onion sauce to flavour the meat.

This sauce can also be brushed on broiled or barbecued fish steaks.

In a large saucepan or deep skillet, heat the oil over medium-low heat. Cook the onions, stirring often, for 20 to 25 minutes, until tender but not browned. Add the garlic and cook for 2 to 3 minutes, until lightly golden. Stir in the vinegar, water, tomato paste, and salt. Simmer gently for about 5 minutes, until the sauce is slightly thickened. Sprinkle in the parsley and paprika and immediately pour the sauce over the prepared meat or fish. Cover and let stand for at least 30 minutes before serving.

MAKES ABOUT 1½ CUPS (375 ML)

¼ cup (60 mL) olive oil

5 onions, thinly sliced

6 cloves garlic, minced

2 Tbsp (30 mL) white wine vinegar

2 Tbsp (30 mL) water

1 Tbsp (15 mL) tomato paste

Fine salt, to taste

⅓ cup (80 mL) chopped fresh parsley

Pinch paprika

PARSLEY DRESSING

Molho de Salsa

MAKES ABOUT 1½ CUPS (375 ML)

1 clove garlic, coarsely chopped

¼ tsp (1 mL) fine salt

Pinch coarsely ground
    black pepper

½ small onion, finely chopped

¼ cup (60 mL) chopped
    fresh parsley

⅓ cup (80 mL) white wine vinegar

⅔ cup (160 mL) olive oil

Dash piri-piri sauce or
    Tabasco sauce

Pour this tangy parsley dressing over boiled octopus, cod, barbecued stickle-back, or lobster. Or serve it with a simple dish of fish and boiled potatoes to absorb the zesty flavour. This traditional green dressing is made according to taste: some people like to double the garlic and parsley, others like the addition of half a finely chopped green pepper. I like to include a teaspoon (5 mL) of finely chopped lemon zest. Experiment and come up with your favourite combination.

Using a mortar and pestle, mash the garlic with the salt and pepper until smooth. Add the onion and parsley and mash until paste-like.

Transfer the paste to a small bowl, scraping any bits from the mortar, and whisk in the vinegar, oil, and piri-piri sauce. Taste and adjust the seasonings with salt, if necessary. Serve. Stir before using.

Although a food processor simplifies the procedure, it also makes the sauce too runny. Use an old-fashioned mortar and pestle or a small bowl and the back of spoon to achieve a thicker consistency. This dressing is best made fresh just before using.

FOUR PEPPER SAUCE

Molho de Pimenta

Four Pepper Sauce gives everyday food a dash of colour and taste. Prepare it while your entrée is cooking or make it earlier in the day to allow the flavours to blend before using.

In a large, heavy saucepan or deep skillet, heat the oil over medium heat. Cook the peppers and onion, stirring often, for 6 to 8 minutes, until softened. Add the tomatoes and garlic and gently stir to mix. Reduce the heat to medium-low, cover, and cook, stirring occasionally, for about 10 minutes, until the peppers are tender.

Add the vinegar, pimento paste, and cinnamon, and stir to combine. Taste and adjust the seasonings with salt and pepper. Turn off the heat, cover, and let stand on the stovetop for 30 minutes.

Before serving, return the skillet to medium-high heat and heat through. If a smoother texture is desired, purée the sauce briefly in a food processor before serving.

> For a spectacular dish, toss the sauce with 8 oz (240 g) of Manila clams during the last 5 minutes of cooking and cook until the clams open. Use the sauce (with or without clams) to smother grilled, baked, or pan-fried boneless pork loin, chicken, sirloin tip steak, or fish fillets for a meal full of Azorean flavour. It's also delicious simply spooned over fresh bread as a light snack.

MAKES ABOUT 4 CUPS (1 L)

¼ cup (60 mL) olive oil

2 yellow bell peppers, seeded, cored, and sliced

2 red bell peppers, seeded, cored, and sliced

½ hot red banana pepper, seeded, cored, and sliced

½ hot yellow banana pepper, seeded, cored, and sliced

2 large onions, sliced

1 cup (250 mL) peeled, seeded, and chopped tomatoes

2 cloves garlic, minced

1 Tbsp (15 mL) white wine vinegar

1 tsp (5 mL) pimento paste

Pinch ground cinnamon

Pinch each fine salt and coarsely ground black pepper

PIRI-PIRI HOT SAUCE AND LEMON PIRI-PIRI SAUCE

Molho Piri–Piri

MAKES ABOUT ½ CUP (125 ML)

PIRI-PIRI HOT SAUCE

2 piri-piri peppers or 1 small
    hot red pepper, seeded and
    stems removed

½ cup (125 mL) olive oil

The Portuguese have a passion for piri piri, the explosive tiny Angolan pepper, and use it almost daily in their cooking. Piri-piri sauce is often brushed directly onto barbecued meats. Although bottled piri-piri sauce or Tabasco sauce is available in stores, it is not as flavourful as the homemade brew. Two easy-to-make recipes are provided here.

If you cannot find the piri-piri pepper, substitute any hot red pepper. Remember that in most cases, the smaller the pepper, the hotter it will be. Use gloves to chop peppers and don't touch your mouth or eyes while working with them. For a less-spicy sauce, seed the peppers.

In many of the recipes in this book, its quantity has been toned down; use at your own risk.

PIRI-PIRI HOT SAUCE

Place the peppers in a small jar with a tight-fitting lid. Pour the oil over the peppers, leaving a ½-inch (1 cm) headspace. Seal. Store in the refrigerator for 1 week before using. Once opened, it will keep for up to 1 month in the refrigerator.

MAKES ½ CUP (125 ML)

LEMON PIRI-PIRI SAUCE

⅓ cup (80 mL) butter

2 Tbsp (30 mL) lemon juice

¼ tsp (1 mL) piri-piri sauce or
    Tabasco sauce

1 Tbsp (15 mL) pimento paste
    (optional)

LEMON PIRI-PIRI SAUCE

In a saucepan, heat the butter, lemon juice, piri-piri sauce, and pimento paste over low heat until the butter melts and the sauce is heated through.

One of the many uses for lemon piri-piri sauce is to season shrimp. Simply grill shrimp for 3 to 4 minutes, until no longer pink inside, then brush with lemon piri-piri sauce, serving the remaining sauce alongside.

TOMATO SAUCE WITH PORT WINE

Molho de Tomate com Porto

This tomato sauce is essential to many dishes in Portuguese cooking. Chef José Alves of Via Norte in Toronto uses a version of this sauce to lend flavour to his stew, rice, and roasted-potato dishes. I like to keep some on hand to lend a homey layer of flavour to my stews and casseroles, often using it to replace the tomatoes called for in recipes. If you can, use San Marzano tomatoes. The thick, meaty tomatoes provide the best results.

In a large saucepan, heat the oil over medium-high heat. Cook the onion and garlic, stirring occasionally, for 8 to 9 minutes, until beginning to brown and soften. Add the wine and port, increase the heat to high, and cook for 2 to 3 minutes. Add the tomatoes with juices and 2 cups (500 mL) water. Season with salt and pepper, to taste. Reduce the heat to medium and simmer for 20 minutes or until slightly thickened. Reduce the heat to medium-low and cook for 5 to 10 minutes, stirring occasionally. Add up to ½ cup (125 mL) more water if the sauce is thickening too quickly. Take off the heat. Using a fork or potato masher, break up the tomatoes. Add the basil and set aside for 15 to 20 minutes before using. Adjust the seasonings with salt and pepper just before serving. Will keep in the refrigerator for up to 4 days.

MAKES ABOUT 2 CUPS (500 ML)

2 Tbsp (30 mL) olive oil

1 onion, finely diced

4 cloves garlic, minced

½ cup (125 mL) dry white wine

2 Tbsp (30 mL) port

1 large can plum tomatoes (28 oz/796 mL)

1 bunch fresh basil, chopped

½ tsp (2 mL) fine salt (approx.)

Coarsely ground black pepper, to taste

RED PEPPER AND OLIVE RELISH

Pimenta Vermelha e Azeitonas Picadas

MAKES ABOUT 1⅔ CUPS (410 ML)

1 large red bell pepper

2 cups (500 mL) finely diced
   red onions

⅔ cup (160 mL) finely
   chopped parsley

⅓ cup (80 mL) finely chopped
   cured Moroccan olives (or any
   black cured olives)

½ cup (125 mL) + 3 Tbsp (45 mL)
   olive oil (approx.)

2 Tbsp (30 mL) raspberry, sherry,
   or white wine vinegar

Fine salt and coarsely ground black
   pepper, to taste

This relish lends a vibrant, fresh taste to grilled tuna, skate fish, or octopus. Brazilian-born Angelita Flors, who assists in the kitchen at Via Norte, a Portuguese restaurant in Toronto, loves to spoon the relish on fried eggs, boiled sweet potatoes, chouriço, or warm buttered cornbread. Her passion for the relish inspired me to use it to boost the flavours of otherwise simple dishes. Do the same in your kitchen: Add a dollop over garlic toast with a warmed sliver of Serra da Estrela cheese (or any other semi-soft cheese). Or make a pressed sandwich with cheese, prosciutto, and a spoonful of relish.

For best results, make this relish a full day ahead of time and allow the flavours to meld. For an extra punch of flavour, heat the relish in a small pan with one or two teaspoons (5 or 10 mL) of raspberry vinegar just before using. Cut all vegetables in a uniform size before mixing.

Grill the whole red pepper on a greased grill set to high (or 4 inches / 10 cm from hot coals) for 2 to 3 minutes per side or until blackened in parts. Plunge the pepper into ice water and set aside for about 5 minutes. Using a sharp knife, peel and discard the skin, seeds, and white membrane of the pepper. Finely dice the pepper and add to a large bowl (you should have about ⅔ cup/160 mL). Add the onion, parsley, olives, ½ cup (125 mL) oil, and vinegar, stirring well after each addition. Add salt and pepper, to taste. Transfer to a preserving jar or container with a tight-fitting lid. If needed to adequately cover the vegetables, add an additional 2 or 3 Tbsp (30 to 45 mL) of oil. Cover and set aside until ready to use or cover and refrigerate for up to 10 days. Bring to room temperature for 30 minutes before using. Serve spooned over grilled fish, meat, or eggs. For best results, make 24 hours before using to allow the flavours to blend.

MOONSHINE HOT SAUCE

Molho Picante com Aguardente

This hot sauce is a delicious accompaniment to barbecued chicken or fish or sandwiches that need a little extra heat. The orange-coloured spicy and creamy seasoning improves its flavour with age, although it can be used directly after making it.

To protect your face and hands from the hot seeds, wear plastic gloves and a face mask when preparing the chilies and do not touch your eyes or mouth.

Place all of the peppers in a medium-sized saucepan. Cover with water and bring to a boil over medium-high heat and cook for 2 to 3 minutes. The peppers should retain their bright-red colour. Drain and cool in a colander.

In a food processor or food mill, combine the garlic, 1 Tbsp (15 mL) Aguardente, oil, salt, mustard, lemon juice, and white wine vinegar; mix well. Add the drained hot peppers and purée the pepper mixture to make a smooth, creamy, orange-coloured paste. Transfer to a small preserving jar or container with a tight-fitting lid, add the bay leaves, and cover and refrigerate for 1 week before using. Just before serving, taste and add up to 1 Tbsp (15 mL) more Aguardente and season with salt and pepper. Add the rosemary and parsley and mix well. Will keep for up to 3 months in the refrigerator.

MAKES ABOUT 1 CUP (250 ML)

80 small Thai chilies, cut into half, seeded and stems removed (about 1 cup/250 mL)

1 head garlic, peeled (about 10 to 12 cloves)

1 to 2 Tbsp (15 to 30 mL) Aguardente or brandy (approx.)

2 Tbsp (30 mL) olive oil

½ tsp (2 mL) fine salt

1 Tbsp (15 mL) Dijon mustard

2 Tbsp (30 mL) lemon juice

1 Tbsp (15 mL) white wine vinegar

2 bay leaves, crumbled

Fine salt and coarsely ground black pepper, to taste

5 sprigs fresh rosemary

⅓ cup (80 mL) chopped fresh parsley

RED PEPPER PIMENTO PASTE SEASONING

Pimenta Moida, Calda de Pimentos

MAKES ABOUT 3 CUPS (750 ML)

ORIGINAL PIMENTO PASTE

1 lb (500 g) hot red banana
   peppers (4 to 6)

1 lb (500 g) shepherd peppers
   (about 3)

¼ cup (60 mL) fine salt

3 tsp (15 mL) olive oil

Ever since Maria José Martins, a friend I made while collecting recipes, learned to make pimento paste at home, she hasn't been able to go back to eating the store-bought variety. The ruby-coloured homemade red pepper paste has a chunkier texture and sweeter finish. The seasoning paste, known as *pimenta moida*, is used to lend an Azorean-style kick and colour to more traditional Portuguese dishes. It's an Azorean flavouring not typically used by Portuguese mainlanders. Maria José adds a few spoonfuls to her beef stew and roasted chicken dishes, along with some of her favourite Portuguese fla-vourings, such as garlic, wine, bay leaves, and olive oil. Use red bell peppers if shepherd peppers are unavailable.

I have included two recipes for pimento paste here. The first version was included in my first book. It is bright red and has a fresher, sweeter-pepper flavour. The second version was provided by Maria José; it is boiled and reduced, which makes for a slightly more potent pepper taste. Both are excel-lent recipes and can be kept in the refrigerator for up to one month or in the freezer for up to three months.

ORIGINAL PIMENTO PASTE

Rinse the peppers under cold running water and drain in a large colander. Wearing plastic gloves (for handling the hot peppers), core, seed, and cut the peppers into approximately ¼-inch (6 mm) strips (about 8 strips per half shepherd pepper and about 6 strips per banana pepper). Set aside.

Bring a large cooking pot of water to a full boil over high heat and add the peppers. Return to the boil and cook for about 1 minute. Drain the peppers in a colander and set aside to cool.

When cool enough to handle, process the peppers using a food processor or food mill to form a somewhat smooth paste with some chunks of pepper remaining.

Place the peppers in a large bowl; add the salt and mix well. Cover and refrigerate for 3 days, stirring occasionally. Ladle into 3 hot 1-cup

(250 mL) sterilized jars, leaving 1 inch (2.5 cm) of headspace. Cover each jar with 1 tsp (5 mL) of oil. Seal and store in the refrigerator until ready to use. Will keep in the refrigerator for up to 1 month after opening.

BOILED SWEET PEPPER PIMENTO PASTE

Rinse the peppers under cold running water and drain in a large colander. Wearing plastic gloves (for handling the hot peppers), core, seed, and cut the peppers into approximately ¼-inch (6 mm) strips (about 8 strips per half shepherd pepper and about 6 strips per half hot pepper). Set aside.

Process the peppers using a food processor or food mill to form a somewhat smooth paste with some chunks of pepper remaining.

Place the peppers and salt in a heavy saucepan over medium-high heat and bring to a boil. Reduce the heat to medium and simmer for about 10 minutes or until the mixture forms a thick sauce.

Ladle into 3 hot 1-cup (250 mL) sterilized jars, leaving 1 inch (2.5 cm) of headspace. Cover each jar with 1 tsp (5 mL) of oil. Seal and store in the refrigerator until ready to use. Once opened, it will keep in the refrigerator for up to 1 month.

Making pimento paste is often a family affair. An assembly line of children of all ages, husbands, and wives wearing gloves and face masks seed and slice bushels of peppers at a time, often on a four to one ratio—four bushels of hot peppers to one bushel of sweet. Smaller proportions are provided in this recipe. Although you can use store-bought pimento paste, homemade has a thicker consistency and contains no seeds. The peppers commonly used in these recipes are often called "long red hots" or "hot banana peppers" and are 4½ to 6 inches (11 to 15 cm) long.

MAKES ABOUT 3 CUPS (750 ML)

BOILED SWEET PEPPER
PIMENTO PASTE
1 lb (500 g) red hot peppers
   (4 to 6)
1 lb (500 g) shepherd peppers
   (about 3)
¼ cup (60 mL) coarse salt
1 Tbsp (15 mL) olive oil

TOMATO JAM

Doce de Tomate

MAKES ABOUT 2 CUPS (500 ML)

2 lb (1 kg) ripe tomatoes
    (preferably roma), chopped
    into large chunks (about
    6 cups/1.5 L)
2 cups (500 mL) granulated sugar
Two 2-inch (5 cm) cinnamon sticks

Tomato jam is a creative testament to Portuguese farmers' frugal nature. Plentiful tomatoes from the fall's harvest are boiled up to make this delicious jam. *Doce de tomate*, which means "tomato sweets," pairs nicely with Creamy Fresh Cheese (page 49) and cornbread, makes a wonderful spread for crackers, or dresses up grilled cheese. For the more adventurous, spoon some onto your burger or your favourite sandwich.

The tomatoes go into the pot with skin and seeds intact (similar to the beginnings of tomato sauce); the end result is a rich, ruby-coloured spread that is easily mistaken for strawberry jam.

The amount of sugar used in the original recipe given to me by a family friend was two pounds (1 kg), which is the same amount as the tomatoes. In this version I have reduced it by less than half. The jam maintains its texture but has a fruitier taste than the original recipe.

In a Dutch oven, bring the tomatoes, sugar, and cinnamon to a boil over high heat. Reduce the heat to medium-high and cook at a vigorous boil until the tomatoes are softened, the tomato mixture is reduced in bulk, and the mixture has a sauce-like consistency, about 10 minutes. Reduce the heat to medium-low and cook for 40 to 45 minutes, stirring as needed and reducing the temperature further if the mixture sticks to the bottom of the pan (keep an eye on the jam near the end of the cooking time). Maintain a low to medium boil. The mixture will take on a rich, ruby colour and be glossy in appearance near the end of cooking.

TEST FOR DONENESS AFTER 50 MINUTES TO SEE IF THE JAM IS SET Drip about 1 tsp (5 mL) of the jam onto a plate and let cool momentarily. Tilt the plate; the jam should not run. If the jam runs, return the pot to a low-to-medium simmer. Repeat the test every 5 minutes until the jam has set.

When the jam is ready, remove the cinnamon sticks and discard. Ladle into 2 hot 1-cup (250 mL) sterilized jars, leaving 1 inch (2.5 cm) of headspace. Seal the jars.

PROCESS THE JARS IN A HOT-WATER CANNER Place filled jars in the bottom of a large canning pot filled with boiling water (water should cover the jars by 1 inch/2.5 cm). Cover the pot and bring to a full boil; boil for 5 minutes. Carefully remove the jars and allow to cool completely, about 3 to 4 hours or overnight. Check the seal: the lid of jar should be depressed. Store in a cool, dark place. Once opened, refrigerate and consume within 2 weeks.

As this makes a small quantity of jam (about 2 cups/500 mL), I usually forgo the canning process and keep one jar in the refrigerator and give one away.

QUINCE MARMALADE SLICES

Fatias de Marmelada

MAKES ABOUT THREE 2-INCH (5 CM) STRIPS AND ABOUT 30 CUBES

7 quince, peeled
(about 2 ½ lb/1.25 kg)
4 cups (1 L) granulated sugar

In Portugal, quince is made into a marmalade paste, cooked until very thick, and then poured into pots and jars and placed outdoors to sun-dry. It is left to thicken under the Portuguese sun until you can cut it into cubes. In North America, where the sun is not that warm in the late summer and fall when quince is available, the paste is cooked in a low oven until the desired consistency is reached before cutting into thick strips.

While the quince is boiling it looks, feels, and acts like lava. Cover your arms and clothing, as well as the floor around the pot. The boiling mixture makes a loud sticking noise as the mixture slaps against the pot (really!).

Quarter the quince and remove the seeds and core. Set aside.

Bring a large cooking pot or stockpot to a boil over medium-high heat; add the quince and return to a boil. Boil at high heat, partially covered, for 40 minutes or until the quince is fork-tender.

Drain the quince in a colander. Transfer to a food processor and purée until smooth, stopping twice to scrape down the sides of the work bowl.

Place the puréed quince in a large heavy saucepan or Dutch oven. Add the sugar and stir until well blended. Place over high heat and bring to a boil; cook at a high boil for about 10 minutes. The mixture will splatter during high cooking; wear gloves and cover you arms. Reduce the heat to low and continue cooking for about 1 hour and 30 minutes total, stirring every few minutes or as needed. While cooking, tiny bubbles will develop along the sides of the pan and the mixture will sizzle after stirring, ensuring steady, slow cooking. The marmalade is ready when the mixture is visibly thickened and dried out.

Meanwhile, line a 9-inch (23 cm) square baking pan with parchment paper and grease with butter. Spoon the mixture into the baking dish; using a spatula, evenly spread over the pan. Place on the lowest rack in your oven and bake at 175°F (80°C) for about 45 minutes. Bake until dry and firm enough to cut. Let cool to room temperature. Cut into 2-inch (5 cm) strips.

Wrap in plastic wrap. Refrigerate and consume within 2 weeks.

Fatima, a friend and fellow Portuguese food lover, recalls that the quince marmalade slices her mother placed between two slices of fresh Portuguese bread was one of her favourite sandwiches as a child. In restaurants in Portugal, quince marmalade sandwiches are topped with a slice of Serra da Estrela cheese and better known as "Romeo and Juliets." An appetizer variation on this sandwich is Quince and Serra Bites (page 68). You can also serve this marmalade with cheese and Bolachas Maria cookies (a packaged cookie that is the Portuguese version of the Marie biscuit).

PORT SAUCE

Molho de Vinho do Porto

MAKES ABOUT ¾ CUP (185 ML)

2 cups (500 mL) water

1 cup (250 mL) granulated sugar

⅓ cup (80 mL) port

This port sauce is usually made to accompany thick slices of golden French toast slices called *Rabanadas* (page 358). Just before serving, pour some of this sauce onto the bread slices and serve the rest on the side for everyone to add to taste. (Do not worry about the alcoholic content; it burns off while the sauce is cooking.)

In Portuguese homes, the recipe is flavoured with cinnamon sticks and orange peel. I skip the additional flavourings as I prefer the intense, smoky flavour of the reduced port.

To prevent crystallization of sugar when cooking, be sure to use a clean saucepan and do not use a spoon to stir the sauce; instead, swirl the pan to blend the ingredients and don't stray too far from the stovetop while it is simmering.

In a heavy saucepan, bring the water, sugar, and port to a boil over medium-high heat. Reduce the heat to medium-low and simmer for 40 to 45 minutes or until the sauce is amber and thickened. Stay close to the saucepan during the last 5 to 10 minutes when the mixture is very foamy.

TEST THE THICKNESS OF THE SAUCE AT ABOUT 40 MINUTES Drip 1 tsp (5 mL) onto a cold plate and let cool for 1 or 2 minutes. The sauce should have a sticky consistency. I prefer a thick sauce and stronger flavour. For a thinner sauce, remove from the heat after 30 to 35 minutes of cooking.

Serve warm. (The sauce can be made ahead but note that it continues to thicken with time; warm just before using in a *bain-marie* by placing the sauce in a pot in a bigger saucepan full of hot water.)

Store any unused portions in a jar and refrigerate for up to 1 week.

Use this rich sauce to dress up any dessert. Try serving this rich sauce with Pumpkin Fritters (page 314), Pear Cream Tart (page 344), Apple Cake (page 331), or Sponge Cake (page 335) with berries and coffee-flavoured ice cream. You can also add it to waffles or, similar to a toffee sauce, pour over pound cake.

FRUIT CHUTNEY

Chutney de Frutas

MAKES ABOUT 1²/₃ CUPS (410 ML)

APPLE CHUTNEY

Peel from ½ a large lemon or
    orange, slivered (remove as
    much of the bitter white pith
    as possible)

1 cup (250 mL) granulated sugar

½ cup (125 mL) + 1 to 2 Tbsp
    (15 to 30 mL) white wine
    vinegar (approx.)

1 Tbsp (15 mL) whole pink
    peppercorns

1 cup (250 mL) water

3 Granny Smith apples,
    peeled, cored, and cut
    into fat matchsticks

Portuguese fruit chutney is a creative blend inspired by the different fruits that the Portuguese found around the globe in their worldly travels. This recipe is inspired by watching forward-thinking chef José Alves of Via Norte in Toronto combine chutneys with traditional favourites. Typically paired with barbecued cod or salmon, chutney heightens the flavours of mild-tasting fish. It can also be used to brighten broiled or grilled chicken and is delicious as a side order to Mozambique Curried Shrimp (page 118) and Cod and Apples (page 154). Green-apple chutney also pairs nicely with the mild flavour of Serra da Estrela cheese on a fruit and cheese platter.

I adapted the same recipe that I use to make green-apple chutney in the winter for the sweet mango readily found in the summer. Ripe mangoes added a significant amount of natural sweetness and, as a result, my chutney tasted more like jam, so I had to make some adjustments. Be sure to keep tasting all throughout the cooking process and in particular at the end of the reduction. You may need to add an additional tablespoon (15 mL) of vinegar, so adjust as desired. The chutney should taste slightly acidic and not be too sweet.

APPLE CHUTNEY

In a large skillet, add the lemon peel, sugar, ½ cup (125 mL) vinegar, peppercorns, and water; stir. Bring to a boil over medium-high heat and simmer for 6 to 8 minutes or until the mixture is reduced by about half; stir occasionally. Add the apples and return to a boil; reduce to medium heat and cook 3 to 4 minutes further, until the apples are tender. Taste and add the additional 1 to 2 Tbsp (15 to 30 mL) of vinegar, if needed. The sugar and vinegar should be somewhat balanced. The liquid should be reduced and remain clinging to the fruit. Set aside and cool to room temperature before serving. (If time allows, set aside for 24 hours to allow the flavours to fully meld.)

Will keep in the refrigerator for up to 2 weeks. Bring to room temperature before serving.

MANGO CHUTNEY

In a large skillet, add the lemon peel, sugar, ½ cup (125 mL) vinegar, peppercorns, and water; stir. Bring to a boil over medium-high heat and simmer for 6 to 8 minutes or until the mixture is reduced by half; stir occasionally. Add the mangoes and return to a boil; reduce the heat to medium and cook for 3 to 4 minutes further or until the mangoes are tender. Taste and add an additional 3 to 4 Tbsp (45 to 60 mL) of vinegar, if needed. The sugar and vinegar should be somewhat balanced. The liquids should be reduced and remain clinging to the fruit. Set aside and cool to room temperature before serving. (If time allows, set aside for 24 hours to allow the flavours to fully meld.)

Will keep in the refrigerator for up to 2 weeks. Bring to room temperature before serving.

MANGO CHUTNEY

Peel from ½ a large lemon or orange, slivered (remove as much of the bitter white pith as possible)

⅔ cup (160 mL) granulated sugar

½ cup (125 mL) + 4 Tbsp (60 mL) white wine vinegar (approx.)

1 Tbsp (15 mL) whole pink peppercorns

1 cup (250 mL) water

2 mangoes, peeled and cut into matchsticks

BREADS

Pães

Not until I tasted Portuguese-style sourdough buns fresh from a local Portuguese baker and served to me by my father-in-law did I realize that bread could be extraordinary. The bread, chewy on the inside and crispy on the outside, was like nothing I had ever tasted before. Soon after, I learned of densely textured and hearty-flavoured Portuguese cornbread. At first I ate it toasted. When I got used to its moist and heavy texture, I skipped the toasting and dipped pieces in olive oil. It wasn't until much later that I learned of the wide variety of cornbread available at some baker's. (The heartier versions have a greater corn flour to wheat flour ratio.) I do not think I ate much of anything other than bread when I first began visiting my in-laws. I remember one aunt chiding "all she eats is bread" as if there were something wrong with that.

About the same time that I first learned of these amazing breads, I had another Portuguese bread experience. In Azorean tradition, my mother-in-law had made a promise to the church concerning her son's health. Upon a positive outcome she was to bake and offer bread to the church community. Far from wealthy, my hard-working in-laws bought flour, yeast, and sugar and gathered friends and family at a local Portuguese bakery for a day of baking. Using the professional ovens and working space donated by the bakery, hundreds of loaves of bread were mixed, kneaded, and baked. The following Sunday after church I watched, awestruck, as the loaves were given out to churchgoers or anyone else who wanted one. Within 30 minutes the loaves disappeared.

These experiences sealed my love affair with Portuguese bread. I grew to love Cornbread (page 304), Sweet Egg Bread (page 310), and Milk Bread (page 307)—breads that were usually baked or purchased for special occasions such as Easter or Christmas. My husband and I would scour the Portuguese community in Toronto looking for the best Flat Cornbread (page 303) that only a select few bakers in the city prepare. (The baker who originally supplied the community with this special flat cornbread gave away his recipe and sold his business when he retired. The new baker, of Asian decent, is the only commercial baker who makes this bread in Toronto.) Looking for the best Portuguese breads here in the city has been worth the journey. Along the way we tasted some outstanding breads and treats.

Portuguese bread is so loved that it is a shame to throw it out. Clever and frugal Portuguese cooks rejuvenate day-old bread in a variety of dishes. It's an essential feature in soups like Seafood and Bread in Broth (page 77) and Bread and Egg in Garlic and Coriander Broth (page 78). In Collard Greens, Cornbread, and Garlic Stir-Fry (page 269), day-old breadcrumbs tossed in olive oil are used in place of rice. Portuguese dough is also often paired with other Portuguese delicacies, such as in Chouriço Bread (page 308) and Sardine Pizza (page 318). It's interesting to note that many of the meals that feature bread as the main ingredient were invented on farms. Portuguese gaspacho (page 80) came about in the fields where a hearty, quick meal was necessary in order to continue a labourer's day of hard work.

Crusty Buns (page 302) are another much-loved treasure. The bread is used to make *tostas mistas*, grilled cheese with ham—standard fare at Portuguese bakeries. The buns are an essential beginning for many other amazing Portuguese sandwiches. For an easy chicken sandwich, split the buns and fill them with Portuguese rotisserie chicken, pan drippings, Original Pimento Paste (page 221), mayonnaise, pickled vegetables (page 221), and lettuce.

Whenever I have a loaf of bread on hand, no matter how fresh, I like to warm it up. If I am lucky enough, I might have a piece of São Jorge cheese or chouriço on hand. The sausage is easily warmed in a hot pan. I smear the bread in the chouriço-spiced oil that spills out and wrap the bread around the chouriço. I know I will soon find my husband in the kitchen beside me, standing up over the sink savouring every last bite.

Portuguese bread, either fresh from the bakery or baked from one of these easy-to-follow recipes, is worth the effort and makes for wonderful, comforting meals.

BREADS
Pães

CRUSTY BUNS

Papo-Secos

MAKES 18 BUNS

1 tsp (5 mL) granulated sugar

2 cups (500 mL) lukewarm water

1 package active dry yeast
(1 Tbsp/15 mL)

5 cups (1.25 L) all-purpose flour

1 Tbsp (15 mL) fine salt

1 Tbsp (15 mL) lard

Basic white dough is used to make dozens of shaped breads. Although more time-consuming to make than kaisers and other breads that are shaped by machine, the traditional Portuguese crusty buns, shaped by hand, are a labour of love.

In a measuring cup, dissolve the sugar in ½ cup (125 mL) of lukewarm water. Sprinkle in the yeast and let stand for about 10 minutes, until foamy.

In a large bowl, combine the flour and salt. Using your fingers, rub in the lard until well blended. Stir the yeast mixture vigorously with a fork and stir into the flour mixture. Gradually mix in the remaining 1½ cups (375 mL) lukewarm water to make a stiff dough.

Turn out the dough onto a lightly floured surface and knead for about 10 minutes, until smooth and elastic.

Gather the dough into a ball and place in a lightly greased bowl, turning to grease all over. Cover and let rise in a draft-free place for 1½ hours or until doubled in bulk.

Punch down the dough and divide into 18 pieces. On a well-floured board, using the palm of your hand, lightly flatten each piece into a 3-inch (8 cm) round. Using the side of your hand, press down on the dough firmly to make an impression in it without separating it. Fold the sides in to the centre and pinch the ends to form slight points. Arrange about 2 inches (5 cm) apart on well-greased baking sheets. Dust with flour. Cover and let rise in draft-free place for about 45 minutes or until doubled in bulk.

Bake 1 sheet at a time on the top rack of a preheated 500°F (260°C) oven for 12 to 15 minutes, until the buns are well browned and sound hollow when tapped on the bottom. Transfer to wire racks to cool.

These buns are best eaten the same day they are made. If not using immediately, wrap the cooled buns in plastic wrap. Will keep for up to 2 days at room temperature.

FLAT CORNBREAD

Bolos de Milho

This specialty from the island of Pico is a special treat with *queijo fresco* (Fresh Creamy Cheese on page 49) or the sharper-tasting São Jorge cheese, but the hearty corn flavour also goes well with Portuguese appetizers or egg dishes.

In a large heavy cooking pot or Dutch oven, bring 8 cups (2 L) of water and the salt to a boil. Turn off the heat. Using a wooden spoon, stir in the corn and semolina flours slowly and steadily to prevent clumping. Stir until smooth. Set aside to cool completely.

Divide the mixture into 3 equal portions. Transfer one-third to a bowl. Make a well in the centre and, using your hands, work in ½ cup (125 mL) of the all-purpose flour and ¼ cup (60 mL) water (the dough will remain sticky and soft). Gather into a ball and roll onto a work surface coated with corn flour. Repeat with the remaining 2 portions.

With the palm of your hand, lightly flatten each ball to a 10 inch (25 cm) circle ½ inch (1 cm) thick. Slide the circles onto a greased baking sheet, sprinkle with the corn flour, and bake on the middle rack of a preheated 475°F (240°C) oven for 30 minutes. Broil for 5 minutes, turn off the heat, and leave in the oven for 5 minutes or until the top has brown spots and the bottom is golden brown. (You might have to reduce the heat when making the second or third breads if the oven gets too hot.) Cool on wire racks.

These flatbreads are best eaten the same day they are made. If not using immediately, wrap the cooled flatbreads in plastic wrap. Will keep in the refrigerator for up to 2 days.

MAKES THREE 10½-INCH (26 CM) FLATBREADS

8 cups + ¾ cup (2 L + 185 mL) water

2 tsp (10 mL) fine salt

2½ cups (625 mL) white or yellow corn flour

2½ cups (625 mL) semolina flour

1½ cups (375 mL) all-purpose flour

1 cup (250 mL) corn flour (approx.)

CORNBREAD

Pão de Milho

MAKES 1 LARGE OR
2 SMALL LOAVES

1¼ cup (310 mL) fine white
    or yellow cornmeal

3 tsp (15 mL) fine salt

1¼ cups (310 mL) boiling water

2 tsp (10 mL) granulated sugar

1 cup (250 mL) lukewarm water

2 packages active dry yeast
    (2 Tbsp/30 mL)

3¼ cups (810 mL) all-purpose flour

½ cup (125 mL) white or yellow
    corn flour (approx.)

Corn is an important crop in Portugal, and it provides the grain for the country's staple, cornbread. In many of the villages in the Azores on All Saints' Day, each family proudly places one bushel of their corn crop against the church wall, where an auction is held for the prized corn. Everyone joins in the fun and contributes as generously as they can afford. The money is donated to the town parish, and a special prayer is said for each contributing family.

In a large bowl, blend the cornmeal and salt. Add the boiling water and stir until smooth. Let cool for 10 minutes until lukewarm.

Meanwhile, in a measuring cup, dissolve the sugar in lukewarm water. Sprinkle in the yeast and let stand for about 10 minutes, until frothy. Stir the yeast mixture vigorously with a fork and stir into the cornmeal mixture. Gradually mix in the all-purpose flour, until well combined. Turn out onto a well-floured surface and knead for 10 minutes or until smooth and elastic.

Gather the dough into a ball, place in a lightly greased bowl, and turn to grease all over. Cover and let rise in a draft-free place for about 1½ hours or until doubled in bulk.

Punch down the dough. Shape into a round loaf or two small ones. Roll the dough in the corn flour until well covered. Place the loaf on a well-greased baking sheet or 8-inch (20 cm) cake pan. Cover and let rise in a draft-free place for 45 minutes or until doubled in bulk. Sprinkle with additional corn flour just before baking.

Bake in a preheated 450°F (230°C) oven for 30 to 45 minutes, until the loaves sound hollow when tapped on the bottom and are golden brown and crusty on top. Transfer to a wire rack to cool.

This bread is best eaten the same day it is made.

This recipe makes a dense homestyle bread. If you find the cornbread too moist, try toasting it—it's a delicious accompaniment to most Portuguese meals.

CORN CAKES

Bolinhos de Farinha de Milho

MAKES ABOUT 40 CAKES

6 cups (1.5 L) white corn flour

⅔ cup (160 mL) all-purpose flour

½ cup (125 mL) granulated sugar

1 Tbsp (15 mL) baking powder

2 tsp (10 mL) fine salt

6 eggs, lightly beaten

2 ⅔ cups (660 mL) boiling water

1 cup (250 mL) milk

Vegetable oil for frying

Serve these sweet corn fritters warm from the griddle and slathered with butter with Peas and Eggs in Tomato and Red Peppers (page 66) or with Tomato and Egg Spread (page 35). Although white corn flour is traditionally used, yellow corn flour works just as well.

In a large bowl, combine the corn flour, all-purpose flour, sugar, baking powder, and salt. Pour the eggs, boiling water, and milk over the dry ingredients, stirring after each addition until smooth.

In a large skillet, heat the vegetable oil to cover the skillet by ½ inch (1 cm) over medium heat. Pour 2 Tbsp (30 mL) of the batter (for small fritters) into the hot skillet. Cook for 2 to 3 minutes or until golden brown on the bottom. Turn, reduce the heat to medium-low, and cook for about 2 minutes, until cooked through. Transfer the corn cakes to a plate lined with paper towels. Keep warm until ready to serve. Repeat with the remaining cakes.

These are best eaten the same day they are made.

MILK BREAD

Pão de Leite

Delicious milk bread is almost sweet, a natural foil for fresh jam. For the best results, make sure the ingredients are at room temperature. The shaping of these breads may take a little practice but is simple. They can also be made into smaller buns, which are great for sandwiches.

In a measuring cup, dissolve 1 tsp (5 mL) of the sugar in the lukewarm water. Sprinkle in the yeast and let stand for about 10 minutes, until frothy.

In a large bowl, whisk together the eggs and milk. Stir the yeast vigorously with a fork and stir into the egg mixture. Combine the remaining ½ cup (125 mL) sugar and salt. Add to the milk mixture. Using your hands if necessary, gradually mix in enough flour to make a soft dough; add the last cup (250 mL) gradually. Knead in the butter.

Turn out the dough onto a lightly floured surface and knead until smooth and elastic, about 10 minutes. Shape the dough into a ball and dust liberally with flour. Place in a lightly greased bowl and turn to grease all over. Cover and let rise in a draft-free place for 2½ hours or until doubled in bulk. Punch down the dough; turn out onto a lightly floured surface.

Divide the dough into 3 equal pieces. Shape each portion into a ball. Place on a lightly floured surface, cover, and let rise in a draft-free place for 1 hour or until doubled in bulk.

To shape the bread, fold it in half. Repeat with the remaining 2 balls. Place the loaves on a greased baking sheet, cover, and set aside in a draft-free place for 30 minutes or until doubled in bulk. Brush with the egg yolks.

Bake the loaves in a preheated 375°F (190°C) oven for 40 to 45 minutes or until the bread is lightly browned. Cover with foil for the last 20 minutes of baking time. The bread should sound hollow when tapped on the bottom. Transfer to a wire rack to cool.

If not using immediately, cool the bread completely and wrap in plastic wrap. Will keep for up to 3 days at room temperature.

MAKES 3 LOAVES

1 tsp (5 mL) + ½ cup (125 mL) granulated sugar

½ cup (125 mL) lukewarm water

1 package active dry yeast (1 Tbsp/15 mL)

2 eggs

3 cups (750 mL) whole milk

2 tsp (10 mL) fine salt

10 cups (2.5 L) all-purpose flour (approx.)

½ cup (125 mL) butter, softened

3 eggs (yolks only)

CHOURIÇO BREAD

Pão de Chouriço

MAKES 3 LOAVES

1 tsp (5 mL) granulated sugar

2 cups (500 mL) lukewarm water

1 package active dry yeast
   (1 Tbsp/15 mL)

5 cups (1.25 L) all-purpose four

1 Tbsp (15 mL) fine salt

4 Tbsp (60 mL) lard

1½ lb (750 g) chouriço

3 to 4 Tbsp (45 to 60 mL) butter

2 egg yolks

1 Tbsp (15 mL) water

In the south of Portugal, bakers bring their own wood stoves on wheels to fairs and flea markets, where they sell these popular snacks steaming hot from the oven.

In a measuring cup, dissolve the sugar in ½ cup (125 mL) of the lukewarm water. Sprinkle in the yeast and set aside for about 10 minutes, until foamy.

In a large bowl, combine the flour and salt. Using your fingers, rub in 2 Tbsp (30 mL) of the lard until well combined. Stir the yeast mixture vigorously with a fork and add to the flour mixture. Gradually add the remaining 1½ cups (375 mL) lukewarm water and mix with your hands to make a stiff dough.

Turn out the dough onto a lightly floured surface and knead for about 10 minutes, until smooth and elastic.

Gather the dough into a ball and place in a lightly greased bowl, turning to grease all over. Cover and let rise in a draft-free place for 1½ hours or until doubled in bulk.

In a saucepan, cover the chouriço with water and simmer over medium heat for 10 minutes; drain. Using a sharp knife, remove the skin and slice the chouriço into ⅛-inch (3 mm) slices. Set aside.

Turn out the dough on a well-floured surface. Punch down and divide into 3 equal pieces. With a rolling pin, flatten each portion into a circle about 10 inches (25 cm) in diameter.

In a small bowl, combine the butter and the remaining 2 Tbsp (30 mL) lard. Melt in the microwave on high for about 15 seconds or until melted. Brush each circle with the mixture. Divide the cooked chouriço slices evenly and arrange on the dough circles, leaving a ½-inch (1 cm) border. Roll each circle up jelly-roll fashion, lightly pinching the edges to contain the chouriço. Roll up the dough crosswise, tucking in the ends and smoothing into a ball.

Place the breads on well-greased baking sheets. Cover and let rise in a draft-free place for 1 to 1½ hours or until doubled in bulk.

In a small bowl, beat the egg yolks and water with a fork; brush over the breads.

Bake in a preheated 425°F (220°C) oven for 25 to 30 minutes or until browned and the breads sound hollow when tapped on the bottom. Transfer to wire racks to cool.

This bread is best eaten the same day it is made. If not using immediately, cool the bread completely and wrap in plastic wrap. Will keep in the refrigerator for up to 2 days.

This bread can also be baked in a cigar shape with a raw egg, chopped parsley, and mozzarella cheese tucked inside before baking—an excellent breakfast for when you are on the run.

SWEET EGG BREAD

Folar ou Massa Sovada

**MAKES TWO 8-INCH
(20 CM) LOAVES**

1 tsp (5 mL) + 1 cup (250 mL)
    granulated sugar

½ cup (125 mL) lukewarm water

1 package active dry yeast
    (1 Tbsp/15 mL)

½ tsp (2 mL) fine salt

1 Tbsp (15 mL) finely grated
    lemon zest

5 eggs

5 cups (1.25 L) all-purpose
    flour (approx.)

½ cup (125 mL) butter, softened

2 egg yolks

This Easter specialty is a sure sign of spring in the Portuguese community. In families where there is an avid bread maker, the airy egg bread is served throughout the year to accent special dinners. It is delicious slathered with butter and homemade jam as a light snack with tea.

This bread is baked on fresh banana leaves in the Azores. In this recipe, lemon peel has been added for extra flavour. You can also make single-serving buns to use for sandwiches with cheese or jam.

For best results, make sure the ingredients are at room temperature. Because of the long rising time, it is important that the bread is allowed to rise in a draft-free place.

In a measuring cup, dissolve 1 tsp (5 mL) of the sugar in the lukewarm water; sprinkle in the yeast and let stand for about 10 minutes, until frothy.

In a large bowl, combine the remaining 1 cup (250 mL) sugar, salt, and lemon zest. Using a wire whisk, swiftly mix in the eggs one at a time until all the eggs have been added and the mixture is foamy. Briskly stir the prepared yeast with a fork and stir into the egg mixture. Using a wooden spoon, gradually beat in enough flour to make a stiff dough.

Using your hands, knead in the butter 2 Tbsp (30 mL) at a time, kneading until the dough is soft and slippery, about 10 minutes (most of the butter should be absorbed at this stage). The dough should be soft and spring back when touched in the centre. Cover and let rise in a draft-free place for about 4 hours.

Punch down the dough; turn out onto a lightly floured surface. Divide the dough into 2 pieces. Shape each portion into a ball and place in a greased 8-inch (20 cm) cake pan or in the centre of a greased baking sheet. Cover and let rise in a draft-free place for about 3 hours or until doubled in bulk.

Cut a cross in the top of each loaf, brush with the egg yolks, and bake on the bottom rack of a preheated 350°F (175°C) oven for 40 minutes. Bake until golden brown and the loaves sound hollow when tapped on the bottom.

If not using immediately, cool the bread completely and wrap in plastic wrap. Will keep for up to 3 days at room temperature.

CINNAMON BREAD

Bolinhos de Canela

MAKES 3 LOAVES

1 tsp (5 mL) + ½ cup (125 mL) granulated sugar

½ cup (125 mL) lukewarm water

1 package active dry yeast (1 Tbsp/15 mL)

3 eggs

¼ tsp (1 mL) ground caraway

1 Tbsp (15 mL) ground cinnamon

1 tsp (5 mL) fine salt

2 tsp (10 mL) finely grated lemon zest

½ cup (125 mL) raisins

½ cup (125 mL) pine nuts

1 cup (250 mL) water

5 cups (1.5 L) all-purpose flour

1 egg yolk

Traditionally, slices of this cinnamon-scented sweet bread were passed out to children on All Saints' Day in little towns outside of Lisbon. They are a delicious treat to bake any time of the year.

In a measuring cup, dissolve 1 tsp (5 mL) sugar in ½ cup (125 mL) lukewarm water. Sprinkle in the yeast and let stand for about 10 minutes, until frothy.

In a large bowl, whisk together the eggs, caraway, cinnamon, salt, lemon zest, raisins, and pine nuts. Stir in the 1 cup (125 mL) water. Stir the yeast mixture vigorously with a fork and add it to the egg mixture.

In a bowl, combine the remaining ½ cup (125 mL) of sugar and the flour. Using a wooden spoon, gradually beat the dry ingredients into the egg mixture to make a soft dough.

Turn out the dough onto a floured surface and knead until smooth and elastic, about 10 minutes. Place in a lightly greased bowl, turning to grease all over. Cover and let rise in a draft-free place for 1½ to 2 hours or until doubled in bulk.

Punch down the dough; turn out onto a lightly floured surface. Divide the dough into 3 pieces. Shape each portion into a ball and place on a greased baking sheet. Cover and let rise in a draft-free place for 1 hour or until doubled in bulk.

Brush with the egg yolk. Bake the loaves in a preheated 375°F (190°C) oven for 20 to 25 minutes, until golden brown and the bread sounds hollow when tapped on the bottom. Transfer to wire racks to cool.

If not using immediately, cool the bread completely and wrap in plastic wrap. Will keep for up to 3 days at room temperature.

PUFF PASTRY

Massa Folhada

Flaky, buttery puff pastry is the base for countless Portuguese sweets, savoury pies, and tartlets. Puff pastry is not difficult to make, but it is time-consuming. Frozen pastry is an acceptable shortcut.

In a large bowl, combine the flour and salt. Make a well in the centre. Pour in the water and stir briskly with a wooden spoon until the dough holds together. Turn out the dough onto a lightly floured board. Using your hands, knead until the dough is smooth. Cover and let rest for 20 minutes.

Roll out into a 16- × 10-inch (40 × 25 cm) rectangle about ¼ inch (6 mm) thick. Set aside.

Place the butter on a floured board. Using a floured rolling pin, pound the butter until 1 inch (2.5 cm) thick. Fold the butter in half. Continue pounding and folding, sprinkling the board with enough flour to keep the butter from sticking, until the butter is soft and pliable but not melting (if it gets too soft, refrigerate it for 20 to 30 minutes). Carefully roll or pound the butter into approximately a 12- × 6-inch (30 × 15 cm) rectangle. Set aside.

Place the dough on a lightly floured board with the short end toward you. Place the butter in the centre of the dough, leaving about a 2-inch (5 cm) border on all sides. Gently fold one-third of the dough rectangle over the centre; then repeat and fold the other side one-third over the centre. Using a rolling pin, press the short ends together to seal. Roll out the dough lengthwise into a 24- × 12-inch (60 × 30 cm) rectangle (you will be able to see flecks of butter when the dough stretches out). Fold the dough into thirds; press the short ends together to seal, and rotate the dough. (If the butter begins to melt and the dough becomes difficult to work with, refrigerate for 20 to 30 minutes in between rolling out the dough.) Wrap the dough in waxed paper, place on a baking sheet, and refrigerate for 30 minutes.

Repeat the rolling and folding 3 more times, refrigerating for 30 minutes each time. The dough can be refrigerated for up to 2 days or frozen for up to 3 months.

MAKES 1½ LB (750 G) DOUGH

3½ cups (875 mL) all-purpose flour
Pinch fine salt
1¼ cups (310 mL) cold water
1⅓ cups (330 mL) butter

For quick and tasty Portuguese snacks or appetizers, cut the pastry pieces into strips and wrap around slices of chouriço or pieces of sardine, or simply brush with Olive Paste (page 65) or Red Pepper Pimento Paste Seasoning (page 286) and olive oil, and bake until golden brown.

PUMPKIN FRITTERS WITH CINNAMON SUGAR DUST

Bolinhos de Jerimu

MAKES ABOUT 20 FRITTERS OR 10 BAKED PUMPKIN CAKES

½ cup (125 mL) all-purpose flour

¾ cup (185 mL) granulated sugar

2 Tbsp (30 mL) ground cinnamon

2 tsp (10 mL) baking powder

2 cups (500 mL) pumpkin pulp (facing page)

2 eggs, separated

Vegetable oil for deep-frying

Pumpkin fritters, a delicacy from the north of Portugal, are enjoyed in the fall when pumpkins are plentiful. Each family has a treasured recipe. Some creative cooks add one quarter cup (60 mL) locally grown pine nuts, toasted, in addition to one quarter cup (60 mL) of raisins to their batter.

The secret to making these fritters is to squeeze out as much water from the cooked pumpkin as you can using clean kitchen towels; the result is a thick pumpkin pulp. If you like, you can serve these pumpkin fritters for dessert with a dollop of ice cream and drizzle a few drops of your best port overtop. For an even more decadent treat, serve with Port Sauce (page 292).

In a bowl, combine the flour, ¼ cup (60 mL) of the sugar, 1 Tbsp (15 mL) of the cinnamon, and baking powder. Set aside.

In a large mixing bowl, place the pumpkin pulp. Add the egg yolks, one at a time, beating well after each addition. Add the flour mixture and beat until well combined.

In a separate bowl, beat the egg whites until stiff peaks form. Gently fold into the pumpkin batter just until combined.

In a large skillet, heat vegetable oil to a depth of about 2 inches (5 cm) to 375°F (190°C). Using 2 spoons, drop about 1 Tbsp (15 mL) of the batter into the oil, flattening slightly using the back of a spoon (you can cook 4 to 5 fritters at a time). Cook for about 5 to 6 minutes, turning once, until golden brown all over. If necessary, adjust the heat to keep the fritters from browning too quickly. Drain on paper towels. Repeat with the remaining dough.

Combine the remaining ½ cup (125 mL) sugar and 1 Tbsp (15 mL) cinnamon. While still warm, toss the fritters with the cinnamon sugar. Serve warm or at room temperature.

TO MAKE PUMPKIN CAKES Spoon about 2 Tbsp (30 mL) of the batter into greased muffin tins and bake in a preheated 350°F (175°C) oven for 15 minutes. Remove from the pan while still warm and roll into the cinnamon sugar.

PUMPKIN PULP

PUMPKIN PULP
1 medium to large pumpkin
   (about 5 lb/2.2 kg)

Using a sharp knife, peel and halve the pumpkin. Remove the seeds, pulp, and stringy membrane. Cut it into small pieces and cover with water; boil over medium-high heat for about 25 minutes or until tender. Drain and set aside until cool enough to handle. Place the pumpkin in a clean kitchen towel and squeeze out as much water as you can from the cooked pumpkin. You should have about 2 to 2½ cups (500 to 625 mL) of pumpkin pulp. Mash or purée the pulp in a blender or food processor, or put through a food mill.

SWEET BREAD WITH COCONUT

Pão de Deus

MAKES 12 BUNS

1 tsp (5 mL) + ½ cup (125 mL)
    granulated sugar

½ cup (125 mL) lukewarm water

1 pkg active dry yeast
    (1 Tbsp/15 mL)

¼ cup (60 mL) butter, softened

6 eggs

⅓ cup (80 mL) port

4½ to 5 cups (1.125 to 1.25 L)
    all-purpose flour (approx.)

COCONUT TOPPING

1 cup (250 mL) finely grated
    fresh coconut or unsweetened
    dried flaked coconut

3 Tbsp (45 mL) granulated sugar

3 eggs, separated

½ cup (125 mL) sifted
    icing sugar (approx.)

This recipe for "Bread of God," egg bread with coconut garnish, is found in most Portuguese bakeries. Sometimes the bread is braided into a ring and the coconut filling is stuffed into the bread in addition to being strewn over top. This recipe was inspired by Ana Vieira, an avid baker who was determined to create her own version by combining some of her sweet bread recipes using her imagination. This bread is mildly sweet, which makes this a perfect breakfast treat with Quince Marmalade Slices (page 290) and butter.

TO MAKE THE DOUGH In a measuring cup, dissolve 1 tsp (5 mL) of the sugar in the lukewarm water; sprinkle in the yeast and let stand for about 10 minutes, until frothy.

Meanwhile, in a large bowl, combine the butter and the remaining ½ cup (125 mL) of sugar and blend well. Using a wire whisk, swiftly mix in the eggs, one at a time, until all the eggs have been added and the mixture is foamy. Whisk in the port. Briskly stir the yeast with a fork and stir into the egg mixture.

Using a wooden spoon, gradually beat in enough of the flour to make a soft, slightly sticky dough (about 4½ cups/1.125 L). Turn out onto a floured surface and knead for about 10 minutes or until smooth and elastic, dusting with enough of the remaining ½ cup (125 mL) flour to prevent sticking. The dough should be soft and spring back when touched in the centre. Shape the dough into a ball and place in a lightly greased bowl, turning to grease all over. Cover with plastic wrap and set aside to rise in a warm, draft-free place for 1 to 1½ hours or until doubled in bulk and an impression remains when a finger is pressed into the dough.

Punch down the dough; turn out onto a lightly floured surface. Divide the dough into 12 equal pieces. Shape each piece into a somewhat flattened ball and place onto a greased baking sheet. Cover and set aside in a draft-free place for 45 to 60 minutes or until doubled in bulk.

TO MAKE THE COCONUT TOPPING Combine the coconut, sugar, and egg whites and set aside.

In another small bowl, beat the egg yolks with a fork and set aside.

TO BAKE THE BUNS Brush each bun with the egg yolks. Spread about 1 to 2 Tbsp (15 to 30 mL) of the coconut filling over the top-centre of each bun. Bake in a preheated 375°F (190°C) oven for 15 to 20 minutes or until the bread is lightly browned. For a light-coloured bun, loosely cover with foil for the last 5 to 10 minutes of baking. Dust the buns with icing sugar. Transfer to a wire rack to cool. Best served warm and eaten the same day they are made.

If not using immediately, cool the buns completely and wrap in plastic wrap. Will keep in the refrigerator for up to 2 days.

SARDINE PIZZA

Pizza de Sardinhas

MAKES 1 PIZZA OR
4 APPETIZER SERVINGS

1 small ball pizza dough
(1½ lb/750 g store-bought
dough or half of the Crusty
Buns dough recipe, page 302)

1½ lb (750 g) sardines, scaled,
gutted, bones and heads
removed, and quartered

1 tsp (5 mL) fine salt

4 Tbsp (60 mL) olive oil (approx.)

1 large onion, thinly sliced

2 cloves garlic, minced

2 Tbsp (30 mL) chopped
fresh parsley

3 Tbsp (45 mL) pimento paste
(optional)

Fine salt and coarsely ground
black pepper, to taste

Martin Silva, a Portuguese newscaster at CHIN radio in Toronto, introduced me to sardine pizza. He remembers having the savoury treat when he was a young child, usually around the time his parents cultivated their crops. His grandmother would place the sardines on some freshly risen dough and bake it in the oven, just until the dough and the sardines were cooked.

I added onions, garlic, and parsley for a subtle boost of flavour. You can experiment with tomatoes, olives, or other vegetables to suit your preferences. The availability of frozen sardines throughout the year ensures you can make this any time you like. Sardines offer a healthy dose of omega-3 fatty acid and give you one more reason to include this pizza as one of your favourite snacks.

Gather the dough into a ball and place in lightly greased bowl, turning to grease all over. Cover and let rise in a draft-free place for about 45 minutes to 1 hour or until doubled in bulk.

Turn out the dough into a large rectangular baking pan, approximately 11- × 16-inch (28 × 40 cm), and, using your hands, press the dough flat all over, forming a slightly raised edge. Cover and let rise in a draft-free place for about 30 minutes.

Rinse the sardines under cold running water and pat dry with paper towels; lightly salt and set aside (if using pimento paste, reduce the amount of salt by half). Brush 2 Tbsp (30 mL) of the oil over the base of the pizza dough. Scatter the dough evenly with half of the onions and top with the sardines. Sprinkle with garlic, parsley, and pimento paste (if using). Top with the remaining onions and 2 Tbsp (30 mL) oil.

Bake in a preheated 500°F (260°C) oven for 10 to 12 minutes or until the crust is golden. Remove from the oven and, using a fork, check that the bottom of the pizza dough is golden brown. Transfer to a wire rack to cool for about 5 to 10 minutes before cutting into squares and serving.

DESSERTS

Doces

Countless decadent Portuguese desserts are based on a combination of eggs, cream, and port. Almost every restaurant serving a Portuguese clientele has a house special featuring flan. White Chocolate Flan (page 329), a refreshing variation, is featured in this chapter. Crème Brûlée (page 362), Cream from Heaven (page 352), and Chocolate Mousse (page 330) are equally favoured and reflect the Portuguese fondness for sinfully decadent desserts. The simple steps outlined in this chapter will help you make these outstanding classic desserts at home.

Homestyle desserts usually include Cinnamon Rice Pudding (page 326), Sweet Vermicelli Pudding (page 327), Sponge Cake (page 335), Easy Doughnuts (page 361), and Rosa's Almond Anise Cookies (page 349). These treats are flavoured with a hint of lemon, orange, cinnamon, or almonds and, often, a little bit of port.

Finding home cooks to make some of the more decadent cream-based recipes was a challenge. Talking to some bakers and catching a quick glance at the pudding and chocolate mix-packages at Portuguese grocery stores explained why so few of the decadent desserts were made at home. In our fast-paced, very busy life, few people have time to temper eggs to make perfect custards and even less time to whip eggs and melt chocolate for chocolate mousses. Although none of the recipes in this book use instant puddings numerous home cooks do use these.

One Portuguese friend, Ana Vieira, noted that café culture, enjoyed by so many in Portugal, is thriving in Portuguese Canadian bakeries. Although she loves baking, as a young woman in Portugal she rarely baked. She recalls that in Portugal the much smaller ovens required a well-supplied propane tank. Due to the cost, planning, and the work involved to keep the tanks filled, it's not hard to understand why many people were not able to bake at home. In Canada, she does not think twice about baking to her heart's content.

The recipes in this section reflect the Portuguese's adventurous spirit. Ingredients such as oranges and coconut, tropical flavours found in their travels to Africa and Brazil, were brought back in recipes such as Orange Cake with Orange Topping (with coconut sauce) (page 332), Moist Coconut Drops (page 350), and Coconut Pudding with Meringues and Chocolate Streaks (page 328).

Much-loved as well, almonds flavour endless treats. Almost everyone I know has a treasured recipe for Almond Tart (page 346) or cookies such as Rosa's Almond Anise Cookies (page 349).

Fresh fruit also makes for a simple yet outstanding dessert. Port-Soaked Pineapple with Mint and Lemon (page 343), Strawberries Marinated in Port (page 357), and fruit salad just skim the surface of the delicious fruit offerings in Portuguese homes and restaurants.

One key sweet that almost all experienced Portuguese cooks make is a rich and decadent Port Sauce (page 292). Port sauce can be made in minutes and kept warm in a *bain-marie*. It's traditionally made to accompany French Toast Slices in Port Cinnamon Sauce (page 358), but you can also pour it over sponge cake and fruit for an elegant dessert. The amber sauce is versatile. Use it to add a touch of rich flavour to Pumpkin Fritters with Cinnamon Sugar Dust (page 314), Pear Cream Tart (page 344), or Apple Cake (page 331). Although almost as sinful as the desserts themselves, a little of its decadence goes a long way.

DESSERTS
Doces

CINNAMON RICE PUDDING

Arroz Doce

MAKES 4 TO 6 SERVINGS

2 cups (500 mL) whole milk

2 cups (500 mL) water

Peel from 1 lemon

One 2-inch (5 cm) cinnamon stick

¼ tsp (1 mL) fine salt

½ cup (125 mL) short-grain
    or Arborio rice

½ cup (125 mL) granulated sugar

2 egg yolks

Ground cinnamon

A prized batch of *arroz doce* provides a sweet ending for many family meals. This homestyle recipe produces a thin version of rice pudding, with savoury juices enveloping the flavourful rice. It can be served in parfait glasses with a dollop of whipped cream. More modern cooks, with less time to spare, use vanilla pudding diluted with milk and water for extra flavour. I prefer the subtle lemon and cinnamon used in the recipe below, which is a classic flavour combination adored throughout Portugal and its colonies.

In a heavy saucepan, combine the milk, water, lemon peel, cinnamon stick, and salt; cover and bring to a boil. Stir in the rice. Reduce the heat to medium-low and cook, uncovered, for 35 to 40 minutes, or until almost tender, stirring often and scraping down the sides of pan. Add the sugar and continue cooking over low heat for 5 minutes, until the rice is tender and almost all the liquid is absorbed. Remove from the heat.

Beat the egg yolks until light and stir vigorously into the rice until well combined. Return to the heat, stirring constantly for 1 minute, until slightly thickened.

Remove the cinnamon stick and lemon peel. Spoon the pudding into parfait glasses and sprinkle with ground cinnamon. Serve at room temperature or cover and refrigerate for up to 4 days.

Azoreans from São Miguel serve a more traditional thick pudding. It is spread out on a flat serving dish and decorated with cinnamon sprinkled through paper doilies. Children sometimes prefer it served on a slice of sweet bread as a treat. If you would like the more traditional-style pudding, use 1 cup (250 mL) less liquid. When making this rice, stir and scrape down the sides of the pan often when cooking, to prevent it from sticking. Cook about 5 to 10 minutes less than the instructions given in the recipe above.

SWEET VERMICELLI PUDDING

Aletria Doce

This pasta dessert, pudding similar to rice pudding, originates from the north of Portugal and is traditionally served at Christmastime. Family friend Martin Silva has fond memories of eating this comforting treat as a child. It is typically served topped with ground cinnamon sprinkled through a lace doily. It is easily dressed up for special occasions with toasted pine nuts, finely chopped fresh or dried figs, and a dollop of whipped cream. Infused with subtle cinnamon and orange flavourings, this pudding is equally delicious warm from the stovetop or at room temperature.

When the noodles cool down, they thicken and stick together, which makes it easier to cut into thick pieces (perfect for a tasty midday snack).

I prefer a thinner consistency, so remove it from the heat while the pudding is still runny and briefly cool it before serving.

In a saucepan over medium-high heat, combine the milk, water, sugar, salt, orange peel, and cinnamon and bring to a boil. Add the pasta and reduce the heat to medium-low. Bring to a low boil and cook for about 4 minutes, stirring often, until the pasta is cooked. If necessary, use 2 forks to separate the noodles to prevent them from clumping while cooking.

In a medium bowl, beat the egg yolks. Remove the noodle mixture from the heat and, in a slow, steady stream, add about ½ cup (125 mL) of the hot noodle mixture to the egg yolks, stirring vigorously to prevent the eggs from curdling. Add this mixture back to the noodles and stir until well combined. Return the saucepan to the stove and cook over low heat, stirring often, for 1 to 2 minutes, until the pudding has thickened slightly. Be sure to remove the pan from the heat while the pudding is still runny; it will continue to thicken after cooking. Remove and discard the orange peel and cinnamon stick. Add the butter and mix well.

Pour into individual parfait glasses or a large serving dish and allow to cool slightly before serving.

MAKES 8 TO 10 SERVINGS

2 cups (500 mL) whole milk
1 cup (250 mL) water
½ cup (125 mL) granulated sugar
1½ tsp (7 mL) fine salt
Peel from 1 orange, cut into strips
One 2-inch (5 cm) cinnamon stick
5 oz (150 g) angel-hair-pasta nests
3 egg yolks
1 Tbsp (15 mL) butter

Nests of angel-hair pasta are sold in specialty Portuguese grocery stores. Very fine Chinese noodles can also be used.

COCONUT PUDDING WITH MERINGUES AND CHOCOLATE STREAKS

Pudim de Côco

MAKES 6 TO 8 SERVINGS

8 eggs, separated

1 cup (250 mL) granulated sugar

2 cups (500 mL) hot whole milk

2 Tbsp (30 mL) anise liqueur, Grand Marnier, or port

1½ cups (375 mL) finely grated fresh coconut or unsweetened dried flaked coconut

1 oz (30 g) bittersweet or semi-sweet chocolate

1 Tbsp (15 mL) toasted coconut

This pudding is a specialty in the Azores, where freshly grated coconut is the key ingredient.

For the fluffiest meringue, whip the egg whites just before piling onto the pudding. To toast the coconut, spread it on a baking sheet and bake in a 350°F (175°C) oven for 5 minutes, shaking the baking sheet occasionally to prevent burning.

In a large bowl, whisk together the egg yolks and ¾ cup (185 mL) of the sugar until blended. Gradually whisk in the milk and anise liqueur. Add the coconut and mix well.

Pour the mixture into a greased 6-cup (1.5 L) baking dish. Set the dish in a larger pan and pour in enough hot water to come halfway up the sides of the baking dish.

Bake in a preheated 325°F (160°C) oven for 25 to 30 minutes, until a toothpick inserted in the centre of the pudding comes out clean.

Just before the pudding is done, beat the egg whites with the remaining ¼ cup (60 mL) sugar until stiff peaks form. Take out the pudding and decoratively pile the egg whites over the coconut pudding in peaks and return the dish to the oven. Broil for 1 minute or until golden. Remove the baking dish from the water and let cool.

In a double boiler, stir the chocolate over hot (not boiling) water until melted. Drizzle over the egg whites and set aside at room temperature to cool completely. Sprinkle with toasted coconut. Refrigerate until chilled, at least 1 hour or up to 2 days.

WHITE CHOCOLATE FLAN

Pudim Flan

This decadent, fresh-tasting dessert is a twist on a Portuguese favourite and includes white chocolate and is prepared with milk and cream (typically, homemade versions of flan are made only with milk).

In a small heavy saucepan, add ⅓ cup (80 mL) of the sugar and cook on medium-low heat, uncovered, for 10 to 15 minutes or until amber. Shake the saucepan occasionally, but do not stir. Remove from the heat and carefully add 2 Tbsp (30 mL) of the port and 1 tsp (5 mL) of the orange zest. When the bubbles subside, stir until smooth. Return to the heat and cook for 5 to 10 minutes or until the hard caramel pieces have dissolved. Using oven mitts and working quickly, spoon the syrup onto the inside walls of a 4-cup (1 L) ring mould or other decorative mould.

In a heavy saucepan, heat the remaining 2 Tbsp (30 mL) port and 3 tsp (15 mL) zest, and the cinnamon stick, milk, and cream. Turn off the heat, add the white chocolate chips, and stir until melted and well combined. Set aside.

In a large bowl, whisk together the whole eggs, egg yolks, and remaining ⅔ cup (160 mL) sugar. Do not let the mixture become foamy or you will have air bubbles in the flan. Whisk in the cream and milk mixture and strain through a fine-mesh sieve. Pour into the caramel-lined mould. Place the mould in a larger pan and pour enough hot water into the pan to come halfway up the sides of the mould (to make a *bain-marie*).

Bake in a preheated 350°F (175°C) oven for 55 minutes or until a toothpick inserted in the centre of the flan comes out clean.

Remove the pan of water from the oven do not remove the mould. Let rest until the water is lukewarm. Remove the mould from the water and let the flan cool completely. (Do not move the flan abruptly or the mould could break.) With toothpicks, carefully loosen the flan from the inside edge of the pan. Refrigerate until chilled, at least 1 hour or up to 1 day.

Just before serving, run a knife around the edge of the pan. Invert onto a large plate and drizzle with the caramel sauce from the mould.

MAKES 6 TO 8 SERVINGS

1 cup (250 mL) granulated sugar

¼ cup (60 mL) port or
    orange liqueur

4 tsp (20 mL) finely grated
    orange zest

One 2-inch (5 cm) cinnamon stick

1½ cups (375 mL) whole milk

1½ cups (375 mL) whipping cream

¾ cup (185 mL) white
    chocolate chips

2 eggs

6 egg yolks

CHOCOLATE MOUSSE

Mousse de Chocolate

MAKES 8 SERVINGS

8 oz (240 g) bittersweet or unsweetened chocolate

¼ cup (60 mL) butter

8 eggs, separated

⅔ cup (160 mL) granulated sugar

2 Tbsp (30 mL) port

Pinch fine salt

TOPPING

1 cup (250 mL) whipping cream

2 Tbsp (30 mL) granulated sugar

1 tsp (5 mL) vanilla

Grated bittersweet chocolate

Chocolate mousse has a special place in the hearts of the Portuguese. Although packaged mixes are stocked in Portuguese supermarkets, nothing compares to this rich and creamy version made the old-fashioned way. Serve this mousse with a bottle of your best port—it is a Portuguese tradition to pour a few spoonfuls on each serving.

Melt the chocolate with the butter in a bowl over hot (but not boiling) water. Let cool.

In a bowl, beat the egg yolks until light; gradually beat in ⅔ cup (160 mL) sugar and port. Beat for about 5 minutes or until the mixture has thickened and the batter falls in ribbons when the beaters are lifted from the bowl. Add the chocolate to the egg yolk mixture. Mix until thoroughly blended.

In a separate bowl, beat the egg whites with salt until stiff peaks form. Add about one-quarter of the egg whites to the chocolate mixture; gradually mix until smooth and well blended. Fold in the remaining egg whites just until combined. Pour into a greased 10-cup (2.5 L) soufflé dish. Cover and refrigerate for 2 hours or preferably overnight.

TO MAKE THE TOPPING In a bowl, beat the whipping cream with the 2 Tbsp (30 mL) sugar and the vanilla. Refrigerate until ready to use.

Using a pastry bag, decorate the mousse with whipped cream and sprinkle with grated chocolate.

APPLE CAKE

Bolo de Maçã

Ana Vieira, a friend and extraordinary baker, shared countless cake recipes with me that celebrate the love of apples that abound throughout Portugal. When creating this recipe, I accidentally marinated the apples with oranges and cinnamon for 30 minutes before combining them with the cake batter, adding a surprising and subtle boost of flavour. The end result is this rich sponge cake, laden with bits of apples, delicious and decadent with or without a dollop of ice cream.

In a bowl, combine the apples, orange zest, and orange juice and stir to combine. Mix 2 Tbsp (30 mL) of the granulated sugar with the cinnamon and sprinkle it overtop of the apple. Set it aside for at least 30 minutes.

In a bowl, combine the flour and baking powder. In a large bowl, using an electric mixer, blend the eggs and the remaining 1 cup (250 mL) sugar. Beat for about 5 minutes or until the mixture thickens and turns pale. Add the flour mixture to the egg batter in alternating batches with the oil. Add the vanilla and stir. Using a spatula, gently fold the apple mixture into the batter just until combined.

Pour the batter into a greased and parchment paper–lined 9-inch (23 cm) square cake pan. Bake in a preheated 350°F (175°C) oven for 50 to 60 minutes or until a tester inserted in the centre comes out clean. Let the cake cool in the baking pan for 10 minutes, then transfer it to a wire rack to cool completely. Carefully run a knife around the edges of the pan. Turn out the cake and remove the waxed paper.

Serve warm or at room temperature with a dusting of icing sugar. Ice cream is optional.

MAKES 6 TO 8 SERVINGS

5 apples, peeled, cored and chopped into small pieces (about 3 cups/750 mL)

Grated zest from 2 medium oranges

¼ cup (60 mL) fresh orange juice

2 Tbsp (30 mL) + 1 cup (250 mL) granulated sugar

2 tsp (10 mL) ground cinnamon

1 cup (250 mL) all-purpose flour

1 tsp (5 mL) baking powder

4 eggs

¾ cup (185 mL) vegetable oil

1 tsp (5 mL) vanilla

Sifted icing sugar

ORANGE CAKE WITH ORANGE TOPPING

Bolo de Laranja

MAKES 8 TO 10 SERVINGS

ORANGE TOPPING

3 oranges

2 Tbsp (30 mL) granulated sugar

¼ cup (60 mL) butter, melted

¼ cup (60 mL) brown sugar

1 tsp (5 mL) finely grated
orange zest

½ cup (125 mL) fresh or
maraschino cherries or
chopped walnuts (optional)

ORANGE CAKE

½ cup (125 mL) butter, softened

1 cup (250 mL) granulated sugar

4 eggs, separated

1 Tbsp (15 mL) finely
grated orange zest

2 cups (500 mL) all-purpose flour

2 tsp (10 mL) baking powder

1 cup (250 mL) fresh orange juice

Pinch fine salt

Sifted icing sugar

COCONUT SAUCE

1 cup (250 mL) granulated sugar

1 cup (250 mL) finely grated
fresh coconut or unsweetened
dried flaked coconut

1 cup (250 mL) whole milk

1 Tbsp (15 mL) port

2 Tbsp (30 mL) finely grated
fresh coconut or unsweetened
dried flaked coconut, toasted

Abundant Portuguese oranges and tangerines make this a colourful, flavourful dessert, but pineapples can be substituted.

My friend Isabel Vieira learned to make coconut sauce from her aunt Céu, who lived in Mozambique most of her life. Perfect for a special occasion, the coconut sauce is a decadent topping, but when I make the cake without it, I still get rave reviews.

TO MAKE THE ORANGE TOPPING Peel the oranges and cut away the bitter pith membrane. Cut the oranges into ¼-inch (6 mm) slices, removing any seeds. Sprinkle with the granulated sugar and set aside for 10 minutes.

In the meantime, in the bottom of a greased 8-inch-square (20 cm) cake pan, spread the melted butter evenly and sprinkle with the brown sugar and orange zest. Decoratively arrange the orange slices overtop, placing the cherries (if using) in between to make a design. Set aside.

TO MAKE THE ORANGE CAKE In a large bowl, combine the butter and sugar until light. Add the egg yolks and orange zest, scraping down the bowl after each addition.

In a bowl, combine the flour and baking powder. Gradually add to the batter, alternating with the orange juice.

In a separate bowl, beat the egg whites with salt until stiff peaks form. With a spatula, gently fold the egg whites into the batter until just combined. Spread the batter into the pan. Bake in a preheated 375°F (190°C) oven for 40 to 50 minutes, until a toothpick inserted in the centre comes out clean and the cake is firm to a light touch. Let the cake cool in the pan for 15 minutes. Dust the serving dish with icing sugar. Run a knife around the inside edge of the pan and turn the cake out onto the serving dish. Let cool completely.

TO MAKE THE COCONUT SAUCE Bring the sugar, 1 cup (250 mL) coconut, and milk to a boil over medium-high heat in a small heavy saucepan. Reduce the heat to medium-low and cook, stirring, for 10 to 15 minutes or until the syrup thickens and reduces. Remove from the heat and cool slightly. Stir in the port.

Using the back of a wooden spoon, make holes in the top of the cake. Drizzle the sauce overtop and set aside for 30 minutes or until the cake soaks up the sauce. Sprinkle with the toasted coconut and serve.

CHRISTMAS FIG CAKE

Bolo de Natal com Figos

2 Tbsp (30 mL) liquid honey

¼ cup (60 mL) rye whisky

¼ cup (60 mL) port

¼ cup (60 mL) cherry liqueur

¼ cup (60 mL) Aguardente

1 cup (250 mL) chopped dried figs

1 cup (250 mL) raisins

1 cup (250 mL) chopped candied fruit

1 cup (250 mL) chopped walnuts

2⅔ cups (660 mL) granulated sugar

1⅓ cups (330 mL) butter, melted and cooled

5 eggs

2⅔ cups (660 mL) all-purpose flour

1 Tbsp (15 mL) baking powder

2 tsp (10 mL) freshly grated nutmeg

Sifted icing sugar

Figs add a refreshing change to the traditional fruit cake. *Aguardente*—Portuguese whisky—can be found at liquor stores that supply Portuguese spirits; you can also substitute brandy. This cake can be made a month ahead of time. To keep the cake moist while it is in the refrigerator, brush it with Aguardente or brandy once a week.

In a skillet, bring the honey, whisky, port, cherry liqueur, and Aguardente to boil over medium-high heat. Add the figs, raisins, candied fruit, and walnuts; simmer gently for 5 minutes. Remove from the heat and cool completely.

In a large bowl and using an electric mixer, beat the sugar and butter until blended. Add the eggs, one at a time, beating well after each addition. Continue beating until the mixture is pale in colour and slightly thickened.

In a bowl, combine the flour, baking powder, and nutmeg.

Beat the flour mixture into the batter until blended. Add the fruit mixture and mix well; spoon into a greased and parchment paper–lined 9-inch (23 cm) tube pan.

Bake in a preheated 350°F (175°C) oven for 1 hour and 15 to 20 minutes or until the top is firm and brown and a cake tester inserted in the centre comes out clean. Tent the cake with foil if it is browning too quickly.

Let the cake cool in the pan for 10 minutes and then invert onto a wire rack to cool completely. When cool, wrap well in foil or plastic wrap and refrigerate for up to 2 weeks. Just before serving, dust with icing sugar.

SPONGE CAKE

Pão de Ló

In Portugal, sponge cake is used as a base for many trifle-style desserts. My husband claims the simplest and most delicious way to serve this is with a scoop of ice cream. For a special occasion, drizzle it with Port Sauce (page 292) and serve with berries.

In the bowl of a stand mixer, beat the eggs with salt until light. Gradually beat in the sugar. Beat for 20 minutes or until the mixture is very thick.

In a small bowl, combine the flour and baking powder. With the mixer at the lowest setting, add the flour mixture to the eggs one heaping spoonful at a time, blending well after each addition and scraping down the sides of the bowl frequently.

Carefully pour the batter into a greased and parchment paper–lined 10-inch (25 cm) tube pan. Bake in a 350°F (175°C) oven for 40 minutes or until the cake springs back to a light touch. Let cool in the pan for 10 minutes. Remove from the pan and peel off the waxed paper. Let cool completely on a wire rack. Dust with icing sugar just before serving.

MAKES 8 TO 10 SERVINGS

9 eggs

Pinch fine salt

1½ cups (375 mL) granulated sugar

1⅔ cups (410 mL) all-purpose flour

¼ tsp (1 mL) baking powder

Sifted icing sugar

CARAMEL CAKE WITH CARAMEL SAUCE

Bolo de Caramelo

MAKES 8 TO 10 SERVINGS

4 eggs, separated

1½ cups (375 mL) granulated sugar

2 cups (500 mL) all-purpose flour

1 Tbsp (15 mL) baking powder

¼ tsp (1 mL) fine salt

1 cup (250 mL) butter, melted
   and cooled

1 cup (250 mL) whole milk

CARAMEL SAUCE

1 cup (250 mL) granulated sugar

¼ cup (60 mL) port or fruit liqueur

2 Tbsp (30 mL) boiling water

1 Tbsp (15 mL) butter

1 cup (250 mL) coarsely
   chopped walnuts

The Portuguese passion for caramel desserts has resulted in hundreds of desserts soaked in the amber sauce. *Bolo de caramelo,* an Azorean specialty, has a double dose of caramel: the caramel-coloured and -flavoured cake is also coated in a golden caramel sauce. Take special care to cook the sauce until very thin or it will harden on the cake.

In a large bowl, beat the egg yolks until light; gradually beat in ½ cup (125 mL) of the sugar. Beat for 3 to 5 minutes, until the mixture has thickened and the batter falls in ribbons when the beaters are lifted from the bowl.

In a small bowl, combine the flour, baking powder, and salt. Add to the egg mixture and mix in alternating batches with the melted butter until smooth. Set aside.

In a heavy saucepan, cook the remaining 1 cup (250 mL) sugar on medium-low heat, uncovered, for 10 to 15 minutes, until amber; shake the saucepan occasionally, but do not stir. Remove from the heat and carefully pour in the milk; when the bubbles subside, stir until smooth. Return to the heat and cook for 10 minutes or until the hard caramel pieces have dissolved. Remove from the heat and slowly whisk into the egg batter until well blended, scraping down the sides as necessary.

In a large bowl, beat the egg whites until stiff peaks form; gently fold into the egg yolk mixture, stirring only until mixed. Divide the batter between 2 greased and parchment paper–lined 9-inch-round (23 cm) cake pans.

Bake in a preheated 350°F (175°C) oven for 40 to 45 minutes or until a cake tester inserted in the centre comes out clean. Let the cake cool in the pan for 10 minutes. Remove from the pan and peel off the waxed paper. Let cool completely on wire racks.

TO MAKE THE CARAMEL SAUCE In a heavy saucepan, cook the sugar on medium-low heat, uncovered and without stirring, for 10 to 15 minutes, until amber; shake the saucepan occasionally. Remove from the heat and carefully pour in the port and water. When the bubbles subside, stir until smooth. Return the pan to the heat and cook for 4 to 5 minutes, stirring occasionally, until the hard caramel pieces have dissolved and the sauce is smooth. Stir in the butter and half of the walnuts. Set aside to cool slightly for 5 to 10 minutes.

While still warm, spread one-quarter of the caramel sauce over the top of 1 cake and place the second cake on top. Spread the rest of the caramel sauce in a thin layer over the sides and top of the cake. Sprinkle with the remaining walnuts.

CUSTARD-FILLED PUFF BALLS

Cavacas

MAKES 36 PUFF BALLS

PUFF BALLS

9 eggs

1 cup (250 mL) vegetable oil

1¾ cups (435 mL) water

2 cups (500 mL) all-purpose flour

½ tsp (2 mL) fine salt

ICING

1 cup (250 mL) sifted icing sugar

2 Tbsp (30 mL) cold whole milk

1 tsp (5 mL) vanilla or anise liqueur

CHOCOLATE FILLING

1 Tbsp (15 mL) cornstarch

3 Tbsp (45 mL) sifted unsweetened
    cocoa powder

1 cup (250 mL) cold whole milk

1¾ cups (435 mL) sifted icing sugar

4 egg yolks

2 Tbsp (30 mL) butter

VANILLA FILLING

1 cup (250 mL) granulated sugar

1 cup (250 mL) water

2 Tbsp (30 mL) + 1 tsp (5 mL)
    cornstarch

1 cup (250 mL) whole milk

6 egg yolks

1 tsp (5 mL) vanilla

1 cup (250 mL) blueberries,
    raspberries, or other berries
    (optional)

Crispy *cavacas* (puff balls) can be filled with sweet or savoury mixtures. In addition to the chocolate and vanilla fillings provided here, you can also fill the puff balls with Chocolate Mousse (page 330) or whipping cream whipped with a little strong coffee. Or try adding two teaspoons (10 mL) vanilla or anise liqueur to the batter when making the puff balls—a boost of flavouring in the shells will pair wonderfully with the chocolate and vanilla fillings.

Fill the puff balls just before serving so the shells stay crispy. The puff balls can also be made ahead and frozen.

TO MAKE THE PUFF BALLS In a large bowl, beat the eggs until foamy. Gradually beat in the oil, water, flour, and salt. Beat for about 3 minutes, until well combined.

Fill 12 greased muffin tins three-quarters full with the batter and place in the oven on the second rack from the top. Bake in a preheated 450°F (230°C) oven for 30 minutes or until the puffs are well browned. Reduce the heat to 300°F (150°C) and bake for 30 more minutes (do not open the oven door). Set aside to cool.

TO MAKE THE ICING Mix the icing sugar, milk, and vanilla until blended. While the puff balls are hot, coat the tops with the icing. Cool the puff balls before filling them.

TO MAKE CHOCOLATE FILLING In a small heavy saucepan, combine the cornstarch and cocoa with ¼ cup (60 mL) of the milk until well blended. Add the icing sugar, egg yolks, and the remaining ¾ cup (185 mL) milk. Whisk until well blended. Cook, stirring, over medium-low heat for 10 to 15 minutes, until thickened. Remove from the heat and stir in the butter. Strain. Cover and let cool.

TO MAKE THE VANILLA FILLING In a saucepan, bring the sugar and water to a boil. Simmer over medium-high heat for 10 to 12 minutes, until the sugar runs like a thread off the end of a spoon. In a small bowl, combine the cornstarch and milk and stir into the sugar mixture. Cook over medium heat, stirring, for 5 minutes, until well blended. Beat the yolks and vanilla until frothy. Remove the saucepan from the heat and add the egg yolks in a slow stream. Return to the heat and cook, stirring, for 5 to 10 minutes, until thickened. Strain through a fine-mesh sieve. Add fruit (if using). Cover and let cool.

TO ASSEMBLE Make a small hole in the side or bottom of each puff ball. Remove any excess dough. Add the filling using a pastry bag or small spoon. Sweet puff balls can be dusted with icing sugar if not already iced.

CUSTARD IN PUFF PASTRY SHELLS

Pastéis de Nata

MAKES 12 PASTRIES

¾ cup (185 mL) granulated sugar

¼ cup (60 mL) water

1 cup (250 mL) cold whole milk

1¼ cup (310 mL) whipping cream

2 tsp (10 mL) finely grated
   lemon zest

One 2-inch (5 cm) cinnamon stick

2 Tbsp (30 mL) cornstarch

3 egg yolks

1 egg

1 lb (500 g) Puff Pastry (page 313)

Ground cinnamon

Portuguese custard tarts originated hundreds of years ago in a café near the tower of Belém, a Lisbon fortress. Bakeries in that area are now renowned for these specialties.

These three-bite desserts can be found in most Portuguese bakeries and grocery stores, and are one of my favourite treats to bring to any occasion.

When making the sugar and liquid reduction, to prevent the crystallization of the sugar, do not use a spoon to stir; instead, swirl the pan over the heat occasionally.

In a small saucepan, combine the sugar and water. Boil over medium-low heat for 10 to 12 minutes or until the sugar is reduced to about ¾ cup (185 mL) of syrup. Set aside for 10 minutes to cool slightly.

In a saucepan over medium-low heat, heat ¾ cup (185 mL) of the milk, and the whipping cream, lemon zest, and cinnamon stick until hot. Set aside to cool briefly.

In a deep skillet, combine the cornstarch and remaining ¼ cup (60 mL) cold milk. Gradually add the hot milk and cream. Bring to a boil over medium heat, whisking until the mixture comes to a boil. Continue cooking for about 1 minute, until thickened. Remove from the heat and set aside for 10 minutes to cool slightly.

In a large bowl, using an electric mixer, beat the egg yolks and egg until well blended. Gradually add the prepared sugar water, followed by the milk and cream mixture, and beat for about 1 minute or until well blended. (Be careful not to form too many air bubbles in the batter or it will not bake well.) Cover with plastic wrap and refrigerate until cold. Strain through a fine-mesh sieve just before using.

Method continues . . .

CUSTARD IN PUFF PASTRY SHELLS
(continued)

On a lightly floured surface, roll out one-half of the puff pastry into a 12-inch (30 cm) square about ¼ inch (6 mm) thick. Cut out six 4-inch (10 cm) circles. Press each circle into a muffin tin (wet fingers will make this easier) and prick all over with a fork. (If the pastry gets too soft, refrigerate for 30 minutes before continuing.) Repeat with the remaining puff pastry and refrigerate until muffin pastry shells are cold. Fill the shells three-quarters full with the custard filling.

Set the oven rack in the middle of the oven. Bake the tarts in a preheated 450°F (230°C) oven for 25 to 30 minutes or until the pastry is golden brown and the filling is bubbly with a few flecks of golden brown. (If the tarts are browning too quickly, cover them loosely with foil.)

Immediately sprinkle the tarts with a few drops of cold water and then sprinkle with cinnamon (the water helps the cinnamon stick). Let stand for 5 minutes. Run a knife around the edge of the muffin tins and carefully remove the tarts (clean the knife in cold water and dry it off after each tart has been removed). Let the tarts cool on a wire rack for at least 1 hour (this allows the bottoms to cool and the custard to set).

Although these tarts are best eaten the same day you make them, you can reheat day-old custard tarts (store-bought and homemade) in a 350°F (175°C) oven for a few minutes. Sprinkle with cinnamon and icing sugar and eat immediately.

PORT-SOAKED PINEAPPLE WITH MINT AND LEMON

Ananás com Vinho do Porto

Grilling has a caramelizing effect that brings out the natural sugar in pine-apple. Liberally brushing with port, just after grill marks appear, lends an extra dose of flavour. A scoop of vanilla or mocha ice cream and a few fresh leaves of mint transform pineapple to make a perfect ending to any meal.

Pineapples appear frequently in restaurants in Portugal. In the Azores, where pineapple grow in abundance, I tasted deliciously decadent thin slices (no grilling or baking) that had been marinating a few hours in a familiar Azorean liqueur, Angelica, and served alongside a sweet potato tart.

Heat a grill to high and grease with vegetable oil (or grill pineapple 4 inches/10 cm from medium-hot coals). Grill the pineapple slices until grill marks appear, about 2 to 3 minutes per side. Using a lifter, transfer the slices to indirect heat and brush both sides generously with port. When the pineapple is warmed through, transfer it to a plate and keep warm.

Place the pineapple pieces into parfait glasses and scatter mint leaves and lemon zest overtop. Serve immediately (with or without ice cream).

MAKES 4 TO 6 SERVINGS

1 ripe pineapple, cored, peeled, and cut into 1-inch-thick (2.5 cm) slices
Vegetable oil for brushing grill
½ cup (125 mL) port
¼ cup (60 mL) chopped fresh mint
Zest from ½ lemon

PEAR CREAM TART

Tarte de Pera

MAKES 6 TO 8 SERVINGS

TART

3¼ cups (810 mL) all-purpose flour

2 Tbsp (30 mL) granulated sugar

1 tsp (5 mL) fine salt

1½ cups (375 mL) butter, softened

1 egg

¼ cup (60 mL) port

CREAMY PEAR FILLING

4 or 5 Anjou pears

2 Tbsp (30 mL) lemon juice

2 tsp (10 mL) + 1 Tbsp (15 mL) granulated sugar

2 eggs

1 tsp (5 mL) ground cinnamon

1 cup (250 mL) 18% cream

2 Tbsp (30 mL) port

½ cup (125 mL) sifted icing sugar

This recipe usually calls for apples, which are plentiful in Portugal. One day I tried using pears instead of the apples and was pleasantly surprised by the flavour combination of pears, port, and cinnamon in this buttery dessert. Since the dough makes enough for two crusts, I suggest you make two tarts. Double the egg and cream filling and make one tart using an equal amount of apples and the other using pears, and judge for yourself which is your favourite.

TO MAKE THE TART SHELL Combine the flour, sugar, and salt in a bowl. Gradually add the butter, 1 to 2 Tbsp (15 to 30 mL) at a time, mixing with a fork until well distributed and the mixture is crumbly. Add the egg, mixing well. Gradually add the port, a spoonful at a time, mixing lightly with a fork until the dough forms a ball. (Alternatively, in a food processor mix the flour, sugar, and salt. Add the butter and process until the mixture becomes crumbly. With the food processor running, through the feed tube, add the egg, followed by the port one spoonful at a time until the mixture forms a ball.)

Wrap the dough in waxed paper and refrigerate for about 20 minutes, until cold. This will allow the pastry to rest and make it easier to work with dough. (Recipe can be prepared ahead to this point, covered, and refrigerated for up to 1 day.)

On a floured surface, roll half of the dough into a 10-inch (25 cm) circle (wrap the remaining half and refrigerate for up to 3 days or freeze for up to 3 months for later use). Transfer to a 9-inch (23 cm) pie pan, flute edges, and place in fridge until ready to use.

TO MAKE THE CREAMY PEAR FILLING Peel and core the pears; cut into thin slices. Toss with the lemon juice so they will not turn brown. Remove the pie crust from the refrigerator and arrange the pear slices decoratively in a circular design on the bottom of the crust; sprinkle each layer with a little sugar (you may need up to 2 tsp/10 mL of sugar). In a bowl, beat the eggs, ground cinnamon, 1 Tbsp (15 mL) sugar, cream, and 2 Tbsp (30 mL) of port.

TO ASSEMBLE Pour the cream mixture over the pears in the pie plate. Bake in a preheated 425°F (220°C) oven for 15 minutes. Reduce the heat to 350°F (175°C) and continue baking for 40 to 45 minutes or until the filling in the centre is golden and set. Let cool in the pan for 10 minutes. Dust with icing sugar just before serving.

Anjou pears, available all year round, are great for cooking. Bartlett, Bosc, and Concorde are equally good for pies and readily available in the fall.

ALMOND TART

Picada de Abelha

MAKES 6 TO 8 SERVINGS

1½ cups (375 mL) slivered almonds

1 cup (250 mL) all-purpose flour

½ tsp (2 mL) baking powder

1 cup (250 mL) butter, softened

½ cup (125 mL) granulated sugar

¼ tsp (1 mL) pure almond extract

2 eggs

3 Tbsp (45 mL) whole milk

½ cup (125 mL) icing sugar, sifted

The passion the Portuguese have for almonds is reflected in the numerous cookies, cakes, and desserts that they enjoy. An abundance of the sweet-tasting, versatile nut grow on trees throughout the Algarve province where Manuela Marujo, a family friend, grew up.

Picada de Abelha "bee sting tart" is a decadent, buttery tart topped with crispy almonds. Manuela concludes that the top of this Portuguese dessert resembles what your skin might look after a bee bite. The tart is delightful to eat and in no other way will remind you of a bee sting.

The dessert should be cooked crispy, with a light-brown finish, so stay close to the oven in the final moments of baking as it can quickly burn. I also like to brush the tops and sides of the tart with heated tomato jam or quince marmalade while the cake is still warm from the oven.

TO TOAST THE NUTS Spread the almonds on a baking sheet. Bake in a preheated 350°F (175°C) oven for 5 to 8 minutes, until browned, shaking the baking sheet occasionally. Set aside to cool.

TO MAKE THE PASTRY BASE Combine the flour and baking powder in a small bowl. In a large bowl, cream ½ cup (125 mL) of the butter and ¼ cup (60 mL) of the sugar. Gradually add the flour mixture. Add the almond extract and eggs, one at a time, beating well after each addition. The dough will have a sticky consistency. Wrap the dough in waxed paper and refrigerate for about 20 minutes or until cold. (This will allow dough to rest and make it easier to work with.)

Remove the dough from the refrigerator and shape it into a disc. Place the dough into a fully greased and parchment paper–lined 9-inch (23 cm) pie plate (almost to the rim). Using your fingertips, pat the dough evenly into the bottom and sides. Using a fork, prick the pastry all over. If the dough is too sticky, return it to the refrigerator for 10 to 15 minutes further, until cold.

Bake on the bottom rack of a preheated 375°F (190°C) oven for 20 minutes. The tart will rise slightly and also have a golden-brown edge. Remove from the oven and set aside.

TO MAKE THE ALMOND FILLING In a small heavy saucepan, heat the remaining ½ cup (125 mL) butter over medium-high heat; when melted, add the remaining ¼ cup (60 mL) of sugar and the milk, and mix well. Cook for about 1 minute at a medium boil, then add the almonds and cook 1 minute further (the almonds should be well coated with the butter sauce). Keep warm.

TO ASSEMBLE THE TART Spread the almond filling onto the pastry base and bake on the top rack of a preheated 375°F (190°C) oven for 8 to 10 minutes or until the tart is golden brown along the edges, the almonds turn light-brown, and the topping looks crisp. (Be careful in the last 2 minutes of baking as the tart could quickly blacken.) Let the tart cool in the pan for 10 minutes. Run a knife around the inside edge of the pan. Turn the tart out onto a serving dish. Dust with icing sugar just before serving.

HONEY COOKIES

Broas de Mel

MAKES ABOUT 5 DOZEN COOKIES

4½ cups (1.125 mL)
    all-purpose flour

2 tsp (10 mL) baking soda

2 tsp (10 mL) baking powder

2 tsp (10 mL) ground cinnamon

Finely grated zest from 2 lemons

½ cup (125 mL) butter, softened

½ cup (125 mL) lard, softened

2 cups (500 mL) granulated sugar

⅔ cup (160 mL) mel de cana

5 eggs

These cookies are a speciality of the island of Madeira, which boasts that it produces the best-tasting sugar cane in the world. Hundreds of cookies, cakes, and liquors are produced with the abundant and delicious sugar-cane extraction. The cookies feature a type of light molasses produced from the sugar cane and known by the islanders as *mel de cana* (sugar-cane honey). It has a lovely, subtle taste suited for baking. If you can't find any, you can substitute honey. I like to substitute a combination of half honey and half molasses for the mel de cana in this recipe.

In a bowl, combine the flour, baking soda, baking powder, cinnamon, and lemon zest; set aside.

In a large bowl, using an electric mixer, beat the butter and lard with the sugar until light and fluffy. Beat in the mel de cana until well combined. Add the eggs, one at a time, mixing well after each addition. Gradually add the flour mixture to the egg batter and blend until a smooth dough forms. Using your hands, shape the dough into a ball and wrap in plastic wrap; refrigerate for at least 1 hour or until firm enough to shape.

Scoop out the dough a tablespoon (approx. 15 mL) at a time and roll into balls using the palms of your hands. Place the balls 2 inches (5 cm) apart on parchment paper–lined or greased baking sheets.

Bake in a preheated 350°F (175°C) oven for 10 to 12 minutes or until firm and the edges and bottoms are golden. Transfer to a wire rack to cool completely.

Store in a cookie tin. Will keep at room temperature for up to 7 days.

These cookies are usually served at Christmastime. The holiday table is set with cookies and homemade fruit liqueurs, ready to greet the family returning from midnight mass on Christmas Eve. If desired, you can dress up these cookies by topping them with a piece of dried fig or half a walnut just before sliding in the oven to bake.

ROSA'S ALMOND ANISE COOKIES

Bolinhos da Rosa com Amêndoa e Anis

Rosa Boaventura, a family friend, admits that due to her busy family life she and her husband do not cook and rarely bake. In spite of this, Rosa knows what she likes. With a lot of testing and tasting, Rosa helped me to re-create almond-flavoured anise cookies that she had at a friend's house long ago and that she claims were the best cookies she'd ever tasted. I'm not sure these ones below are exactly like the cookies Rosa remembers, but these almond-jammed butter cookies are outstanding and, with a dusting of icing sugar, are perfect for any occasion.

TO TOAST THE NUTS Spread the slivered almonds on a baking sheet. Bake in a preheated 350°F (175°C) oven for 5 to 8 minutes, until browned, shaking the baking sheet occasionally. Set aside to cool.

In a large bowl, cream the butter and oil with sugar until fluffy. Add the eggs, one at a time, beating well after each addition. In another bowl, combine the ground almonds, flour, baking powder, and crushed anise seeds. Gradually beat the almond mixture into the butter mixture in alternating batches with the port, until smooth. Add the prepared toasted slivered almonds and mix just until combined. Wrap the dough in waxed paper and refrigerate for 30 minutes or until cold enough to shape.

Using well-greased hands, shape approximately 1 Tbsp (15 mL) of the batter into balls. Either roll in the sliced almonds or place one blanched almond firmly into each cookie. Place onto a greased baking sheet, leaving about 2 inches (5 cm) between cookies. Bake on the lowest rack of a preheated 425°F (220°C) oven for 12 to 15 minutes or until the bottoms and edges of the cookies are golden brown. Transfer to a wire rack to cool for about 20 minutes. Serve with a dusting of icing sugar.

Cool completely and store in a cookie tin.

MAKES ABOUT 5 DOZEN COOKIES

1¾ cups (435 mL) slivered almonds

½ cup (125 mL) butter, softened

1 Tbsp (15 mL) vegetable oil

¾ cup (185 mL) granulated sugar

3 eggs

¼ cup (60 mL) ground almonds

2 cups (500 mL) all-purpose flour

1 tsp (5 mL) baking powder

2 tsp (10 mL) anise seeds, crushed with fingertips

2 Tbsp (30 mL) port

1 cup (250 mL) sliced almonds, skin on, or whole blanched almonds (about 1 almond per cookie)

Sifted icing sugar

MOIST COCONUT DROPS

Coquinhos

MAKES ABOUT 24 COOKIES

1 potato, peeled

½ cup (125 mL) granulated sugar

2 Tbsp (30 mL) whole milk

2 egg yolks

1½ cups (375 mL) finely grated
    fresh coconut or unsweetened
    dried flaked coconut

Manuela Marujo, associate chair of Spanish and Portuguese at the University of Toronto, busy grandmother, and outstanding cook and baker in her spare time, prefers to call these cookies *beijinhos de coco*, which means "coconut kisses." A perfect name for the decadent and delightful coconut treats she makes for friends and family.

The potato keeps these cookies moist. Do not overcook the batter, which requires a hot oven and a careful eye during the last few minutes of baking. By the time the cookies begin to turn golden on the edges, they are ready to be removed from the oven. Just to be sure, I take them out when I think they're done (after nine to ten minutes of baking) and break one in half to check for doneness. To prevent burning the bottoms of the cookies, I bake them on a double layer of baking sheets and spoon them in a double layer of paper baking cups. For special occasions, dip the cookies into melted chocolate while still warm.

TO PREPARE THE POTATO Bake or boil the potato until soft. Either mash the potato or force it through a sieve or potato ricer (you will end up with about ¼ cup/60 mL). Set aside.

In a large bowl, combine the mashed potato, sugar, and milk. Gradually beat in the egg yolks, one at a time, in alternating batches with the coconut, scraping down the bowl to incorporate any pieces stuck to the sides. Cover and refrigerate for about 1 hour. (Alternatively, in a food processor, mix the mashed potatoes with the sugar and milk. Process briefly until well combined. Drop the egg yolks, one at a time, into the potato batter, in alternating batches with the coconut, pulsing briefly until combined and scraping down the sides of the bowl as necessary. Transfer the batter to a mixing bowl, cover, and refrigerate for about 1 hour.)

Spoon about 2 Tbsp (30 mL) of the batter onto doubled-lined baking cups placed onto doubled baking sheets.

Bake in a preheated 425°F (220°C) oven for approximately 10 to 12 minutes. The tops and edges should be toasted to a golden colour. Be careful not to overcook; the insides should remain moist. Transfer to a wire rack and allow the cookies to set before sliding off the cookie sheet. Cool completely and store in a cookie tin.

I prefer the light and fluffy texture of russet potatoes, although other potatoes can be substituted.

CREAM FROM HEAVEN

Natas do Céu

MAKES ABOUT 10 SERVINGS

2 pkgs Bolachas Maria cookies or
   any shortbread or digestive
   cookies (14 oz/400 g or about
   60 cookies)

2 cups (500 mL) whipping cream

6 Tbsp + ⅓ cup (90 mL + 80 mL)
   granulated sugar

6 eggs, separated

Pinch fine salt

3 Tbsp (45 mL) whole milk

3 Tbsp (45 mL) port

Toasted sliced almonds

The creamy and crumbly contrast of textures of *Natas de Céu* "cream from heaven" makes for a lighter-than-air and decadent dessert sure to tempt a wide variety of tastes. The following recipe demystifies the classic sweet. If you are making this for a special occasion, assemble it earlier in the day or the night before serving, leaving you free to enjoy more time with your guests. The additional time in the refrigerator allows the dessert to further set. This classic dessert is delicious and appealing topped with a few fresh raspberries, toasted almond slices, or shaved chocolate.

Place the cookies in a sealed bag. With a rolling pan or the back of a heavy cast iron pan, smash the cookies into a mix of fine and medium crumbs. Set aside.

In a large bowl, using an electric mixer, beat the whipping cream at the highest setting for about 2 to 3 minutes, until frothy. Add 3 Tbsp (45 mL) of sugar a spoonful at a time, blending well after each addition, until stiff peaks form. Set aside in the freezer for about 30 minutes to keep the cream hard.

In another large bowl, beat the egg whites with the salt until soft peaks form. While beating, gradually add 3 Tbsp (45 mL) of sugar, continuing to beat until stiff peaks form. Using a spatula, gently fold the egg white mixture into the whipping cream. Set aside in the refrigerator.

TO MAKE THE EGG YOLK CREAM SAUCE In a medium saucepan on medium-high heat, heat the egg yolks, the remaining ⅓ cup (80 mL) sugar, and the milk and port; mix well using a whisk. Set the pan into a larger pan of boiling water (*bain-marie* style) and whisk the egg yolk mixture until smooth. Keep the heat set on medium-high so that the water in the bottom pan is at a medium boil. Continue whisking and cooking the sauce for about 3 to 4 minutes, until the eggs become somewhat runny and pudding-like (the mixture will continue to thicken off the heat). Remove from the heat, strain through a fine-mesh sieve, and set aside until cool, about 30 minutes. Whisk again just before serving.

TO ASSEMBLE In wide ice-cream sundae or parfait dishes, scatter about
2 Tbsp (30 mL) of the cookie crumbs to cover the bottom of each dish.
Using a spatula or butter knife, top with an even layer (about ½ cup/
125 mL of the cream mixture. Repeat with another layer each of cookie
crumbs and cream. Top with the prepared egg yolk sauce, using a spatula
to cover the cookie crumbs. End with a final sprinkle of cookie crumbs
(you should be able to see the yellow-coloured sauce around the rim of
the dish).

Garnish with the sliced almonds. Individually wrap and refrigerate for
2 hours before serving. Keeps for up to 3 days.

If preferred, the dessert can be prepared in a casserole-style dish
instead of individual servings.

POACHED MERINGUES

Farofias

MAKES 6 TO 8 SERVINGS

3¼ cups (810 mL) cold whole milk

Peel of 1 large orange,
   cut into long strips

4 eggs, separated

6 Tbsp (90 mL) granulated sugar

2 tsp (10 mL) cornstarch

¼ teaspoon (1 mL) ground
   cinnamon, for dusting

Poached Meringues is another way that eggs and milk are combined to make a Portuguese classic. I love how the egg whites puff up during poaching, looking somewhat like clouds. And the presentation is beautiful: fluffy egg whites sprinkled with cinnamon in subtle contrast to the custardy bottom (especially apparent when served in a glass dish).

It is best to eat this dessert the same day it is made. Poached egg whites wilt overnight.

In a deep heavy skillet over medium-low heat, bring 3 cups (750 mL) of the milk and the orange peels to a simmer. Remove from the heat and set aside.

In a large bowl, using an electric mixer, beat the egg whites until soft peaks form. Add 3 Tbsp (45 mL) of the sugar and continue to beat until stiff peaks form.

Return the milk to low heat and bring to a low boil. Using 2 spoons, shape the meringue into large ovals, about 3 to 4 inches (8 to 10 cm) in length, and drop into the milk (you can cook 2 meringues at a time). Poach each meringue for 1 to 2 minutes per side, or until firm. The meringues will quickly expand. Using a slotted spoon, carefully transfer the cooked meringues into a colander placed over a bowl to catch the excess milk draining from the meringues. Continue shaping and poaching the remaining meringues. Transfer to a large flat dish, arranging in a single layer, and set aside.

Using a fine-mesh sieve, strain the milk used to simmer the meringues into a heavy saucepan; discard the orange peel. Stir in the remaining 3 Tbsp (45 mL) of sugar. In a small bowl, combine ¼ cup (60 mL) cold milk with the cornstarch; to it, add about ¼ cup (60 mL) of the hot milk and whisk to combine. Slowly pour the cornstarch milk into the pan with the hot milk and whisk to combine. Cook over medium-low heat, whisking continuously, for 3 to 4 minutes or until the mixture begins to thicken enough to coat the back of a spoon.

In a separate bowl, lightly beat the egg yolks. Very gradually, add about ½ cup (125 mL) of the hot milk to the yolks, whisking rapidly to prevent curdling. Add the yolk and milk mixture to the saucepan and cook over medium-low heat for 3 to 4 minutes or until the custard has thickened to a pudding-like consistency (do not boil). Transfer the hot custard into a large shallow heatproof bowl and set aside for about 10 minutes to cool slightly.

Discard any liquid that has been pooling around the meringues and, using a slotted spoon, gently place the meringues on top of the custard.

Sprinkle with cinnamon just before serving. Serve warm or chilled.

STRAWBERRIES MARINATED IN PORT

Morango da Avó Ana

It is worth waiting the required 24 hours for the strawberries in this dessert to take on the delicate, not-too-sweet finish of the port marinade. Served over ice cream or with sweetened whipped cream or mascarpone, they are fit for any special occasion.

Avoid washing strawberries as this makes them soggy. Simply wipe the strawberries with a towel to remove any dirt or grit before slicing. A variety of fruit, such as pineapple and blueberries, are excellent additions to the strawberries. Cut the fruit into uniform pieces and toss them in the strawberries just before serving.

In a large decorative serving bowl, place about 1½ cups (375 mL) of the strawberries in an even layer. Sprinkle with 1 Tbsp (15 mL) of sugar. Repeat the layers until all of the strawberries have been used up. Pour the ¼ cup (60 mL) port over the strawberries (the port will not cover the strawberries; the strawberry juices will extract during marinating). Cover and set aside in the refrigerator for 24 hours. Do not disturb the layered strawberry dish.

To serve, spoon the fruit into dessert cups and drizzle with some of the sauce. Garnish each serving with a mint leaf.

To make a thicker port sauce, strain the strawberries and port and set the strawberries aside. Place the marinating liquids in a small saucepan over medium heat and boil for 3 to 5 minutes, until reduced by about one-third or it reaches the desired consistency. Set aside to cool. Pour the sauce over the strawberries and serve immediately.

MAKES ABOUT 6 SERVINGS

5 cups (1.25 L) hulled and thickly sliced strawberries

3 Tbsp (45 mL) granulated sugar

¼ cup (60 mL) port + additional port for serving

6 fresh mint leaves

FRENCH TOAST SLICES IN A
PORT AND CINNAMON SAUCE

Fatias Douradas ou Rabanadas

**MAKES 12 PIECES OF
FRENCH TOAST**

1 day-old French loaf

2 cups (500 mL) port

2 cups (500 mL) whole milk

5 Tbsp (75 mL) ground cinnamon

6 eggs

2 cups (500 mL) granulated sugar

Vegetable oil for frying

Fatias dourada, which means "golden slices," is typically prepared on the morning of Christmas Eve at my friend Fatima Silva's house. The golden bread slices, piled high into a pyramid, drip and form a delicious cascade of sugar, cinnamon, and port wine.

Brief frying gives the slices of bread a crispy outer layer while retaining its creamy milk and port centre. Make sure the bread is at least one day old so that it can tolerate the soaking without falling apart.

Cut the bread into 1½-inch (4 cm) slices and set aside. You should have about 12 slices of bread without the ends, depending on the loaf size.

Prepare 3 shallow bowls large enough to dip one bread slice at a time. In 1 bowl, place the port; in another bowl, combine the milk and 2 Tbsp (30 mL) of the cinnamon; in the third bowl, whisk the eggs. Set aside.

In a flat dish, combine the sugar and the remaining 3 Tbsp (45 mL) of cinnamon.

In a large skillet, heat oil to cover the skillet by ½ inch (1 cm) of oil to 375°F (190°C).

Dip each bread slice, on both sides, first in the port, then in the milk mixture, and lastly into the egg. The bread should be wet but not soggy. If the bread becomes too soggy or heavy in either the port wine or milk mixtures, gently squeeze out the excess liquid from the bread before dipping into the eggs. Using two forks, carefully place the egg-dipped bread slices into the hot oil, 2 to 3 slices at a time. Cook for 1 to 2 minutes per side or until browned all over; if necessary, adjust the heat to keep the bread slices from browning too quickly. Briefly drain each piece on paper towels and then roll in the cinnamon sugar, coating all over, while the bread is still hot. Repeat the process with the remaining bread slices. If necessary, add more oil or, if the oil is becoming too dark with bits of cinnamon, change the oil midway through frying.

Place 4 slices of cinnamon toast on a serving dish and build layers of overlapping slices to form a 4- or 5-tiered pyramid. Set aside for at least an hour before serving to allow the syrup to drip and pool.

If desired, serve with Port Sauce (page 292) or Strawberries Marinated in Port (page 357) and sweetened whipped cream.

The French toast-like dessert can be made less potent for children: omit the port and make a separate port wine sauce for the adults.

Around Christmastime, thick slices of fatia dourada bread can be purchased at Portuguese bakeries to make this golden bread dessert. I always have trouble finding the bread and as a result just use Sweet Egg Bread (page 310) or French loaf. Egg or raisin bread make excellent variations.

BAKED MERINGUES

Suspiros

MAKES ABOUT 30 MERINGUES

6 egg whites
2 cups (500 mL) granulated sugar
1 tsp (5 mL) vanilla

Suspiros means "breaths"—an appropriate name for these airy meringues that melt in your mouth. For festive occasions, the meringues are painstakingly piped onto baking sheets and decorated with candy sprinkles before baking or dipped into melted chocolate when cool. Dust with icing sugar or cocoa powder before serving.

To achieve the right crispy texture, make these the evening before you wish to serve them and leave them in the oven overnight to dry out.

In a large bowl, using an electric mixer, beat the egg whites. Gradually beat in the sugar and vanilla until firm glossy peaks form.

Using a spoon or piping bag, form the meringue into approximately 2-inch (5 cm) spirals placed 1 inch (2.5 cm) apart on 2 baking sheets lined with foil or parchment paper. Bake in a preheated 225°F (105°F) oven for 1 to 1¼ hours or until crisp but not browned (if the meringues begin to turn brown, cover with foil or parchment paper). To test for doneness, taste one; if it is still chewy in the centre, return the meringues to the oven for a further 25 to 30 minutes. Set aside for 1 hour to cool before serving. Store in an airtight container for up to 2 weeks.

EASY DOUGHNUTS

Filhozes ou Malassadas

These doughnuts are made for Shrove Tuesday and to celebrate the day before the beginning of Lent in the Roman Catholic faith. They are called *Filhozes* in the Azores and *Malassadas* in mainland Portugal.

Toss the doughnuts in cinnamon sugar while they are still warm. These doughnuts are often made by the rather laborious yeast method. This baking powder version is just as delicious, and it is foolproof.

In a saucepan over medium heat, combine the milk and cinnamon stick. Bring almost to a boil. Turn off the burner and set aside for at least 2 hours or overnight (refrigerate if using the next day) to intensify the milk flavour. Discard the cinnamon stick before using.

In a small shallow bowl, combine ¼ cup (60 mL) of the sugar and the ground cinnamon. Set aside.

In a large bowl, whisk the eggs until foamy. Beat in the remaining ½ cup (125 mL) of the sugar and the salt until well combined. In a separate bowl, combine the flour and baking powder. In alternating batches with the cinnamon-flavoured milk, gradually beat the flour mixture and milk into the egg batter until smooth.

In a large skillet, heat vegetable oil to a depth of 4 inches (10 cm) to 375°F (190°C). Using 2 spoons, place the batter in the hot skillet in 2 Tbsp (30 mL) portions (you should be able to cook 3 to 4 at a time); immediately lower the heat to medium-low to keep the doughnuts from browning too quickly. Cook for about 10 minutes per batch, turning once, until golden brown all over. Drain on paper towels. Repeat with the remaining batter. While the doughnuts are still hot, roll them in the prepared cinnamon sugar, coating them evenly all over.

Serve warm. These are best eaten the same day they are made.

> If there are any leftovers, I like to heat them briefly in a microwave and then split them in half and spread with jam.

MAKES 36 DOUGHNUTS

2 cups (500 mL) whole milk
One 2-inch (5 cm) cinnamon stick
¾ cup (185 mL) granulated sugar
1 Tbsp (15 mL) ground cinnamon
5 eggs
1 tsp (5 mL) fine salt
4 cups (1 L) all-purpose flour
4 tsp (20 mL) baking powder
Vegetable oil for deep-frying

CRÈME BRÛLÉE

MAKES ABOUT 10 INDIVIDUAL
BRÛLÉES

3 cups (750 mL) whipping cream

1 cup (250 mL) whole milk

Peel from 1 orange

1 vanilla bean split lengthwise
    or 1 tsp (5 mL) vanilla

10 egg yolks

¾ cup (185 mL) granulated sugar

¼ cup (60 mL) port

½ cup (125 mL) granulated sugar
    (approx.)

Although not officially a Portuguese dessert, crème brûlée is so loved that it has been adopted at restaurants that cater to the Portuguese palate. It is easy to see why: it has a creamy texture and a sinfully decadent taste.

Lucia Charlery, a consulting chef at Via Norte in Toronto who makes some amazing desserts, says the secret to achieving a deeper layer of flavour is to boil the cream mixture in advance and set it aside in the refrigerator. The mixture will be more intensely infused with the orange and vanilla flavourings the longer it is left to marinate. You do not need to boil the cream mixture again before assembling the brûlées; just heat it up and continue with the recipe below.

In a heavy saucepan, combine the whipping cream, milk, orange peel, and vanilla, mixing well after each addition. Cook over medium-high heat and bring to a boil, stirring just enough to prevent the cream from scorching, for 6 to 7 minutes. When the mixture comes to a rolling boil, with bubbles forming on the sides of the pan, remove the pan from the heat. Set aside for 20 minutes or up to 8 hours in the refrigerator if you have the time.

Using an electric mixer, beat the egg yolks and sugar for 1 to 2 minutes or until pale and beginning to thicken. Add the port, mix well, and set aside until ready to use.

Heat the cream mixture until hot (you don't need to boil it). Pour it slowly into the egg yolks, whisking constantly. Using a fine-mesh sieve, strain the mixture and discard the peel, cinnamon pieces, and vanilla bean. Pour the mixture into individual ramekins until about three-quarters full. (A water jug with a lip makes this job much easier.)

Place the ramekins in a large baking pan and pour enough hot water into the baking pan to come halfway up the sides of the ramekins (to create a *bain-marie*). Place in a preheated 350°F (175°C) oven for about 30 minutes. The brûlées are ready when they jiggle in the centre and the top of the custard has set. If not ready, continue baking for 5 minutes and test again. The custard will continue to set slightly after removal from the oven.

Remove the pan from the oven and allow the brûlées to cool in the pan for about 15 minutes. Remove the ramekins from the water to cool completely. Cover each ramekin with plastic wrap and refrigerate for 4 to 6 hours (can be made up to 24 hours ahead of time).

Sprinkle 1 tsp (5 mL) of sugar evenly over each ramekin. Transfer the ramekins to a baking sheet. Place the baking sheet on the second rack from the top and broil for approximately 4 minutes (watch closely during last minute of broiling as the sugar can easily burn). Remove from the oven when the sugar is melted and forms a golden glass finish. Cool before serving.

CHESTNUT BRÛLÉE

Creme de Castanhas Caramelizado

MAKES ABOUT 6 SERVINGS

1 lb (500 g) chestnuts, fresh
and shelled, or canned

1¼ cups (310 mL) whipping cream

2 egg yolks

½ cup (125 mL) granulated sugar

Grated zest of 1 orange

2 Tbsp (30 mL) orange liqueur
or port

2 Tbsp (30 mL) brown sugar

**ORANGE AND PORT
WHIPPED CREAM**

1 cup (250 mL) whipping cream

3 Tbsp (45 mL) granulated sugar

Zest of 1 orange

1 Tbsp (15 mL) port

Chestnut custard is a cinch to prepare in Portugal, as both frozen chestnuts or canned chestnuts are readily available. This recipe was created by my friend Alexandra Faria's mother, Helena, who has an abundance of chestnuts in the fall. Her property in Leiria (central Portugal) is covered in chestnut trees, and the inventive Helena created this delicious dessert to use up the nutritious starch (chestnuts contain vitamins, minerals, and proteins).

TO PREPARE THE CHESTNUTS Using a sharp knife, make a horizontal slash or a large *X* along the flat side of each chestnut before boiling (this will make shelling the chestnuts easier).

In a large cooking pot, cover the chestnuts with cold water and bring to a boil over medium heat. Simmer for 15 to 25 minutes, until tender. (Peeling and removing the skin becomes more difficult as the chestnuts cool, so keep them in hot water until you are ready to peel them.) Peel the chestnuts and either mash them with a potato masher or purée them in a food processor. Set aside.

In a saucepan over medium heat, heat the cream, stirring continuously (do not let it come to a boil). Set aside. Strain through a fine-mesh sieve just before using.

In a bowl, using an electric mixer, beat the egg yolks and ½ cup (125 mL) sugar for about 1 to 2 minutes or until pale and beginning to thicken. Add the orange zest and liqueur, mix well, and set aside. Add the warm cream to the eggs and beat until well blended. Add the chestnut purée, a little bit at a time, until well combined.

Spoon the mixture into individual ramekins until about three-quarters full. (A water jug with a lip makes this job much easier.)

Place the ramekins in a baking pan large enough to comfortably fit 6 ramekins. Add enough hot water to the baking pan to come halfway up the sides of the ramekin dishes (to make a *bain-marie*). Place in a preheated

350°F (175°C) oven for about 30 minutes. The custards are ready when they jiggle in the centre and the top of each custard is set. If not quite done, continue to bake for 5 minutes and test again. The custards will continue to set slightly after being removed from the oven. Let the ramekins cool in the pan for about 15 minutes, then remove the ramekins from the water and set aside to cool completely. Cover each ramekin in clear plastic and refrigerate for 4 to 6 hours to set (can also be made about 24 hours ahead of time and refrigerated).

Sprinkle the top of each ramekin with 1 tsp (5 mL) of the brown sugar. Arrange the ramekins on a baking sheet and place in the oven on the second rack from the top. Broil for about 4 minutes—watch closely during the last minute of broiling as the sugar can easily burn. Remove from the oven when the sugar is melted and forms a golden glass finish with a few flecks of brown. Set aside to cool.

TO MAKE THE ORANGE AND PORT WHIPPED CREAM Using an electric mixer, beat the cream and sugar until thickened; add the orange zest and port and beat for 1 minute further. Chill.

To serve, add a dollop of whipped cream overtop each custard.

Drizzling the brûlées with the orange-flavoured whipped cream or with Port Sauce (page 292) makes this into a very decadent dessert.

ACKNOWLEDGEMENTS

This book was a pleasure to put together, and I am extremely fortunate to have met many people in the Portuguese community who provided encouragement and made this project possible. In particular, I am extremely thankful for the help of the individuals who were willing to share their passion for food with me. Their continual support in their kitchens and workplaces and in coffee shops discussing food, and their response to numerous phone calls and emails, provided an abundance of information that helped me to write this book.

Special thanks goes to Chef José Alves, Fatima Silva, Alexandra Faria, and Isabel Vieira. All of these people gave more than I ever could have asked for. In addition, I owe a debt of gratitude to Margarida Rocha, Manuela Marujo, Ana Julia de Macedo Sanca (and her cousin Zilena Mendonça), and Ana Cristina Vieira. Thanks to Lucia Charlery for her excellent and generous baking advice. Also thank you to Madalena Azevedo and her daughter, Carmen. Thank you to Domingos Marques for his insight into sardines and to Maria Lourdes and José Coito of Popular Grocery Store who, with their family, talked to me endlessly about Portuguese food. Also I would like to thank Lucy Ataide and her sister, Maria José Martins, Olidia and Victor Hipolito and their family, Rosa Boaventura, Irene Alves, Ana Fenech, Clara Abreu, Raquel Goncalves, Martin Silva, Palmira Almeida, Carla Cardoso, Isabel Antunes, Maria Julia Paim, Margaret Barbosa Pereira, Sarah Almeida, Angelita Flores (who patiently taught me many skills in a professional kitchen), Irene Faria and her stepson, Adam Gomes, Filipe Queiroz (who greeted me with a smile for almost a year when I showed up in his kitchen most Sundays to cook with his wife), and Cristina and Zé Honorato (for their kind hospitality, especially in barbecue and pool season).

In addition, thanks to Jenny Coimbra, Clara Abreu, Ana Cumbre, Fatima Toste, Ana Paula Ribeiro, Esmeralda Pereira, and Marta Rebelo and her mother, Zulmira Rebelo. Also, thank you to my taste testers at Azevedo and Nelson, who gave me their honest opinions about the food I brought in for them. The staff and owners of Portogrill restaurant in Toronto and Bairrada Grill House and Azores Cambridge Bakery were very helpful, along with

Maria and Helio, who ran Estrela do Mar, and outstanding chef Manuel Vilela at Chiado Restaurant. Thanks to *Sol Português*, a Portuguese newspaper in Toronto, who featured an article on my first cookbook.

I am also immensely thankful to friends and family who encouraged me throughout this process. Thanks to Ina Azevedo for badgering her friends for recipes; Idalina Azevedo; my children, Melyssa Azevedo and Matthew Azevedo, for their invaluable advice; my sister, Anna Lotito for sharing her wealth of knowledge about food; Tony Mastragostino; and my parents, Egidio and Teresa Mastragostino, who to this day share their love of food with me. I would like to also thank friends and family who put up with my endless discussions about Portuguese cooking.

Thanks to Whitecap Books, editor Theresa Best, my editor Tracy Bordian and my proofreaders Grace Yaginuma and Jesse Marchand for their invaluable suggestions and support, and for helping to make this wonderful book possible. Thanks also to Michelle Furbacher, art director at Whitecap Books, for her work.

Although they are long deceased, I would like to remember the support of Maria and João Pereira, who opened up their home to me and provided endless recipes and food that fed my body and soul. I will never forget their contribution to *Uma Casa Portuguesa* and, as a result, my love for Portuguese cooking.

Lastly, I would like to dedicate this book to my husband, Antonio Azevedo, who in addition to putting up with endless discussions about food helps me make my dreams come true. Thank you.

INDEX

Baked Fish in Curry and White Wine, 136
Baked or Boiled Cod Dinner, 146–47
Cod and Apples, 154–55
Cod and Cheese Tart, 150–51
Cod and Chickpeas, 152–53
Cod and Potato Soufflé, 148–49
Cod in Cream Sauce, 142–43
Cod with Scrambled Eggs and Olives, 141
Fish Fillets in Batter, 138–39
Fish Soup Alentejo-Style, 86
Fish Steaks in Pimento and Bacon Sauce, 134–35
grilling techniques, 162
Marinated Fish Steaks in Spicy Wine Sauce, 137
Peppercorn and Garlic–Crusted Tuna, 156–57
in Portuguese cooking, 19
Sardine Pizza, 318
Sardine Stew, 163
sauces for, 272–73
Stickleback in Onion Dressing, 140
Trout Wrapped in Prosciutto with Pine Nut Sauce, 158–59
Tuna and Vegetable Salad, 145
Tuna Pudding in Hot Tomato Sauce, 144
Whole European Sea Bass with Fresh Coriander and Lemon Dressing, 160–62
fish stock
Fish Stock, 75
flavouring, 89
flans
in Portuguese cooking, 320
White Chocolate Flan, 329
Flat Cornbread, 297, 303
flavour-enhancing techniques
with beef jus, 9
for fish stock, 89
natural methods, 10–11
for seafood, 97
for steak, 196
flour, in Portuguese cooking, 19
Folar ou Massa Sovada, 310–11
folding techniques, 11–12
Four Pepper Sauce, 281
Frango com Cogumelos Salteados, 188–89
Frango na Pucara, 190–91
French Toast Slices in a Port and Cinnamon Sauce, 358–59
Fresh Tomato and Bread Soup, 80
fritters
Corn Cakes, 306
Pumpkin Fritters with Cinnamon Sugar Dust, 314–15
fruit. See also individual fruits
Christmas Fig Cake, 334
in crêpes, 102

in Custard-Filled Puff Balls, 338–39
in desserts, 322
Fruit Chutney, 294–95
with Sponge Cake, 335
in Strawberries Marinated in Port, 357

G

Galinha à Moda da Terceira, 173
Galinha Angolana, 174–75
Galinha Assada com Pimenta Vermelha e Azeitonas Picadas, 177
Galinha com Molho de Vinho e Limão, 172
Galinha na Brasa, 170–71
game
Partridge Sautéed with Fresh Herbs, 180–81
in Portuguese cooking, 166–67
Quail in Cream Sauce, 184–85
Rabbit and Chouriço, 186–87
garlic
Baked Potatoes with Pimento and Garlic, 244
Bread and Egg in Garlic and Coriander Broth, 78
Collard Greens, Cornbread, and Garlic Stir-Fry, 269–70
Garlic Herb Marinade, 57
Greens, Potatoes, and Eggs in Garlic Oil and White Wine Vinegar, 262–63
Lamb in Wine and Garlic, 213
Lemon and Garlic Pork Cubes, 218–19
Peppercorn and Garlic–Crusted Tuna, 156–57
Pine Nut–Crusted Rosemary and Garlic Rack of Lamb, 214–17
Popular Garlic Olives, 64
in Portuguese cooking, 20
Rice and Broccoli Rabe with Onion and Garlic Oil, 260
Sautéed Garlic Rabe Greens, 261
Spicy Shrimp with Beer and Garlic, 109
Gaspacho, 80
goat
goat's milk, 16, 50
in Lamb in Wine and Garlic, 213
in Portuguese cooking, 20, 197
Golden Crêpes Stuffed with Crab, 102–3
green beans
Green Beans in Light Batter, 52
Green Beans Stewed in Tomato Sauce, 241
Green Eggs, 60–61
Green Onion and Parsley Mini-Omelettes, 34

greens. See also collard greens
Greens, Potatoes, and Eggs in Garlic Oil and White Wine Vinegar, 262–63
in Portuguese cooking, 234
precooking, 261
Sautéed Garlic Rabe Greens, 261
Grelos com Alho, 261
Grilled Octopus in Red Pepper and Olive Relish, 112–13
Grilled Pineapple and Vegetables with Fresh Mint, 264–65
Grilled Sardines, 58
grilling techniques
chicken, 171
fish, 162
grouper
Baked Fish in Curry and White Wine, 136
Fish Steaks in Pimento and Bacon Sauce, 134–35
Marinated Fish Steaks in Spicy Wine Sauce, 137
with Onion Dressing, 140
Seafood Stew, 91–94

H

halibut
Fish Steaks in Pimento and Bacon Sauce, 134–35
Marinated Fish Steaks in Spicy Wine Sauce, 137
herbs
Chicken Simmered with Bacon, Moonshine, and Herbs, 190–91
Orange Duck with Herbs in a Tomato Port Sauce, 194–95
Partridge Sautéed with Fresh Herbs, 180–81
in Portuguese cooking, 10
honey
Honey Cookies, 348
from sugar-cane, 348
hot sauces
Cape Verde Hot Sauce, 89
Moonshine Hot Sauce, 285
Piri-Piri Hot Sauce, 282
hot water bath technique. See bain-marie technique

I

icings, 338
inhames, 27
Iscas de Borrego Fritas, 212

J

jams. See also chutneys; spreads
Tomato Jam, 288–89

K

kidney beans
Beans and Pork Hock in Beer, 232–33

Tripe and Beans Porto-Style, 230–31
kneading techniques, 12

L

lamb
Lamb in Wine and Garlic, 213
Leg of Lamb Stuffed with Mint and Parsley, 210–11
Pine Nut–Crusted Rosemary and Garlic Rack of Lamb, 214–17
in Portuguese cooking, 20, 197
Sautéed Lamb's Liver Portuguese-Style, 212
lard, Portuguese-flavoured, 222
leftovers, uses for
bread, 297
cod, 147
Easy Doughnuts, 361
Fish Fillets in Batter, 138, 274
garlic oil, 265
Marinated Grilled Chicken with Red Pepper and Olive Relish, 274
meat, 34, 206
"old clothes", 197
Orange Duck with Herbs in a Tomato Port Sauce, 194–5
sardines, 62
vegetables, 206
Leg of Lamb Stuffed with Mint and Parsley, 210–11
lemons
Chicken in Batter and Lemon Sauce, 174–75
Chicken in Wine and Lemon Sauce, 172
Lemon and Garlic Pork Cubes, 218–19
Lemon Chicken in Puff Pastry, 178–79
Lemon Piri-Piri Sauce, 282
Port-Soaked Pineapple with Mint and Lemon, 343
in Portuguese cooking, 20
Shrimp Croquettes with Pine Nuts and Lemon Sauce, 46–47
Whole European Sea Bass with Fresh Coriander and Lemon Dressing, 160–62
light dishes
Chicken and Rice Salad, 176
Cod Pancakes, 53
Green Onion and Parsley Mini-Omelettes, 34
quick ideas for, 30–31
Shrimp Croquettes with Pine Nuts and Lemon Sauce, 46–47
limpets, 26
linguiça, 25
liver
Sautéed Lamb's Liver Portuguese-Style, 212